Contents

Front cover: On Tweed in Autumn. Photograph by Bill Currie.
Graphic Design: Emma Goodman
Editing & Production: Louise Couper, Louise Stanton

Published by Pastime Publications Ltd., 6 York Place, Edinburgh EH1 3EP.
Tel: 0131-556 1105. Fax: 0131-556 1129.
First published by The Scottish Tourist Board 1970.
UK & Worldwide Distribution.
Printed & bound in Scotland.

Admiring the catch. A 14 lb salmon from Spey near Boat of Garten

Scottish Game Fishing: the inside story

by Bill Currie

A summer grilse

When you cast your eye over the pages of Scotland for Fishing 1998, you might well be impressed by the huge variety of game fishing which the guide represents. You will see the names of salmon rivers and details of renowned beats. You will see well-known lochs and a very wide variety of streams, lochans and burns, all of which represent the impressive natural resource Scotland has for the fishing visitor. There is a chance that, as you think about where and when to fish in Scotland, you might fall into the trap of thinking that unless you are in the 'serious' class of game fisher with a cheque book to match, leasing named beats or booking boats on the best lochs, you would somehow miss out on what Scottish game fishing has to offer. You would be wrong. In Scottish fishing, the race is not always to the swift nor the battle to the strong.

Let me illustrate this. Last Summer I was having a mixed family and fishing holiday in Inverness-shire. The fishing element was played down. Really, I just packed my rod and trout tackle on the principle that I could not really contemplate travelling in the Highlands without tackle somewhere in the car. So, I was in the role of casual visiting angler. We spent some time in the Great Glen - Scotland's rift valley - which runs from Inverness, down the great waters of Loch Ness, then through Loch Oich and westwards down the long, deep Loch Lochy and the river Lochy to the sea at Fort William.

When I asked at Spean Bridge whether Loch Lochy was any good for trout these days, people made faces and said it was too deep and where it was accessible it had not very many trout in it. Some people said it once was pretty good for medium-sized trout. I arranged with the boarding house I was staying in to cast a fly on its waters. I started on the south side, not far from the main Fort William to Inverness road. Not much moved - although I did have the delight of seeing an otter close by me coming down to fish the loch in the dusk. That reach seemed empty. Over on the other bank, however, I saw, as it were, a different Loch Lochy. There was no main road. Bushes and trees crowded down to the edge of the loch and behind them the hills rose steeply to rocky tops. I felt attracted to this less accessible reach. I drove over the next afternoon and wading under the bankside trees and just rolling my flies out through the ripple I had nine trout of which I kept four. These trout were barbecued the next day on the sands at Ardtoe Bay. That is, for me, an ideal holiday fishing event.

The inside story of Scottish holiday fishing is that a wealth of trout waters in the hills is available at very low cost. The second inside story is that in a very meaningful sense, fisherman's Scotland begins half a mile from the nearest road. Do not expect to fish out of the car window. Also, don't go expecting huge trout. Go looking for loch trout of half a pound or three quarters. The really important thing is to go to Highland and Hebridean lochs with a certain cast of mind. Expect to walk over the moor; expect days mixed with hillscapes, heatherscapes and marvellous vistas of mountain and sea. Above all, expect wild brown trout, - not huge, but sporting. I can tell you, I have been fishing Scottish waters for over half a century and what I have described is one of the undiminished delights of the game

In another sense, small is beautiful in Scotland. I was greatly struck by this when I was fishing a couple of the big-name rivers for salmon in the spring of 1997. We were on big leased beats, quite expensive, and we were not doing at all well. The news came down to us from the far north, however, that the smaller waters of the north coast, particularly Borgie and Halladale as well as the better known Naver and Thurso were catching salmon. Now, these are not

Getting ready for a days fishing on Spey

insignificant waters; nor are they cheap. But they were giving their fishers sport when larger waters further south were toiling.

In planning fishing in Scotland, never be misled into thinking that only the big waters give good sport. There is another aspect of the inside story of Scottish fishing, - how to do well on a restricted budget. I've already mentioned loch fishing, particularly hill loch fishing as tremendous value for money, but the value-for-money principle applies also to salmon fishing. Many of our famous salmon rivers have fairly well defined seasons. For example, Tweed has good spring salmon most years from as early as February to about mid-June. Between June and August, there are many beats which a visitor can book for a fraction of the cost of the fishing in spring or autumn. For example, a Tweed beat which might cost you £100 for a day's fishing in October would probably cost £25 at any time from the late spring to the end of the summer. The same pattern is found on Tay and on Dee. If you think that the price indicates that sport is certain to be poor in summer,

Teviot in autumn near Ancrum

think again. In 1997 we had some excellent waters in summer (in contrast to the drought of the previous year). When good summer water comes, the visiting fisher may find, as one of my fishing friends puts it, "that they are in the five guinea seats."

I had a nice reminder of this when I took a summer day on lower Tweed in 1997 and found that the beat was full of sea trout and had more than a few grilse running. I took home a couple of nice sea trout and ran, but lost, two grilse. The availability of beats on our main rivers in summer is good. Indeed, on Tweed, Tay and Dee, there is often a range of unlet beats to choose from at very reasonable prices. I live in Scotland and I do fish a number of the more prominent beats in their best periods, but I learn again and again that some of the most memorable sport can be picked up in the supposedly low seasons for a fraction of the cost of fishing at prime times. Brown trout in lochs and rivers in Scotland are resident fish, but the wild harvest we get in our sea trout, grilse and salmon represents sport with migratory fish. Our sea trout, grilse and salmon run into our rivers from spring to autumn. Whenever you are 'hunting' migratory fish you are, of course, at the mercy of the weather and of the whole range of complex issues which affect fish traversing hundreds (even thousands) of miles of ocean - as the salmon does - to reach our rivers. Sea trout are more local, although they also range up and down our coastlines in their winter feeding in salt water.

If you are planning holiday fishing, make sure that you include some lochs on your itinerary. Hedge your bets. I have often travelled far in Scotland to fish a salmon river to find that the water was too low to allow running, or the run was late or some other factor like overhead weather made fishing poor or impossible. Of course, guarantees in the natural world are impossible and, for me at least, the element of uncertainty is part of the game. Yet, I nearly always try on my holidays to have lochs to which I can turn if the salmon in the rivers are either unco-operative or just not there. The inside story goes on. Throughout Scotland there are fishing clubs on rivers

Unhooking a good sea trout from the Tweed

and lochs. Almost every river has one; some rivers like Spey, Tweed and Tay - big names in the fishing world - have extensive club waters. Almost all of these clubs issue daily and weekly tickets. You will see details in *Scotland for Fishing*. Some club waters cover miles of good fishing. When the rivers concerned bring in salmon, grilse and sea trout it does not take a genius to work out that the fish running up into the more expensive beats must surely pass through the club waters below. Therefore, if you are on a day-ticket water at the right time, you would certainly be in with as good a chance as anyone.

Many local clubs ask you to stay in the locality for the period of your fishing. But many clubs have no restrictions. Clubs, of course, have their capacities. It may be that only a dozen day tickets per day are issued, - or some similar restriction is applied. In some cases we have been able to refer to this in our fishing details. It is always wise to check by phone before the trip to see whether tickets are available. Despite these administrative issues however, ticket water in Scotland, in rivers and in lochs, is well worth considering.

I am not preaching a philosophy of 'also ran' in this introduction to *Scotland for Fishing*. I am trying to tell the inside story. Within the wide range of Scottish game fishing there is something for everybody. There is also excellent sport and a great experience of Scotland in taking in the so-called lesser hill waters and the island lochs. My heart leaps up just to write these words, because this fishing is absolutely at the heart of enjoying Scotland. The inside story is also about luck, - coupled, as ever, with some good planning. On rivers where the big times are spring and autumn - and I have named a few - a little bit of luck with water conditions can lead to some great sport with migratory fish. Above all, what I advise is not just in the realms of theory; I do this myself and get some fine fishing as a result.

Open Season

The following are the statutory open seasons for fishing for Salmon and Trout in Scotland:

SALMON

River	Rod Season	River	Rod Season
Add	Feb 16 - Oct 31	Fyne	Feb 16 - Oct 31
Aline	Feb 11 - Oct 31	Girvan	Feb 25 - Oct 31
Allan	Mar 15 - Oct 31	Gruinard & Little Gruinard	Feb 11 - Oct 31
Alness	Feb 11 - Oct 15	Halladale	Jan 12 - Sep 30
Annan	Feb 26 - Nov 15	Helmsdale	Jan 11 - Sep 30
Applecross	Feb 25 - Nov 15	Hope	Jan 12 - Sep 30
Awe	Feb 12 - Oct 15	Inver	Feb 11 - Oct 31
Ayr	Feb 11 - Oct 31	Irvine	Feb 25 - Nov 15
Beauly	Feb 11 - Oct 15	Kannaird	Feb 11 - Oct 31
Berriedale	Feb 11 - Oct 31	Kirkaig	Feb 11 - Oct 31
Bervie	Feb 25 - Oct 31	Kishorn	Feb 11 - Oct 31
Bladnoch	Feb 11 - Oct 31	Laxford	Feb 11 - Oct 31
Borgie	Jan 12 - Sep 30	Lochy	Feb 11 - Oct 31
Broom	Feb 11 - Oct 31	Lomond (Clyde)	Feb 12 - Oct 31
Brora	Feb 1 - Oct 15	Moidart	Feb 11 - Oct 31
Carron (E. Ross)	Jan 11 - Sep 30	Morar	Feb 11 - Oct 31
Carron (W. Ross)	Feb 11 - Oct 31	Nairn	Feb 12 - Oct 30
Conon	Jan 26 - Sep 30	Naver	Jan 12 - Sep 30
Cree	Mar 1 - Oct 14	Ness	Jan 15 - Oct 15
Creed	Feb 11 - Oct 16	Nith	Feb 26 - Nov 30
Croe	Feb 11 - Oct 31	Orchy	Feb 12 - Oct 15
Dee (Aberdeenshire)	Mar 1 - Sep 30	Oykel	Jan 11 - Sep 30
Dee (Kirkcudbrightshire)	Feb 11 - Oct 31	Shiel	Feb 11 - Oct 31
Deveron	Feb 12 - Oct 31	Shin	Jan 11 - Sep 30
Dionard	Feb 11 - Oct 31	Spey	Feb 12 - Sep 30
Don	Feb 12 - Oct 31	Stinchar	Feb 24 - Oct 31
Doon	Feb 11 - Oct 31	Strathy	Jan 12 - Sep 30
Dunbeath	Feb 11 - Oct 15	Tay	Jan 15 - Oct 15
Eachaig	Feb 16 - Oct 31	Teith	Feb 1 - Oct 31
Earn	Feb 1 - Oct 31	Thurso	Jan 11 - Oct 5
Esk (North & South)	Feb 16 - Oct 31	Torridon	Feb11 - Oct 31
Ewe	Feb 11 - Oct 31	Tweed	Feb 1 - Nov 30
Findhorn	Feb 12 - Sep 30	Ugie	Feb 16 - Oct 31
Fleet (Kirkcudbrightshire)	Feb 25 - Oct 31	Ullapool	Feb 11 - Oct 31
Fleet (Sutherland)	Feb 25 - Oct 31	Wick	Feb 11 - Oct 31
Forss	Feb 11 - Oct 31	Ythan	Feb 12 - Oct 15
Forth	Feb 1 - Oct 31		

TROUT: The season for trout is from **March 15 to October 6.**
For conservation reasons, some clubs or associations have slightly shorter seasons.

TILLMOUTH PARK

Scottish Tourist Board HIGHLY COMMENDED AA★★★ RAC★★★

LES ROUTIERS HOTEL OF THE YEAR 1997

A renowned retreat for anglers with all requirements catered for, including drying room and facilities for freezing your catch.
All of our 14 ensuite bedrooms have colour TV, tea and coffee making facilities and direct dial telphone. The public rooms are tastefully decorated and open log fires create a relaxing ambience. Billiard room for residents.

Only 15 minutes drive from Kelso.
Brochure and tariff on request.
4 Crowns Highly Commended.
AA Rosette award for food.
Cornhill-on-Tweed, Northumberland TD12 4UU.
Tel: (01890) 882255. Fax: (01890) 882540.

TWEED SALMON FISHING

at Tillmouth Park
Cornhill-on-Tweed, Northumberland

Seven beats each with its own ghillie
and boat with bankside shiel.

Good spring runs February to May
Superb autumn fishing with fish in the 16 to 30lb class.

Improved summer fishing following removal of
Tweed nets, reduced rents, February to July.

For further details or brochure contact: Sole Letting Agents

Sale and Partners
18-20 Glendale Road, Wooler, Northumberland NE71 6DW.
Tel: (01668) 281611. Fax: (01668) 281113.
International Tel: + 44 1668 281611.

THE SALMON RIVERS OF SCOTLAND

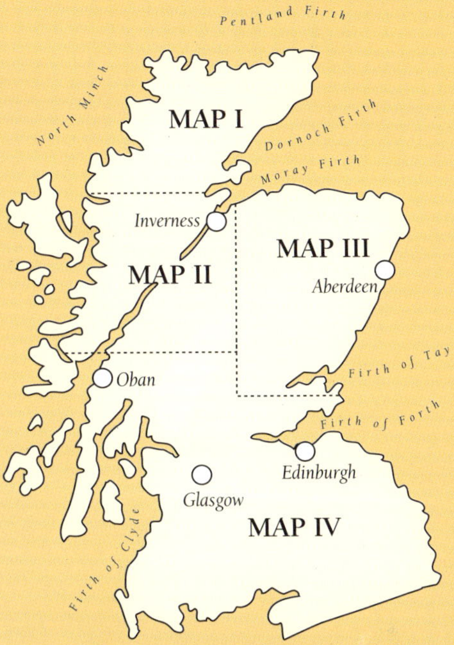

The GLENMORANGIE

FISHERMAN'S CODE

1.

He who'd be a fisher true,
Should know the proper thing to do.
Since brother anglers everywhere,
Are known for courtesy and care.
For love of fishing always mellows,
To love of nature and your fellows.

THE SALMON RIVERS OF SCOTLAND

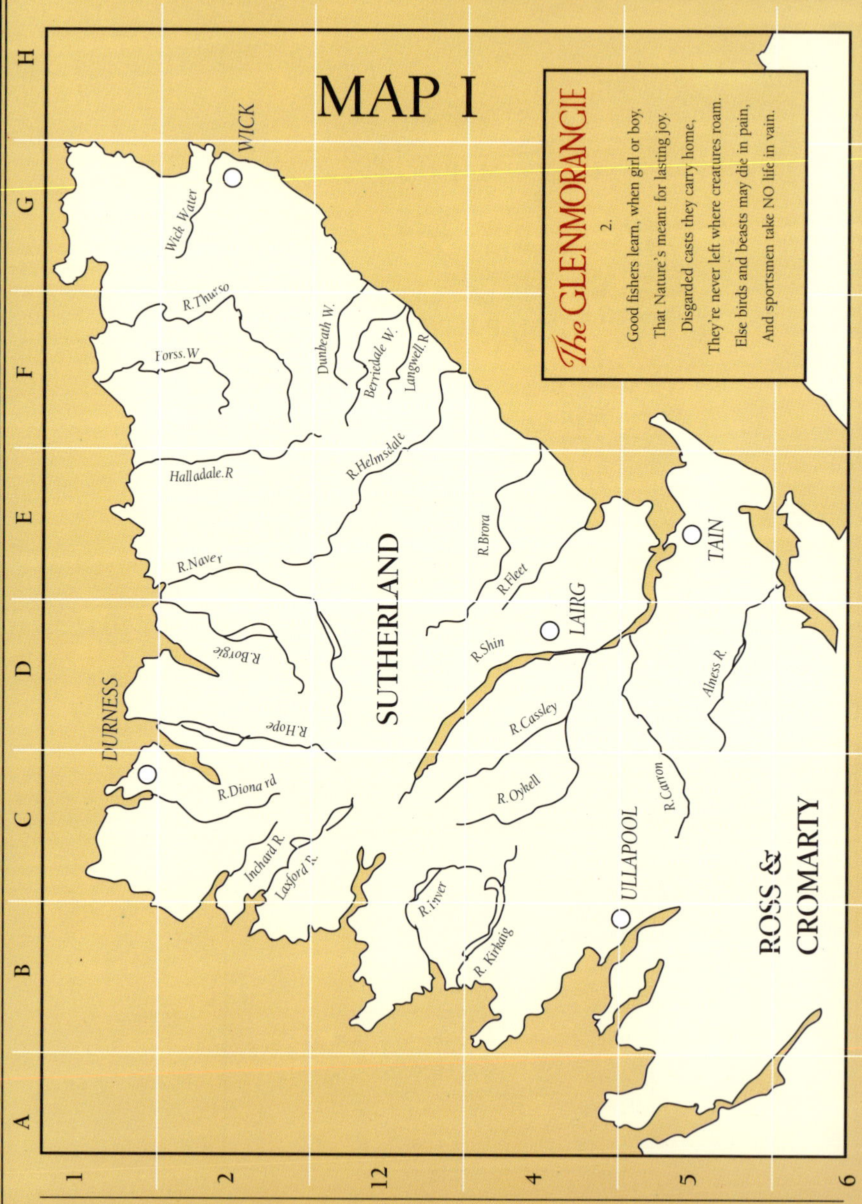

THE SALMON RIVERS OF SCOTLAND

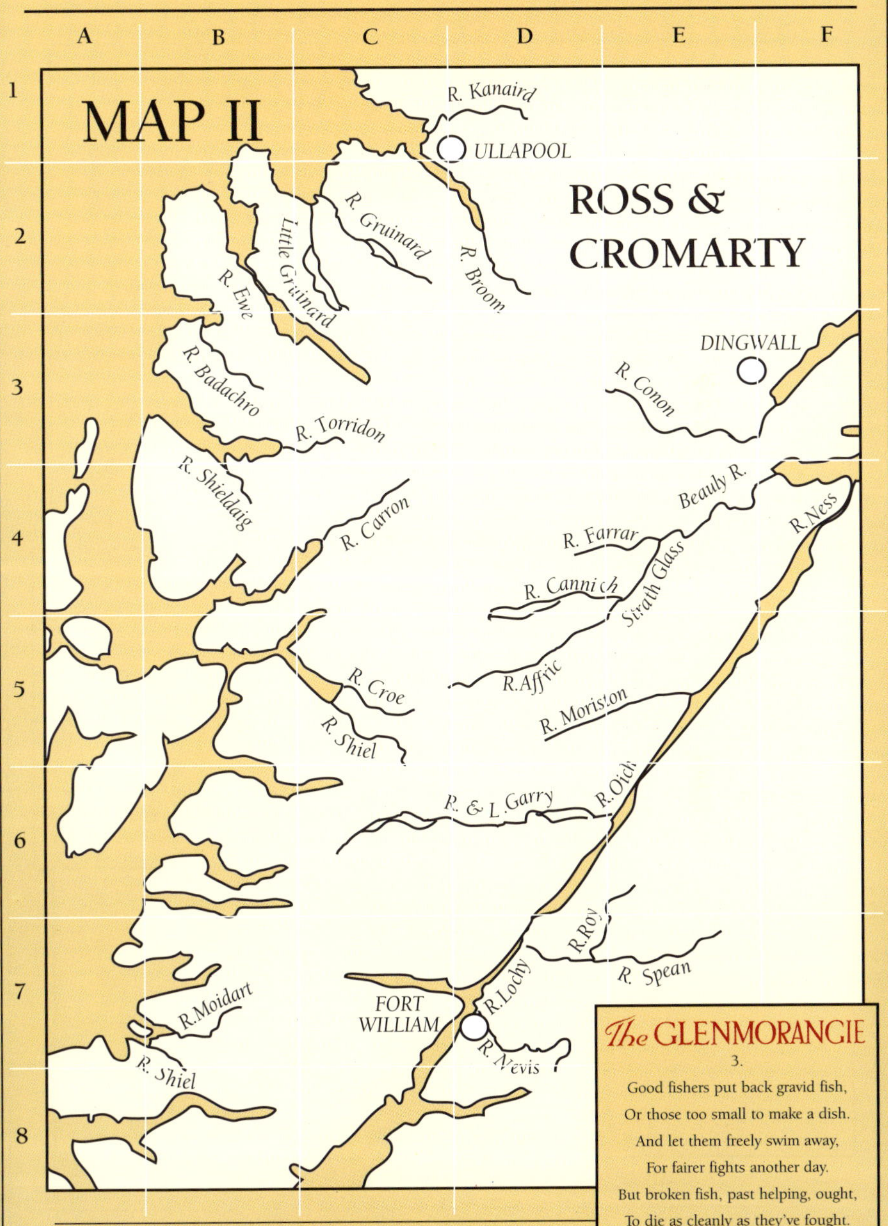

The GLENMORANGIE

3.

Good fishers put back gravid fish,
Or those too small to make a dish.
And let them freely swim away,
For fairer fights another day.
But broken fish, past helping, ought,
To die as cleanly as they've fought.

THE SALMON RIVERS OF SCOTLAND

MAP III

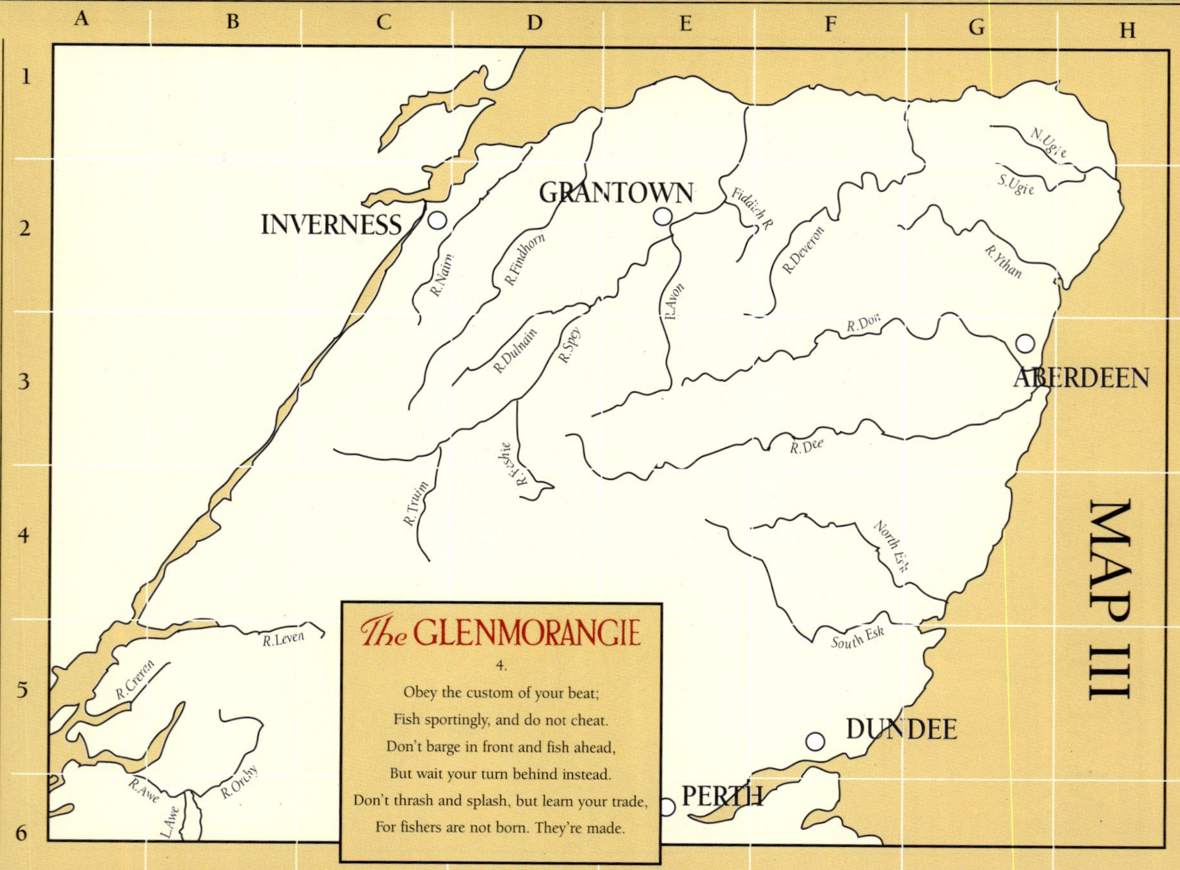

The GLENMORANGIE

4.

Obey the custom of your beat;
Fish sportingly, and do not cheat.
Don't barge in front and fish ahead,
But wait your turn behind instead.
Don't thrash and splash, but learn your trade,
For fishers are not born. They're made.

THE SALMON RIVERS OF SCOTLAND

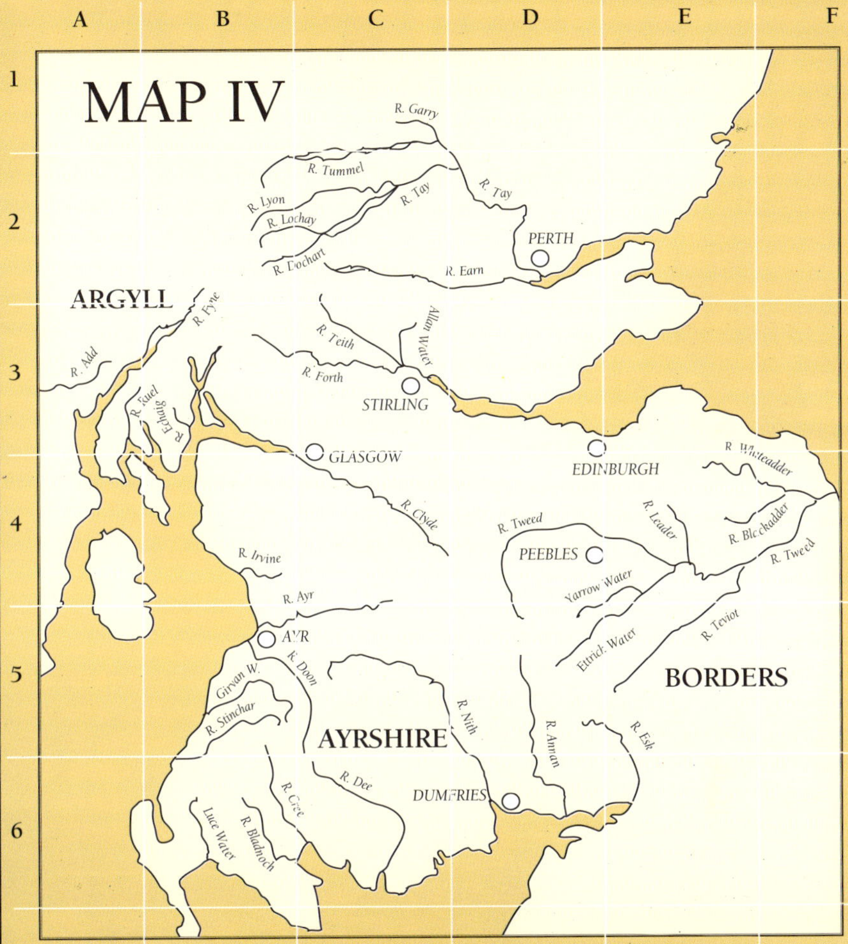

The GLENMORANGIE

5.

And "Manners Makyth Man" it's true,
But manners make the fisher too.
And manners make us toast all three -
"Tight lines!" "Good sport!" "Glenmorangie!"

Michael Daunt 1992

Fishing the Laggan Pool, River Ness.

Fishing Spey in Summer near Grantown.

The West Coast - a new way forward

by Andrew Wallace   photographs by Dr. Colin Bull

Those who regularly fish in Scotland will soon become aware of how very different the west and east coast river systems are. In many respects the west coast is a different country from the point of view of fisheries - a land of long sea-lochs and small spatey rivers running off high, often barren ground or, as in the Outer Hebrides, daisy chains of lochs linked by mere burns.

These rivers have traditionally been the preserve of runs of summer grilse and shoals of sea-trout which surge into the rivers during quick pulses of heavy water brought down by summer thunder-pumps in the hills.

West coast fishing is generally more capricious than that of the east coast and a greater measure of luck and timing is required for success. The consistency of sport that fuels the high prices of the east coast beats is rarely found on the west and this is reflected in both the reasonable cost of fishing and the ability to get hold of good fishing at relatively short notice. Fishing on the west coast is more a game of chance and some might say all the better for it.

But the very nature of this wild part of the country also carries with it a burden of problems for the fisheries manager. The rivers, being small and highly seasonal, are not great income generators. The district fishery boards - the basic unit of fisheries management in Scotland - tend to be small and hard-pressed for funds. And whilst the problems that face these fisheries are often similar in nature to those on the bigger rivers in the east, the resources to cope with them are generally limited.

Three years ago, and prompted partly by the decline in sea-trout stocks on the west coast, the West Highland Sea-Trout and Salmon Group was formed to take a long hard look at how west coast fisheries might be able to better organise themselves. The group, consisting of a wide variety of organisations with an interest in these fisheries, examined the problems and cast around for a solution.

The group found inspiration in a growing number of organisations in Scotland that had started to look rationally and methodically at issues of practical, ground-up,

Juvenile survey work using electro-fishing equipment

Foundation, Spey Research Trust, Tay Foundation and Conon District Fishery Board had all been making considerable progress through the work of their fisheries managers, using practical research techniques and these organisations were starting to come up with answers to questions that people had only been guessing at for years. Where did the spring fish spawn? Were different runs of fish genetically discrete? How much of the system was accessible to fish and where were the blockages?

The slow and painstaking process of coming up with answers to these questions has helped these systems come to sensible decisions about how best to manage stocks and have given them a credibility in the wider world of resource management that had previously been absent.

With the philosophy of integrated catchment management and the appreciation that the health of the land in any catchment surrounding a river is reflected in the health of the river, these Trusts built bridges with organisations such as Scottish Natural Heritage, the Scottish Environmental Protection Agency, the Scottish Office Freshwater Fisheries Laboratory, Scottish Hydro-Electric, the Forestry Commission, farmers etc. - in other words with all those organisations at a local and national level whose work influenced the way these catchments were managed. This has resulted in reliable and authoritative advice coming from river managers on where the problems are and how they might best be solved.

On the west coast the potential for developing these organisations would have been less obvious had it not been for the precedent of the West Galloway Fisheries Trust which demonstrated how four rivers, getting together to co-operate in their management, can be as effective and powerful as some of their bigger brothers on the east coast. The Galloway Trust, a partnership between the Rivers Luce, Cree, Bladnoch and Fleet, has now been operating for nearly a decade and is not only highly regarded by a wide variety of people and organisations but has also got to grips with many of the problems affecting the Trust's rivers.

With the Galloway Trust as a blue-print, the West Highland Sea-Trout and Salmon Group initiated the formation of five further Fisheries Trusts on the west coast: The Western Isles, West Sutherland, Wester Ross, Lochaber and District and Awe Fisheries Trusts. These all came into being in the summer of 1996, each employing a committed and well qualified fisheries biologist cum manager.

The Trusts themselves are made up of a wide variety of representatives from many different parts of the local fisheries community. Local angling clubs, proprietors, fish-farmers, schools and associated businesses are all involved and, as Trustees, have responsibility for the work of the Trusts. This has resulted in a cross-pollination of ideas and an involvement of the community in fisheries affairs.

The five Trust biologists have now been at work for almost a year and are involved in a series of local projects as well as conducting an ongoing juvenile survey programme in all the Trust rivers to try and establish what type of fish are where, and if they are not present, why .The Trusts are also analysing catch statistics in their respective areas and reorganising the way that these statistics are collected by encouraging local and visiting fishermen to supply more information about catches. Also underway are projects with local angling clubs and with schools to encourage children to take an interest in fisheries issues, including the award winning 'Salmon In The Classroom' programme which was initiated by the Galloway Trust.

In 1996 the new Trusts together with the West Galloway Fisheries Trust and the River Clyde Fisheries Management Trust, formed an Association of West Coast Fisheries Trusts (AWCFT) to represent and support its members.This association is now engaged in raising money for the Trusts, ensuring good communication between its members and assisting in the development

Dorsal fin damage by sea lice on a young sea-trout

of projects to look at issues that affect west coast fisheries, such as acidification, fish-farming and the influence of predators. The AWCFT also has a remit to take the message from west coast fisheries to the policy-makers to ensure that these fisheries are properly represented at policy-making level.

With only a year under the Trusts' belt there is still much to do and whilst expectations are likely to be high about what might be achieved, people with an interest in the west coast situation must appreciate that, at the very least, the life-cycle of the salmon requires a minimum of four years before the results of any work might be detected. Given the complexity of the situation on the west coast, it is likely that it will be many years before it is possible to say that action taken at any one given point might have resulted in more fish returning to our rivers.

Fisheries management, particularly for migratory fish, is a long game and much of the value of the Trusts will be in their ability to, over the coming years, put our own house in order, ensuring that returning fish have the best possible opportunity to spawn and their offspring thrive. Migratory fish are inevitably exposed, through much of their lives, to factors way beyond the reach of organisations such as Fisheries Trusts, such as high-seas netting and marine habitat cycles. But there is a very real hope that the case for taking action on some of these issues can be made with far more vigour, if we can demonstrate that we are looking after our home waters in the most effective way possible.

For the future, there are still a few areas on the west coast yet to be covered by the Fisheries Trust and there are moves afoot to look at the development of similar organisations in areas such as South Argyll. As the west coast becomes progressively more organised, the prospect of further co-operation with the east coast rivers increases and, in such an alliance, fisheries management issues in Scotland might assume even greater importance.

For the time being, the Trusts must concentrate on the job in hand and they will need all the support they can get from local and visiting anglers. Those visiting the west coast in 1998 might want to get in touch with the local Fisheries Trust to find out more about the work being conducted in that area, and those who return year after year might want to join the local Trust and receive regular updates on progress through Trust newsletters and reports. It is the opportunity that fishermen now have to get behind local fisheries issues through local Fisheries Trusts, that there now lies the best hope of preserving some of the finest and most intriguing fishing in the country.

GLENMORANGIE

Glenmorangie – Sponsors of the Salmon & Trout Association

During 1996, Glenmorangie launched a three year sponsorship initiative with the Salmon & Trout Association to support their new member recruitment activities at over 50 game-fishing shows and related events across the country. The company also provides a miniature of Glenmorangie 10 Years Old for every new member, helping to make the joining experience even more enjoyable!

Many of the S&TA branch meetings held regularly during the year also benefit from the association with Glenmorangie, through the provision of raffle prizes and the organisation of whisky tastings.

Glenmorangie is Scotland's best selling malt whisky. For over 150 years it has been produced by a small group of dedicated craftsmen at the historic distillery near Tain on the shores of the Dornoch Firth in Ross-shire. The craftsmen – known as 'The Sixteen Men of Tain' – use the best natural products from the surrounding environment for producing Glenmorangie. Water from the nearby Tarlogie Springs and malted barley from the Black Isle help create Glenmorangie's distinctive taste and aroma.

Glenmorangie is proud to support the S&TA and encourages all game-fishing anglers to join the Association in order to safeguard fish stocks and the sport of game-fishing for future generations.

Glenmorangie Launches Rare Limited Edition Claret Wood Finish Malt

It has been a busy year for Glenmorangie with the Company building on its reputation as the whisky industry's expert in cask management, with the introduction of its latest wood finished malt whisky.

Available in extremely limited quantities, Glenmorangie First Growth Claret Wood Finish Single Highland Malt Scotch Whisky is very special indeed.

In 1989, the Distillery Manager selected just eight casks of vintage Glenmorangie which had been laid down to mature in American white oak barrels. The vintage years were between 1976 and 1979.

This Glenmorangie was then transferred into casks which previously contained one of the great first growth clarets from Pauillac, Bordeaux. The whisky was 'finished' for eight further years in these casks, the claret wood enriching the distinctive characteristics of Scotland's favourite malt.

This launch of Glenmorangie First Growth Claret Wood Finish follows on from the success of Glenmorangie Port, Madeira and Sherry Wood Finished Malts which were introduced last year. The technique of 'wood finishing' has been pioneered by the company and it is notably one of the innovations of the malt whisky industry in recent years.

Dr. Bill Lumsden, Manager of the Glenmorangie Distillery commented: "For many years we have been experimenting with the effects of 'finishing' Glenmorangie malt whisky in barrels which have previously held other spirits – Sherry, Port and Madeira for instance. One of our most limited, and most successful trials was this 'finishing' in First Growth Claret Wood.

The result really is extremely special – a marriage of two of the world's most distinguished creations."

The packaging reflects the traditional, handcrafted values of Glenmorangie – Scotland's favourite malt – but also incorporates some elements from fine wines. Each bottle is individually numbered and signed by the Glenmorangie Distillery Manager. A neck tag, sealed with wax, contains tasting notes and the bottle is encased in a wooden box with an engraved brass plaque on the lid.

Glenmorangie Claret Wood Finish is available at Oddbins stores, priced around £89.

20 gift packs to be won in the Glenmorangie Free Prize Draw

Every reader can enter to win one of 20 gift packs of the Glenmorangie Malt Scotch Whisky Collection. This special pack of Glenmorangie miniatures contains all five Glenmorangie 'expressions' – 10 Years Old, 18 Years Old, and the unique range of three new Glenmorangie wood finished single Highland malt whiskies.

The wood finished whiskies have been matured in American oak for 12 years, then racked into casks previously containing port, sherry or Madeira. The second wood enhances the delicate taste of Glenmorangie - Scotland's best selling malt.

The Glenmorangie Collection gift packs are currently available at Oddbins and specialist outlets at a retail price of £15.99.

To enter the prize draw, just fill in your details below, enclosing the entry in an envelope and post it to Glenmorangie at the address shown.

Terms and Conditions:

Original entry forms only - No photocopies will be accepted. One entry per person. Applicants must be 18 years of age. Entries must be received by 30th September 1998. No responsibility can be taken for lost or misplaced entries. Winners will be notified by 30th November 1998. No purchase is necessary.

Glenmorangie plc, 18 Westerton Road, Broxburn, West Lothian EH52 5AQ.

Pastime/Nov 97

Name ______________________________

Address ______________________________

____

Postcode ______________ Date of Birth ______________

☐ Please enter me in the prize draw and send me more information about Glenmorangie.

Research into the age and size structure of brown trout using gill nets

USEFUL ADDRESSES FOR VISITING FISHERMEN

Western Isles Fisheries Trust,
Contact: Mark Bilsby,
Creed Lodge,
Marybank, Stornoway.
Isle of Lewis HS2 9JN.
Tel/Fax: (01851) 701526.
M.Bilsby@BTInternet.com

West Sutherland Fisheries Trust,
Contact: Dr Shona Marshall,
Gardener's Cottage,
Scourie by Lairg,
Sutherland IV27 4SX.
Tel/Fax: (01971) 502259.
Shona@WSFT.Demon.co.uk

Wester Ross Fisheries Trust,
Contact: Dr James Butler,
Rose Cottage,
Eilean Darach Estate,
by Garve,
Wester Ross IV23 2QN.
Wk Tel/Fax: (01854) 633349.
EMail: James@WRFTrust.Demon.co.uk

Lochaber & District Fisheries Trust,
Contact: Dr. Jon Watt,
Arieniskill Cottage,
Lochailort,
Inverness-shire PH38 4LZ.
Tel/Fax: (01687) 470350.
EMail:LDFTrust@Zetnet.co.uk

Awe Fisheries Trust,
Contact: Dr. Colin Bull,
The Ardchonnel Old Schoolhouse,
Eredine,
by Dalmally,
Argyll PA33 1BW.
Tel/Fax: (01866) 844293.
Email: C.BULL@ZETNET.co.uk

West Galloway Fisheries Trust,
Contact: Callum Sinclair,
12A Victoria Street,
Newton Stewart DG8 6BT.
Tel: (01671) 403011.
Fax: (01671) 402248.

River Clyde Fisheries Management Trust,
Contact: Jim MacAloon,
12 Chalmers Crescent,
Murray 7,
East Kilbride G75 0PE.
Tel: (01355) 221724.

The Ballindalloch Beat on the River Avon

The fishing belongs to Ballindalloch Estate, which is situated in Speyside 14 miles north-east of Grantown-on-Spey. The Estate is owned by the Macpherson-Grant family and is centred around Ballindalloch Castle, the family home since 1546, which is now open to the public.

This beautiful river flows out of Loch Avon in the heart of the Cairngorm mountains and joins the famous River Spey beside Ballindalloch Castle. The Estate owns the first six miles of the River Avon (pronounced A'an) from its junction with the River Spey to the march with the Crown Estate at the Alt na Criche burn on the left bank. The Avon is the largest tributary of the Spey and attracts good runs of Salmon, Grilse and Seatrout. These migratory fish normally start appearing in the river in late April and the fishing season ends on the 30th September annually.

The Avon is an intriguing river to fish. The fast flowing clear water does not yield up its secrets easily. The rocky pools have numerous individual lies and the streamy water is particularly attractive for fly fishing. Flies such as Silver Stoat, Garry Dog, Munro Killer, Stoat's Tail and Ally's Shrimp sizes 8 to 12 fished with an 11-14 foot rod are recommended. Spinning is only permitted if the conditions are unsuitable for the fly. Please read the attached Fishing Rules.

Over four miles of the best water with fishing on both banks from Livet Mouth downstream to Fire Pump Pool below the Bridge of Avon have been divided up into six beats known as the Lower Beats. Each beat is fished by two rods on a daily rota system. There are over 30 named pools on these beats all of which may be fished twice during a weeks stay at Ballindalloch. Good access to the river has been provided for vehicles and most beats have smallfishing huts. Guests are provided with maps and rotas and are shown where to fish. There is a fishing Ghillie on hand to help newcomers to the river. From the march with the Crown Estate downstream to the Livet Mouth the fishing is from the left bank only. This stretch of water is known as Beat A and is let separately. Worming is permitted on Beat A up to 31st August.

The fishing is let by the week, but day permits may be issued if there are any rods available. Day permits are normally let on Beat A. Each month of the season has its attractions. In May when the wild cherry blossom is out Strathavon looks at its best and there is the exciting prospect of catching a large fresh run spring salmon. June and July see the main runs of grilse and seatrout and the long hours of daylight in these northern latitudes make it possible to fish all night. In August and September the river holds its full complement of summer fish and large catches can be made if the water conditions are right. For further details contact:

The Estates Office,
Ballindalloch,
Banffshire AB37 9AX
Tel: (01807) 500205
Fax: (01807) 500210

The Delnashaugh Inn

The Delnashaugh Inn also belongs to the Estate. Conveniently situated near the river at the Bridge of Avon, the hotel has established a good reputation with visiting fishermen and has a well-equipped rod room with deep freeze.

The hotel is under the personal supervision of the proprietors David and Marion Ogden, who offer special terms to guests taking a weeks fishing on the River Avon.

Enquiries about accommodation should be addressed to Mr. Ogden at the hotel on Tel.no: **(01807) 500255.**

Delnashaugh Inn

Borgie Lodge Hotel

Borgie Lodge Hotel, located on the north coast of Sutherland is a haven for the discerning angler as there is a great variety of quality fishing on offer to guests. The Borgie is a gem of a salmon river which flows through Loch Loyal, Loch Craggie and Loch Slaim. These lochs provide a necessary safe area for the spring fish, especially in summers of low rainfall. The Borgie Lodge Hotel is set in a quiet secluded Highland glen on the banks of the River Borgie. Peter and Jacqui MacGregor offer their guests a comfortable and welcoming stay.
Telephone for further details:

Borgie Lodge Hotel,
Skerray, Tongue,
Sutherland.
Tel/Fax: (01641) 521332.

The Dumfries & Galloway fishing experience

One of the slogans the Tourist Board uses to promote Dumfries and Galloway is *Scotland's best kept holiday secret*. If you are a convinced salmon or sea-trout fisher, you may disagree with it for the rivers of the region have long been famed for their prodigious runs of sea-trout and greyback Solway salmon. The region has five major game fishing rivers.

Starting in the east of the region, you'll find the ***Border Esk*** - best known for its fighting sea-trout but with equally impressive runs of salmon. Then comes the ***Annan,*** flowing down through beautiful Annandale. Further east still comes the ***Nith***, flowing down Nithsdale, past Sanquahar and Thornhill, through the spectacularly beautiful grounds of Drumlanrig Castle.

Head on westwards, to the ***Urr***, the ***Kirkcudbrightshire Dee***, and the ***Fleet***, these are all worthwhile game fishing rivers with much sporting potential. A little further west is the ***Cree*** which flows down through the Galloway hills to join the Solway Firth. The last major game fishing river to the west is the ***Bladnoch***, flowing into Wigtown Bay. Until very recently

Old Bridge of Urr, on river Urr.

Dumfries and Galloway did not attract many fishermen looking for coarse fishing and the species taken were mainly pike and perch. Things have changed considerably - and whilst there are still very good specimens of pike and perch to be caught - there is also a wide choice of other species providing good sport.

There are waters offering fishing for carp, perch, pike, rudd or tench. There are large bream in ***Castle Loch*** at Lochmaben and carp and tench at ***Craighlaw Fisheries*** near Newton Stewart. Angling for coarse fish has become popular across the region and provides sport for many visiting anglers. ***Loch Ken*** supports a fine stock of large pike and is also noted for its roach.

It is little wonder that the coastline of Dumfries and Galloway has attracted sea anglers from all over Britain for many years. Dogfish, bass, conger, mackerel, and pollack provide good sport in the local waters.

Sea angling around Luce Bay, the Irish Sea and the Mull of Galloway is available on board the "Cimmaron" from Drummore. The boat is equipped for up to 12 persons, D.O.T. and N.F.C.S. qualified skipper.
Tel: (01557) 330337.

If you would like a copy of the Dumfries & Galloway Tourist Board Holiday and Accommodation Guide call the Brochure Request Line: (0990) 134948 (calls are charged at local rates.)

Salmon fishing, the Middle Dee.

Spey in Summer.

Fishing around the Western Islands of Scotland

by Duncan Swinbanks

The waters around the Western Islands of Scotland are teeming with fish. Pollock, coalfish, codling, fast-moving tope shoals of haddock and ton-up skate are typical of what the angler may expect. However, angling varies dramatically throughout the year.

During January, February and March there is little inshore activity. This is fortunate, as the weather can be very unsettled and gales are common place. April can be a bumper month for skate, but only if the angler is fortunate enough to charter a suitable boat and skipper.

It must be emphasised that few angling boats are experienced enough to cope with offshore conditions at this time of year therefore expert advice is essential. April and May are poor months for fish such as cod, haddock and whiting which are spawning. Favourite marks often fail to produce results and if fish are caught they tend to be immature or out of condition. During June, the weather is the best of the year with sunny and calm conditions providing ideal angling opportunities. The deeper offshore marks produce fish, especially giant skate and biting pollock. The absence of summer spur dogfish gives an added advantage of baits left untouched while waiting for their huge cousins. By the advent of summer, most species have finished spawning and the shoals, with the coalfish first to arrive, move inshore to search for food.Small fish inhabit the reefs, while larger specimens feed on the sand eel shoals. By the end of July, bottom fish have dispersed over the fishing grounds and haddock, codling, ling and pollock are numerous. More voracious fish such as spurdogs form hunting packs following the bait fish which move from area to area.

During August and September, summer visitors and warmer water fish frequent the marks. Tope patrol gullies and turbot settle on the banks and halibut and shark can turn up anywhere but as yet their migration patterns remain a puzzle. Boat and shore angling now continues at a peak until November when the water begins to cool and fish move back to the deep. Still, frosty

Big bait, big hook (Seamaster 10/o)

Double Boom and Red Gurnard

days in December can give good catches, especially cod and flatfish. The visiting angler should bring a light and a heavy boat rod; reels loaded with 20 and 50 lbs line. For shore fishing, tackle such as a medium beachcaster and a spinning rod are ideal. The latter is very important as this can be used from the rocks or to sample some of the excellent fresh water sport available. Many island rivers and lochs allow spinning or bait fishing which is the preferred method of angling by a large number of locals. A salmon taken from a small spate river on a worm or a big brownie caught in a hill loch on a spinner is a thrilling experience. The best brown trout fishing tends to be in May and June while salmon arrive from July on until October.

In the clear northern seas, fish baits such as mackerel or sand eel and artificial lures, e.g feathers, spinners etc normally catch most fish. The Western Islands of Scotland form an area of unequalled scenic beauty. Rugged, mist-shrouded peaks, deep heather-sided glens and dark enchanted lochs. The shore is rocky with many inlets and sandy bays and long saltwater lochs strike deep into the countryside. The Islands have a relatively mild climate because of the Gulf Stream. Fortunately for the angler, rain in the coastal zones can be half that of a few miles inland. The effect can be even more noticeable at sea. On many occasions, a day's sunshine can be enjoyed afloat while watching rainclouds hanging over the home port. And remember - if rain and wind do prevent putting to sea there are many rivers and burns which, especially when in spate, yield great catches of salmon and sea trout. The cost of day's fishing on these waters will seldom exceed the price of a boat trip.

Hundreds of thousands of people now visit the Western Islands of Scotland and this has led to many improvements: roads have been upgraded, hotel accommodation increased and roll-on roll-off car ferries introduced. For example, Oban, Gateway to the Islands is now only two and a half hours drive from Glasgow. Developments such as these are widespread and of immense benefit to the angler. Remember, however, that this is a remote and rugged area and although small villages are numerous, larger towns are uncommon. Thus sea-angling centres, boats, tackle shops and suitable accommodation are mainly limited to these towns. However, just about every local is an angler (or knows one) and is never slow to give advice to a willing ear!

Pollack caught on KF Super Spreader 200

Fishing on the 'Road to the Isles'

by John Brown, Chairman of the Rannoch and District Angling Club

I have fond memories of my early days fishing. With a cane as a rod and a green string as a line, a bent pin as a hook and a box full of garden worms I used to take to the water.

I spent some of my happiest days on the local hill burns, especially after heavy rainstorms. We all have our childhood memories. Some of us remember Christmas, though my mind always goes back to the start of the trout fishing season. I started fishing with a cast of two wet flies on the River Tummel below Dunalastair Dam. After studying the movement of fish, I decided to try the art of Dry Fly fishing. After a while I got very keen on this type of fishing and hence began a lifetime hobby, during which I have had some extremely good times, and have often put my rod by the side of Loch Rannoch and let my worries pass me by. Kinloch Rannoch is at the fishing centre of Scotland, and has a very large range of Lochs and rivers. Just down from my garden gate lies the Tummel, a perfect river that runs due east into the Dunalastair reservoir, and a river where I have often been successful with the dry "Greenwell Glory"

The centre of fishing activity has undoubtedly always been the Dunalastair Hotel. Hotel records date back over a hundred years and are full of some more than impressive catches. One fisherman staying at the Dunalastair Hotel one hundred years ago wrote 'Loch Rannoch is a lovely spot and the view from the village is magnificent. You can see the whole length, 12 miles, of the loch and in certain conditions of the atmosphere, the mirage is wonderful; it looks as though the loch were coming right on top of you. He states as equally fine 'Schiehallion' a sugar-loaf mountain towering on the South side, with Dunalastair and Killiekrankie in the distance. The river Tummel flows out of Loch Rannoch and winds its way down to Dunalastair reservoir.'

'To resume my experiences' he states, 'very large trout are occasionally to be caught on the loch. The most consistent areas of the Loch were from Tower bay down to Finnart point. The former being named after a fortress that can still be seen in the middle of the loch and was originally built as a prison.' This gentleman whilst staying at the Dunalastair, also tried dry fly fishing on the Tummel and had some considerable

Dunalastair Hotel

success at Ballinloan and at the 'Doctor's Pool', where he must have seen several good trout rising. I put on a Greenwell and began casting upstream, successfully casting over arising fish. It was not long before I had secured several trout, one fully 1lb in weight.

Before leaving the Dunalastair Hotel and on the subject of "Rannoch", he states 'I must tell you the story of Stuart Campbell, an old highland shepherd'. Stuart had told his friends that he had the faith of St. Peter and was able to walk on water! One evening, and after a good few drams, Stuart announced his intention to cross the 'Doctor's Pool', a very deep place in the River Tummel. Sure enough the next morning, accompanied by his friends of the night before, he went to the pool. He stepped out, confidently, from the river bank, only to get the best ducking that he had ever had. When he rose to the surface, he sang out 'Stuart Campbell, nae mair'! Lovely memories of Loch Rannoch he writes!

The years to 1970 were extremely good for fishing in the Rannoch area though the number of wild brown trout has steadily been declining. The local Rannoch and District Angling Club, of which I am secretary, in conjunction with the Loch Rannoch Conservation Association now has its own hatchery from which we breed young brown trout and, when they are of mature age, release them into Loch Rannoch and Dunalastair reservoir. The hatchery has been up and running now for ten years, consequently the numbers of brown trout in the Loch is on the increase. Loch Rannoch and Loch Garry also hold large stocks of char. These are not so well known fish, though anglers are taking an interest in the fish.

A recent survey carried out by Glasgow University shows large stocks of this species and has concluded that it may well be a fish to watch in the future. In fact, their survey showed that Loch Rannoch was the best loch in Britain and was second to only one in the Northern Hemisphere. The years from 1995 have shown average catches of brown trout are again on the increase and there has been a great deal of large fish caught. The most recent a brown trout of 15lbs 2 ozs taken on a size 10 March Brown fly, caught from the shore of the South side of Loch Rannoch. It would appear that the better than average seasons are beginning to return. So long as anglers obey the regulations that are printed on the permits, Loch Rannoch and surrounding lochs should continue to be a popular Scottish destination. As for me, I still enjoy the odd outing with the local club and am delighted to be able to fish these magnificent waters. Tight lines to all anglers that fish the Rannoch area, it really is, apart from the midges, a beautiful area to fish.

Loch Tummel

'On the Road to the Isles', Loch Tummel is easily accessible on both the North and South shores. It is approximately seven miles long and one mile wide. It contains stocks of brown trout, pike and perch. The average weight of brown trout is 10ozs, but larger fish of two to three pounds are not uncommon. Standard patterned flies are best. Trout of 9 inches must be returned

Loch Bhac

Lies in the Allean Forest. Fishing is managed by Pitlochry Angling Club. It is regularly stocked with both rainbow and brown trout. The average weight is about 1lb, though larger fish of around 4lb have been taken. Standard loch flies such as blae and black and black pernal and Peter Ross are strong favourites. Permits available from Mitchell's Tackle Shop, Pitlochry or from J. Brown, The Square ,Kinloch Rannoch. Fish under 10 inches must be returned. Fly Fishing only.

Loch Kimardochy

This loch lies in the area of Kinloch Rannoch on the Road to Schiehallion and is, again, managed by Pitlochry Angling Club. It is regularly stocked with brown trout, the average weight being about 1lb. Fishing is by boat only and electric outboards are not allowed. Standard loch pattern flies are best, with black flies as favourites. Permits are available as for Loch Bhac. Fish under 10 oz must be returned. Fly fishing only.

Dunalastair Water

Dunalastair Water is a flooded area of the river Tummel between Kinloch Rannoch and Tummelbridge. It holds stocks of large brown trout, pike and perch. It is approximately one and a half miles long by half a mile wide and is quite shallow in places. The average weight is about 2 lbs but recently fish of 6lbs have been taken. It is regularly stocked by brown trout from the hatcheries managed by Loch Rannoch Conservation Association. Standard loch flies are best with Peter Ross and Zulu's favourites along with black flies. Dunalastair is a lovely place to fish as it lies at the foot of Schiehallion, the fairy mountain. Permits are available from Dunalastair Estate and Dunalastair Hotel. Fly fishing only for trout and fish under 10 inches must be returned. Please note boat fishing only. Boats available from Dunalastair Hotel.

River Tummel

River Tummel flows from Loch Rannoch to Loch Tummel and has some splendid pools for trout fishing. The river is ideal for the dry fly angler. Trout fishing by fly only. Fish under 10 inches must be returned.

Loch Rannoch

Continuing on the Road to the Isles, Loch Rannoch is eleven miles long and a mile wide. It is easily accessible by road on the North and South Shores. It is managed by Loch Rannoch Conservation Association and holds stocks of brown trout, perch, pike and char. It is regularly stocked with trout from LRCA's hatcheries. The average weight is about 1lb, but many larger trout have been taken. 1997 saw a brown trout weighing 15lb 2ozs being caught on Loch Rannoch on a March Brown no.10 fly. Standard loch pattern flies are best with Wickam's fancy, Grouse and Claret, and Peter Ross as favourites along with black flies. Bank permits for fly fishing are available from shops and hotels in Kinloch Rannoch. Boats are available from Loch Rannoch Hotel. The Dunalastair Hotel displays many fine specimens of large fish caught locally over the past 100 years. Loch Rannoch still proves the most popular loch with anglers. Fish under 10 inches must be returned.

Brown trout 15 lb 2 oz taken on a size 10 march brown fly from Loch Rannoch

Loch Eigheach

Again on the Road to the Isles, Loch Eigheach west of Loch Rannoch, close to Rannoch Station is approximately two miles long by three quarters of a mile wide. It is managed by Rannoch and District Angling Club. Bank fishing only by fly is permitted. The average weight is about 5ozs. Many larger trout to about 7lbs have been taken over the years. Standard loch flies are best with Grouse and Claret and Green, along with black flies are favourites. Fish under 9 inches must be returned. The loch also has a small number of perch. Permits are available from a number of local outlets.

Loch Laidon

Loch Laidon is a long, narrow loch, which flows from Glencoe in the west towards Rannoch Station in the east. It is surrounded by moorland and is a true paradise for nature lovers. It holds large stocks of brown trout. The average weight is about 5ozs, though much larger trout have been taken out. Standard loch flies are best with fish taking almost any pattern. Permits are available from numerous sources in the Rannoch Station area. No size or catch limits in operation.

Ferox anglers at Rannoch

The Artic Char of Loch Rannoch

More than a century after Sir James Maitland first described an unusual form of Arctic char, which he named Salvelinus struanensis, in Loch Rannoch, Perthshire, scientists from the Freshwater Fisheries Laboratory at Pitlochry found that he had missed at least another.

Exploratory netting with modern, fine-meshed gill nets, able to be set to fish sunk along the bed as well as floating at the surface, revealed the presence of two distinct types of char which later studies showed were genetically distinct from one another. Maitland's struanensis form, a small-headed, claret-coloured morph which feeds mainly on zooplanktonic Cladocera, was still present.

The other type of char, a paler fish with larger head and jaws, was shown to eat a wider range of invertebrates and also other fish. Whereas the claret char ranges the open water in a pelagic life-style, the pale char is benthic (bottom-living) in habit, tending to stay a little deeper than its main competitor the brown trout, which also feeds on the same wide range of animals living on the bed of the loch, as well as on plankton and insect larvae in the open water and on insects emerging at the surface or blown in from the surrounding land. While most of the trout remain quite small (about 250-300g), some grow much larger and become specialist predators (ferox), feeding to some extent cannibalistically but mainly on the char. Each year, a few large ferox weighing 5-7kg are caught in Loch Rannoch by specialist anglers patiently trolling with large natural and artificial fish baits, but many fruitless hours are spent trying to catch them. Even so, specimens of up to 10kg were recorded last century and, who knows, some of this size may still be present as even bigger ferox than this have been caught recently in Loch Awe. Other fish species found in Loch Rannoch include perch and pike, which are relatively scarce and localised and salmon and eels which only reach the loch in small numbers, passing numerous natural and man-made barriers on their journey up from the sea by the River Tay and its major tributary the Tummel. Three-spined sticklebacks and minnows make up the remaining species, but char are probably the most common fish in the loch.

After the initial study in the 1980s established the presence of the two main forms, further research by the Department of Zoology of the University of Glasgow, has shown that the pale, bottom-feeding char living in the main body of the loch and in the smaller basin at its head, near Bridge of Gaur, are themselves separable by careful body measurements. The Glasgow University studies also confirmed that the three types spawn separately in different areas of the loch, only in the autumn/early winter, unlike the two forms of char in Lake Windermere, one of which spawns in autumn, the other in late winter. The claret char of Loch Rannoch lay their eggs in gravel redds along the shelving sides of the main loch, whereas the pale char living in the same main basin spawn in gently flowing water such as the Dall Burn. Likewise, the pale char living in the basin at the head of the loch spawn in shallow, running water in the lower River Gaur. By setting fyke-nets for ripe specimens at spawning time, fertilised eggs were obtained for rearing trials which showed striking behavioural differences between the progeny of the different forms, providing further evidence of their genetic divergence. At the same age, the claret, pelagic-feeding, shoaling form made greater use of the water column in the tanks and were less aggressive to one another than the pale form which normally feeds on the bed of the loch.

Although there are many examples in the scientific literature from other countries of multiple forms of char within the same water body, the complex of char forms in Loch Rannoch was the first example of this phenomenon found in Scotland. Since then, divided populations of char have been identified in several other large Scottish lochs and char resembling the pale form from Rannoch have been captured in Lochs Tummel and Ericht.

Few people are aware that we have at least two hundred char populations in this country, or know much about them. As the name "Arctic" suggests, they are well-adapted to the rigorous environment of northerly and alpine fresh waters. In fact they are a circumpolar species which also exists in sea-going form extending southwards to the approximate limit of sea ice in winter. South of this limit only freshwater-resident populations occur. Thus, while we have no sea-run char nowadays, they must have been common during the Pleistocene retreat of the last ice age.

With general climate warming, all of our char populations became landlocked, although some in lochs in the Hebrides are only just above sea level. The species is much rarer farther south in the UK and Ireland, although notable among them and mentioned earlier are those of Lake Windermere in the English Lake District which have been extensively studied by the Freshwater Biological Association, now part of the Institute of Freshwater Ecology. There is still a small char fishery for the table market in Windermere, the traditional

plumb-line and small, brightly flashing spoons, although most of the char are now taken by the prosaic means of maggot-baited hooks and swim-feeder cast out from the shore. In contrast, the pale char from Loch Rannoch has pale flesh with little taste, but the claret form is excellent, the flesh colour often being bright orange, although they are fairly small, with a mean weight of only about 150g. Even so, char of this size are popular for the table in other countries, notably in Iceland and Norway, where there is a strong tradition of commercial netting of freshwater lakes and where ice-fishing is a great social occasion during winter. Our ice tends to be a little more precarious.

At present, perhaps partly through ignorance of their existence, or due to their specialised feeding behaviour, relatively few char are caught by anglers at Loch Rannoch, yet many are taken by fly-fishing in neighbouring Loch Garry where, on some days it is necessary to fish deep to find them, while on others, typically on still, summer evenings, they shoal in great numbers at the surface. Although often abundant, the char in most Highland lochs tend to be small like those from Rannoch and for many years the British rod-caught record was only about a kilo (Loch Insh). However, with the recent development of cage rearing of Atlantic salmon smolts and rainbow trout in freshwater lochs, resulting in an increase in local biological productivity and a new direct source of food in the form of pellets which fall through the meshes, there has been a steady increase in the char record. The present provisional record is one of more than 10 pounds (ca. 4.55kg) from Loch Arkaig in Inverness-shire.

Not surprisingly, there is a developing interest in intensive artificial culture of char as the species has been found to thrive in cool water in crowded freshwater tanks and cages and, as already stated, it is highly marketable. Sadly, although this is an interesting development which may support some extra employment in the Highlands, it increases the risk of losing some of the rich genetic diversity of char forms which have developed in long-term geographic isolation, like those only recently discovered in Loch Rannoch, through the unconsidered or accidental release of cultivated and introduced strains. Anglers can help to identify waters which still contain particularly interesting types of char and by supporting efforts to conserve these beautiful and intriguing fish for future generations.

For further information contact:
A. F. Walker,
The Freshwater Fisheries Laboratory,
Pitlochry,
Perthshire PH16 5LB.

Useful Addresses in Scottish Sport Fisheries

Scottish Tourist Board	23 Ravelston Ter, Edinburgh EH4 3EU. Tel: 0131-332 2433.
Department of Agriculture & Fisheries for Scotland	Pentland House, 47 Robb's Loan, Edinburgh EH14 1TY. Tel: 0131-244 6015.
Inspector of Salmon Fisheries	Pentland House, (Room 407) 47 Robb's Loan, Edinburgh EH14 1TY. Tel: 0131-244 6227.
S.O.A.F.D.	Officer in Charge, Freshwater Fisheries Laboratory, Faskally, Pitlochry PH16 5LB. Tel: (01796) 472060. Fax: (01796)473523.
S.O.A.F.D. Marine Laboratory	P.O. Box 101, Victoria Rd, Aberdeen AB11 8DB. Tel: (01224) 295511.
Scottish Environment Protection Agency	1 South St, Perth PH2 8NJ. Tel: (01738) 627989.
Scottish Sports Council	Caledonia House, South Gyle, Edinburgh EH12 9DQ. Tel: 0131-317 7200.
Scottish Natural Heritage	12 Hope Ter, Edinburgh EH9 2AS. Tel: 0131-447 4784.
Forest Enterprise	Howard Hart, Information Officer, 231 Corstorphine Rd, Edinburgh EH12 7AT. Tel: 0131-314 6494.
Scottish Hydro-Electric plc	10 Dunkeld Rd, Perth PH1 5WA. Freephone: 0800 300000.
Scottish Anglers' National Association	Administrative Office, Caledonia House, South Gyle, Edinburgh EH12 9DQ. Tel: 0131-339 8808.
Federation of Highland Angling Clubs	K. MacDonald, Secretary, 13 Swanston Ave, Inverness IV3 6QW. Tel: (01463) 240095.
Institute of Ecology and Resource Management, REIM (Forestry),	University of Edinburgh, Darwin Buildings, The Kings Buildings, Mayfield Rd, Edinburgh EH9 3JU. Tel: 0131-650 1000.
Institute of Aquaculture	University of Stirling, Stirling FK9 4LA. Tel: (01786) 473171.

BORDERS

RIVERS AND LOCHS

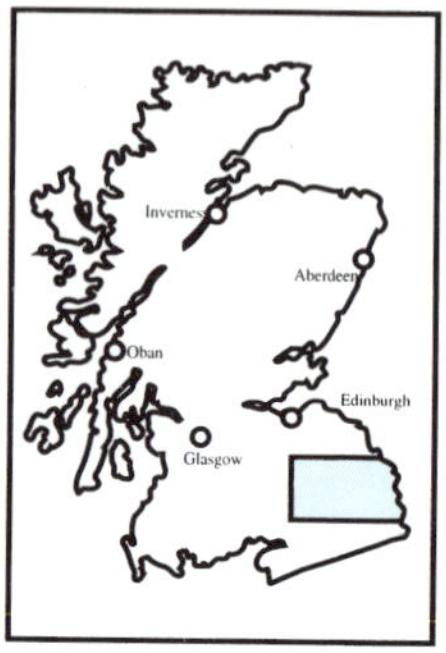

Area Tourist Board
Scottish Borders Tourist Board
Director of Tourism,
Scottish Borders Tourist Board,
70 High Street,
Selkirk TD7 4DD.
Tel: (01750) 20555.

River Purification Board
Tweed River Purification Board
Burnbrae,
Mossilee Road,
Galashiels.
Tel: (01896) 752425.

Water	Location	Species	Season	Permit available from	Other information
Blackadder (Map IV F4)	Greenlaw	Brown Trout	1 Apr. to 6 Oct.	Greenlaw Angling Club T. Waldie, 26 East High St., Greenlaw TD10 6UF. All hotels.	No bait fishing until 1st May. Sunday fishing. No spinning.
Bowmont Water	Morebattle	Trout Grayling	15 Mar. to 6 Oct.	Keith Rothwell, Eildon View, Mainsfield Ave., Morebattle TD5 8QP. Tel: (01573) 44247.	No ground baiting. No Sunday fishing from Primeside Mill up.
Eden Water	Kelso	Brown Trout	1 Apr. to 30 Sep.	Forrest & Sons, 40 The Square, Kelso. Tel: (01573) 224687. Intersport, 43 The Square, Kelso. Tel: (01573) 223381. Border Hotel, Woodmarket, Kelso TD5 7AX. Tel: (01573) 224791.	Fly only. No spinning. Restricted to 3 rods.
	Gordon	Brown Trout	15 Mar. to 6 Oct.	J.H. Fairgrieve, Burnbrae, Gordon. Tel: (01573) 410357.	No spinning. No Sunday fishing.
Ettrick & Yarrow (Map IV E4)	Bowhill	Salmon Trout	1 Feb. to 30 Nov. 15 Mar. to 30 Sep.	Buccleuch Estates Ltd., Estate Office, Bowhill, Selkirk. Tel: (01750) 20753.	Tweed Rules. No Sunday Fishing.
	Selkirk	Brown Trout	1 Apr. to 30 Sep.	P. & E. Scott (Newsagent), 6 High Street, Selkirk. Tel: (01750) 20749.	Night fishing (15 May to 14 Sep.). Week ticket only. No minnows or spinning. No Sunday fishing.
Ettrick (Map IV D5)	Ettrick Bridge	Brown Trout Salmon	1 Apr. to 30 Sep. 1 Feb. to 30 Nov.	Ettrickshaws Hotel. Tel: (01750) 52229.	Packed lunches and flasks for residents. Permits also available for other waters.
Kale Water	Eckford	Trout Grayling	1 Apr. to 30 Sep.	Mr. Graham, Eckford Cottage, Eckford, Kelso. Tel: (01835) 850255.	No Sunday fishing.
	Morebattle	Trout Grayling	15 Mar. to 6 Oct.	Keith Rothwell, Eildon View, Mainsfield Ave., Morebattle TD5 8QP. Tel: (01573) 44247. Templehall Hotel, Morebattle.	No ground baiting. No Sunday fishing.

Water	Location	Species	Season	Permit available from	Other information
Leader Water (Map IV E4)	Lauderdale	Trout	15 Mar. to 6 Oct.	M. & I. Rattray (Newsagent), Lauder. J.S. Main, Saddler, 87 High Street, Haddington. Tel: (01620) 822148. Lauder Post Office. Tower Hotel, Oxton, by Lauder. Tel: (01578) 750235. Anglers Choice, 23 Market Square, Melrose TD6 9PL. Tel: (01896) 823070.	No spinning. Sunday fishing. No grayling fishing.
Leader Water/ Tweed	Earlston	Trout	15 Mar. to 30 Sep.	Earlston Angling Assoc., C.T. Austin, 23 Summerfield, Earlston. Tel: (01896) 849548. D. & B. Welsh Newsagents, The Square, Earlston. E. & R. Anderson Newsagent, The Square, Earlston. Tel: (01896) 849330. Anglers Choice, 23 Market Square, Melrose. Tel: (01896) 823070. Hotels and pubs.	No Sunday fishing. Other restrictions as per permit.
Liddle Water	Newcastleton	Sea Trout	1 May to 30 Sep.	J.D. Ewart, Fishing Tackle Shop, Newcastleton. Tel: (01387) 375257.	Day and weekly tickets available.
	South Roxburgh-shire	Salmon Sea Trout Brown Trout	1 Feb. to 31 Oct. 15 Apr. to 30 Sep. 1 May to 30 Sep.	Esk & Liddle Fisheries, R.J.B. Hill, Bank of Scotland Buildings, Langholm. Tel: (013873) 80428. George Graham, Hagg-on-Esk, Old School, Canonbie. Tel: (013873) 71416.	Spinning allowed until 14 April and otherwise only when water is above markers at Newcastleton, Kershopefoot and Penton Bridges. No Sunday fishing.
Lyne Water	Tweed Junction to Flemington Bridge	Trout Grayling	1 Apr. to 30 Sep.	Peeblesshire Trout Fishing Assoc., D.G. Fyfe, 39 High Street, Peebles.Tel: (01721) 720131. Tweeddale Tackle Centre, 1 Bridgegate, Peebles.Tel: (01721) 720979. Sonny's Sports Shop, Innerleithen.Tel: (01896) 830806. Tweed Valley Hotel, Walkerburn EH43 6A A.Tel: (01896) 870636. J. Dickson & Son, 21 Frederick Street, Edinburgh.Tel: 0131-225 4218. Crook Inn, Tweedsmuir.Tel: (01899) 880272.	No Sunday fishing. No spinning. No bait fishing April & September. Tickets also cover Tweed.
Oxnam Water	Morebattle	Trout Grayling	15 Mar. to 6 Oct.	Keith Rothwell, Eildon View,Mainsfield Ave., Morebattle TD5 8QP. Tel: (01573) 44247.	No ground baiting. No Sunday fishing from Bloodylaws up.
Teviot (Map IV E5)	Above Chesters	Salmon Sea Trout	1 Feb. to 30 Nov.	The Pet Store, Union Street, Hawick. Tel: (01450) 373543.	All rules and regulations on ticket. Limited to 9 rods on 3 beats per day. (9 day tickets Mon–Fri. 6 visitor season tickets only on application to:) Mr. R. Kohler, Hawick Angling Club, 8 Twirlees Terrace, Hawick. Tel: (01450) 373903.

Water	Location	Species	Season	Permit available from	Other information
	Eckford	Salmon Sea Trout Brown Tro	1 Feb. to 30 Nov. 15 Mar. to 30 Sep.	Mr. Graham, Eckford Cottage, Eckford, Kelso. Tel: (01835) 850255.	No Sunday fishing. Limited to 4 day permits. Bait and spinning 15 Feb. to 15 Sep. only. Spinning for trout and grayling prohibited.
Teviot Cont.	Jedforest	Salmon Trout	1 Feb. to 30 Nov. 1 Apr. to 30 Sep.	Jedforest Angling Assoc., J. Tait, 9 Boundaries, Jedburgh TD8 6EX. Tel: (01835) 863871. Shaws (Newsagent), 10 Canongate, Jedburgh. Tel: (01835) 863245.	No Sunday fishing. Salmon: 6 rods per day. Spinning 15 Feb. to 14 Sep. Fly only 15 Sep. to 30 Nov. No Sunday fishing.
	Kelso	Brown Trout Grayling	1 Apr. to 30 Sep.	Forrest & Sons, 40 The Square, Kelso. Tel: (01573) 224687. Intersport, 43 The Square, Kelso. Tel: (01573) 223381. Border Hotel, Woodmarket, Kelso TD5 7AX. Tel: (01573) 224791.	No Sunday fishing. Restrictions on spinning. No maggots or ground bait. Size limit 10".
Teviot (and Ale Slitrig Borthwick Rule)	Hawick	Brown Trout Salmon	15 Mar. to 30 Sep. 1 Feb. to 30 Nov.	The Pet Store, 1 Union Street, Hawick. Tel: (01450) 373543.	All rules and regulations on ticket.
Tweed (and Teviot) (Map IV F4)	Kelso	Brown Trout Coarse Fish	1 Apr. to 30 Sep.	Forrest & Sons, 40 The Square, Kelso. Tel: (01573) 224687.	
Tweed (Map IV F4)	Peeblesshire (substantial stretch of river)	Trout Grayling	1 Apr. to 30 Sep.	Peeblesshire Trout Fishing Assoc., Blackwood & Smith w.s., 39 High Street, Peebles EH45. Tel: (01721) 720131. Tweed Valley Hotel, Walkerburn EH43 6AA. Tel: (01896) 870636. F. & D. Simpson, 28/30 West Preston Street, Edinburgh EH8 9PZ.Tel: 0131-667 3058. J. Dickson & Son, 21 Frederick Street, Edinburgh. Tel: 0131-225 4218.	No spinning. No bait fishing April & September. No Sunday fishing. Tickets also cover Lyne Water. Fly only on Tweed from Lynefoot upstream. New catch and release policy for native trout. Bag limit for stocked trout.
	Clovenfords (Peel Water)	Salmon Sea Trout	1 Feb. to 30 Nov.	J.H. Leeming ARICS, Salmon Fishing Agent, Stichill House, Kelso TD5 7TB.. FREEPHONE: 0800 387675. Office: (01573) 470280. Fax: (01573) 470259.	Half mile single bank. 2 rods. Spinning or fly 15 Feb. to 14 Sep. Fly only 15 Sep. to 30 Nov.
	Coldstream (West Learmouth Beat)	Salmon Grilse Sea Trout	1 Feb. to 30 Nov.	J.H. Leeming ARICS, Salmon Fishing Agent, Stichill House, Kelso TD5 7TB. 24hr Information Service. FREEPHONE: 0800 387675. Office: (01573) 470280. Fax: (01573) 470259.	2/3 of a mile of south bank. Average catch 238 fish. No spinning before 15 Feb. or after 15 Sep.
	Cornhill	Salmon Sea Trout	1 Feb. to 30 Nov.	Tilmouth Park Hotel, Cornhill-on-Tweed, Northumberland TD12 4UU. Tel: (01890) 882255.	No Sunday fishing. Boats and ghillies available. Special terms for residents.
	Galashiels (Fairnilee Beat)	Salmon Sea Trout	(salmon) 1 Feb. to 30 Nov.	J.H. Leeming ARICS, Salmon Fishing Agent, Stichill House, Kelso TD5 7TB. 24hr Information Service. FREEPHONE: 0800 387675. Office: (01573) 470280.	3.5 miles single bank. . Ghillies, rod room, hut, boat and full facilities. No spinning before 15 Feb. or after 15 Sep.

Water	Location	Species	Season	Permit available from	Other information
Tweed cont.		Trout	1 Apr. to 30 Sep.	Messrs. J. & A. Turnbull, 30 Bank Street, Galashiels. Tel: (01896) 753191. Anglers Choice, 23 Market Square, Melrose TD6 9PL. Tel: (01896) 823070.	No Sunday fishing. Day tickets available on Saturdays. No spinning.
	Galashiels (Boleside Beat)	Salmon Sea Trout	Feb. to Nov.	J.H. Leeming ARICS, Salmon Fishing Agent, Stichill Ho e, Kelso TD5 7TB. 24hr Information Service. Tel: 0800 387675 .Office: (01573)470280. Fax: (01573) 470259.	1.5 miles of double bank with 9 named pools Boleside is regarded as one of the top Tweed beats. Average catch: 419. 2 boats available.
	Galashiels (Netherbarns Beat)	Sea Trout Salmon	Feb. to Nov.	J.H. Leeming ARICS, Salmon Fishing Agent, Stichill House, Kelso TD5 7TB. 24hr Information Service. FREEPHONE: 0800 387675. Office: (01573) 470280. Fax: (01573) 470259.	The beat forms the bottom part of Boleside Fishings and is about half a mile of double bank fishing. Average catch 33 .No boats.
	Horncliffe (Tweedhill Beat)	Salmon Sea Trout	1 Feb. to 30 Nov.	J.H. Leeming ARICS, Salmon Fishing Agent, Stichill House, Kelso TD5 7TB. 24hr Information Service. FREEPHONE: 0800 387675. Office: (01573) 470280. Fax: (01573) 470259.	3 miles of single bank. Some tidal water. Average catch 115 fish.
	Innerleithen (Traquair Beat)	Salmon Sea Trout	1 Feb. to 30 Nov.	J.H. Leeming ARICS, Salmon Fishing Agent, Stichill House, Kelso TD5 7TB. 24hr Information Service. FREEPHONE: 0800 387675. Office: (01573) 470280. Fax: (01573) 470259.	2 miles above and 1 mile below Innerleithen Bridge. Ghillie, fishing hut and good access to both banks. Average catch Oct/No 46 salmon and sea trout. No spinning before 15 Feb. or after 15 Sep.
	Nr. Kelso (Hendersyde Beat)	Salmon Sea Trout	1 Feb. to 30 Nov.	J.H. Leeming ARICS, Salmon Fishing Agent, Stichill House, Kelso TD5 7TB. 24hr Information Service. FREEPHONE: 0800 387675. Office: (01573) 470280. Fax: (01573) 470259.	The water is split into two beats which are fished 3 days in rotation with the opposite bank. Thus 2 rods are able to fish 1 mile of double bank fishing. Average catch 265 fish.
	Kelso	Brown Trout	1 Apr. to 30 Sep.	Border Hotel, Woodmarket, Kelso TD5 7AX. Tel: (01573) 224791.	Fly only. No spinning. Restricted to 3 rods.
	Ladykirk	Brown Trout	19 Mar. to 8 Oct.	Victoria Hotel, Norham. Tel: (01289) 382237.	No spinning. No ground baiting. Fly only above Norham Bridge to West Ford. No Sundays.
	Melrose	Trout Grayling	1 Apr. to 6 Oct.	Melrose & District Angling Assoc., Anglers Choice, 23 Market Square, Melrose. Tel: (01896) 823070.	No spinning. No ground baiting. No Sunday fishing. Minnow fishing not permitted. Spinning reels of all types prohibited.
	Melrose (Ravenswood Tweedswood)	Brown Trout	1 Apr. to 30 Sep.	Anglers Choice, 23 Market Square, Melrose. Tel: (01896) 823070.	Fly fishing only.
	Melrose (Ravenswood Beat)	Salmon Sea Trout	Feb. to Nov.	J.H. Leeming ARICS, Salmon Fishing Agent, Stichill House, Kelso TD5 7TB. 24hr Information Service. FREEPHONE: 0800 387675. Office: (01573) 470280. Fax: (01573) 470259.	1.5 miles of right bank with 7 named pools. The beat lies in a wooded gorge, having no road beside it. Average catch 85 fish. 1 boat available.

Water	Location	Species	Season	Permit available from	Other information
Tweed cont.	Melrose (Pavilion)	Salmon Sea Trout	1 Feb. to 30 Nov.	Anglers Choice, 23 Market Square, Melrose. Tel: (01896) 823070.	Fly only: 1 to 15 Feb., and 15 Sep. to 30 Nov. 16 Feb. to 14 Sep fly and spinning.
	Nest	Salmon Sea Trout Trout	1 Feb. to 30 Nov. 1 Apr. to 30 Sep.	Tweed Valley Hotel, Walkerburn EH43 6AA. Tel: (01896) 870636.	Private salmon/sea trout beat approx. 1.75 miles, 4 rods. Fly only 15 Sep. to 30 Nov. Trout and grayling permits available to all.Week or day letsSpring/Summer.Week lets only Oct & Nov.
	Norham (Ladykirk Beat)	Salmon Grilse Sea Trout	1 Feb. to 30 Nov.	J.H. Leeming ARICS, Salmon Fishing Agent, Stichill House, Kelso TD5 7TB. 24hr Information Service. FREEPHONE: 0800 387675. Office: (01573) 470280. Fax: (01573) 470259.	3 miles of the north bank. Boats and ghillies provided. Average catch 196 fish. No spinning before 15 Feb. or after 15 Sep.
	Norham (Pedwell Beat)	Salmon Grilse Sea Trout	1 Feb. to 30 Nov.	J.H. Leeming ARICS, Salmon Fishing Agent, Stichill House, Kelso TD5 7TB. 24hr Information Service. FREEPHONE: 0800 387675. Office: (01573) 470280. Fax: (01573) 470259.	1.5 miles single bank. Average catch of 62 fish. No spinning before 15 Feb. or after 15 Sep.
	Peel	Salmon Sea Trout	1 Feb. to 30 Nov.	Tweed Valley Hotel, Walkerburn EH43 6AA.Tel: (01896) 870636.	Private 2-rod salmon beat on south bank. Week or day lets Spring/Summer. Week lets only October and November. Angling course, September.
	Peebles (Wire Bridge Pool to Nutwood Pool – excluding Kailzie)	Salmon Grilse Sea Trout	21 Feb. to 30 Nov.	Peeblesshire Salmon Fishing Assoc. Seasons:Blackwood & Smith w.s., 39 High Street, Pee bles.Tel: (01721) 720131Day Permits: Tweeddale Tackle Centre, 1 Bridgegate, Peebles EH45 8RZ. Tel: (01721) 720979.	Strictly fly fishing only. No Sunday fishing. Other regulations on tickets.
	St. Boswells (Bemersyde Beat)	Salmon Grilse Sea Trout	1 Feb. to 30 Nov.	J.H. Leeming ARICS, Salmon Fishing Agent, Stichill House, Kelso TD5 7TB. 24hr Information Service. FREEPHONE: 0800 387675. Office: (01573) 470280. Fax: (01573) 470259.	1 mile of excellent water. Average catch 188 fish. Must be a good walker and wader as parts are difficult and access to the river bank not available to cars.
		Brown Trout	1 Apr. to 30 Sep.	Dryburgh Abbey Hotel, St. Boswells. Tel: (01835) 822261. Anglers Choice, 23 Market Square, Melrose. Tel: (01896) 823070. Mr. Stuart Robb (Newsagent), St. Boswells.	Fly only 1 Apr. to 1 May. No bait fishing until 1 May. No Sunday fishing. No spinning tackle. No coarse fishing allowed outside season. Access to restricted beats by special permits only.
	Tweedsmuir	Brown Trout Grayling	1 Apr. to 30 Sep.	Crook Inn, Tweedsmuir. Tel: (01899) 880272.	All rules and regulations on permits.
	Walkerburn	Salmon Sea Trout Trout	1 Feb. to 30 Nov. 1 Apr. to 30 Sep.	Tweed Valley Hotel, Walkerburn EH43 6AA. Tel: (01896) 870636.	Salmon tickets for hotel guests only after 14 Sep. Special salmon and trout weeks tuition. Trout and grayling permits available to all.

Water	Location	Species	Season	Permit available from	Other information
Tweed cont.	Haystoun (Beat 1.5 miles)	Salmon Sea Trout	15 Feb. to 30 Nov.	Fraser's Salmon Fishing & Hire Ltd., 16 Kingsmuir Crescent, Peebles. Tel: (01721) 722362.	No spinning in autumn – fly only. No Sunday fishing. Rods limited to 6 per day. Part-time ghillie included in permit price. 8 named salmon pools.
	Kingsmeadow (Beat [3/4] mile)	Salmon Sea Trout	15 Feb. to 30 Nov.	Fraser's Salmon Fishing & Hire Ltd., 16 Kingsmuir Crescent, Peebles. Tel: (01721) 722362.	Spinning allowed 15 Feb. to 14 Sep. Rods limited to 2 per day. Part-time ghillie included in permit price. 5 named salmon pools.
Whiteadder & Dye & Tributaries	30 miles	Brown/ Rainbow Trout	15 Mar. to 30 Sep.	Whiteadder Angling Assoc., Mr. Cowan, Crumstane, Duns. (Bailiff). Tel: (01361) 883235. J.S. Main, Saddlers, 87 High Street, Haddington. Tel: (01620) 822148.	No Sundays. Fly only before 15 Apr. Worm from 15 Apr. only. Minnow from 1 May only. Size limit 8 inches.
Whiteadder (Map IV F4)	Allanton	Trout	15 Mar. to 30 Sep.	Berwick & District Angling Association, Mr. D. Cowan,129 Etal Road, Tweedmouth,Berwick-upon-Tweed Tel: (01289) 306985.	Fly only before May. No spinning. No threadline. No maggot fishing. No ground baiting. 9 inch min.

LOCHS & RESERVOIRS

Water	Location	Species	Season	Permit available from	Other information
Acreknowe Reservoir	Hawick	Brown Trout	15 Mar. to end Sep.	The Pet Shop, 1 Union Street, Hawick. Tel: (01450) 373543. Mr. D Smith, "Wellogate Bank", Wellowgate Brae, Hawick. Tel: (01450) 373142.	Ticket covers all other trout waters managed by Hawick Angling Club. Boat available from Pet Shop. Fly fishing only.
Alemoor Loch	Hawick	Brown Trout Perch Pike		As Acreknowe	Bank fishing only.
Alton Loch	2 miles N. of Hawick	Brown/ Rainbow Trout	1 Mar. to 31 Oct.	At loch only. Further details from: Mr. Morand, Flat 7, 3 Quay Walls, Berwick-upon-Tweed, Tel: 0836 339757 (mobile).	Average weight of fish caught: 1.5 to 3 lbs. Fly fishing only. 4 boats plus 4 on bank. Sessions: Day 8am-4pm;Evening 430pm-dusk.
Clearburn Loch	Nr. Hawick	Trout		Tushielaw Inn, Ettrick Valley, Selkirkshire. Tel: (01750) 62205.	Boat supplied free.
Clerklands Loch	Nr. Selkirk	Rainbow/ Brown Trout	15 Mar. to 30 Sep.	Clerklands Fly Fishery, Nr. Selkirk. Tel: (01835) 870757.	Trout Master available. Open daily.Trout 2lb 8oz.
Coldingham Loch	Reston	Brown/ Rainbow Trout	15 Mar. to 6 Oct.	Dr E.J. Wise, West Loch House, Coldingham. Tel: (01890) 771270.	Fly only. 4 boats (max 8 rods). 4 bank rods. Sunday fishing. Advance booking essential.
Eildon Hall Loch	Melrose	Brown/ Rainbow Trout	15 Mar. to 30 Oct.	Langlands Service Station, Newtown, St. Boswells. Tel: (01835) 23310.	2 sessions: 9am to 4pm, 4pm to dusk. Sunday fishing. Bag limit 3 trout per session.
Fruid Reservoir	Tweedsmuir	Brown Trout	1 Apr. to 30 Sep.	Crook Inn, Tweedsmuir. Tel: (01899) 880272.	Fly, bait, spin.

Water	Location	Species	Season	Permit available from	Other information
Hass Loch	Nr. Letham	Rainbow Trout	1 Apr. to 31 Oct.	Jedforest Filling Station, Cleathaugh, Camptown. Tel: (01835) 840330.	Loch is regularly stocked. Bank fishing for 7 rods per session. Sessions: Day 9am to 5 pm, Evening 5pm to 11pm. Fishing 7 days per week.
Heather-hope Reservoir	Hownam	Trout	15 Mar. to 6 Oct.	Keith Rothwell, Eildon View, Mainsfield Ave., Morebattle TD5 8QP. Tel: (01573) 44247. The Garage, Morebattle. Templehall Hotel, Morebattle. Tel: (01573) 440249.	No ground baiting. No Sunday fishing.
Hellmoor Loch	Hawick	Brown Trout		As Acreknowe.	No boat. No competitions. Limit 6 trout.
Knowes-dean Reservoir	Selkirk	Brown/ Rainbow Trout	15 Mar. to 31 Oct.	J. & A. Turnbull, 30 Bank Street, Galashiels. Tel: (01896) 753191.	Bag limit 3 fish. 2 sessions per day. Advance booking advisable.
Loch Lindean	Selkirk	Brown Trout	Apr.–Oct.	P. & E. Scott, Newsagent, 6 High Street, Selkirk TD7 4DA. Tel: (01750) 20749.	2 boats available.
Loch of the Lowes and St. Mary's Loch	Selkirk	Brown Trout Pike Perch Eels	1 Apr. to 30 Sep. 1 May to 30 Sep.	St. Mary's A.C. per Sec., N. MacIntyre, "Whincroft" 8 Rosetta Road, Peebles EH45 8JU. Tel: (01721) 722278. Gordon Arms Hotel, Yarrow. Countrylife, 229 Balgreen Road, Edinburgh. Tel: 0131-337 6230. Hook, Line & Sinker, 20 Morningside Road, Edinburgh. Tel: 0131-447 9172. Tibbie Shiels Inn, St. Mary's Loch, Yarrow, Selkirk. Tel: (01750) 42231. Anglers Choice, 23 Market Square, Melrose. Tel: (01896) 823070. Glen Cafe (lochside). Tweeddale Tackle Centre, 1 Bridgegate, Peebles. Tel: (01721) 720979. Mikes Tackle Shop, 46 Portobello High Street, Edinburgh. Tel: 0131-657 3258.	Fly fishing only, until 30 April thereafter spinning and bait allowed. Club fishing apply Secretary or keeper. Sunday fishing. Weekly permits and rowing boats from keeper, Mr. Brown (01750) 42243. Outboard engines of up to 5 h.p. may be used, but none available for hire. No float fishing. Loch of the Lowes is bank fishing only. River Tweed Protection order applies. Club memberships available.
Megget Reservoir	Tweedsmuir	Brown Trout	1 Apr. to 30 Sep.	Tibbie Shiels Inn, St, Mary's Loch, Yarrow, Selkirk. Tel: (01750) 42231.	No bait fishing. 6 Boats available. Max. bag limit 10 fish.
Peebles-shire Lochs	Tweed Valley	Brown/ Rainbow Trout	Apr. to Oct.	Tweed Valley Hotel, Walkerburn EH43 6AA. Tel: (01896) 870636.	Stocked private lochans. Wild brown trout loch.
Portmore Game Fisheries	Peebles-Eddleston	Wild Brown Trout Rainbow Trout	1 Apr. to 31 Oct.	Portmore Game Fisheries at the loch. Tel: (01968) 675684.	Average weight of fish caught: 2lbs. Popular flies: Lures at beginning; from May, dry & wet. Boats are available, contact: Steve McGeachie at number opposite.

Water	Location	Species	Season	Permit available from	Other information
Purdom Stone Reservoir (Map IV D6)	Hoddom & Kinmount Estates Ecclefechan	Brown Trout	1 Apr. to 15 Sep.	The Water Bailiff, 1 Bridge End Cottage, Hoddem, Lockerbie. Tel: (01576) 300488.	Fly fishing only.
Sunlaws Trout Pond	Morebattle	Rainbow Trout	All year.	Sunlaws House Hotel, Kelso. Tel: (01573) 450331.	2 sessions: 10am–4pm, 5pm–dusk. Bag limit 4 per day, 3 per evening. From end Oct. to start Apr., 1 day session only, 10am–3.30pm.
Synton Loch	Hawick	Brown Trout		As Acreknowe Reservoir.	Boats available from Pet Store, 1 Union Street, Hawick. Fly only.
Talla Reservoir	Tweedsmuir	Brown Trout	1 Apr. to 30 Sep.	Crook Inn, Tweedsmuir. Tel: (01899) 880272.	Fly fishing only. 2 boats.
Upper Loch	Bowhill	Brown/ Rainbow Trout	1 Apr. to 31 Oct.	Buccleuch Estate Ltd., Estate Office, Bowhill, Selkirk. Tel: (01750) 20753.	Fly only. 2 rods per boat and limit of 8 fish per boat. Boats available on: Tues all season; Mondays during June, July and August. Evening fishing available.
Watch Reservoir	Longformacus	Brown Trout Rainbow Trout	15 Mar. to 30 Sep. All year.	W.F. Renton, The Watch Fly Reservoir. Tel: (01361) 890331 & (01289) 306028.	Sunday fishing. Fly only. Strictly no use of bait/maggots, etc.
West Water Reservoir	West Linton	Brown Trout	1 May to 30 Sep.	Contact: 0131-445 6300.	2 boats. Fly fishing only. Boat fishing only.
Whiteadder Reservoir	Gifford	Brown Trout	1 Jun. to 30 Sep.	Goblin Ha Hotel, Gifford. Tel: (01620) 810244.	Bank fishing 1 Jun. to 30 Sep. Sunday fishing. Fly fishing only. 4 boats are available.
Willies-truther Loch	Hawick	Brown/ Rainbow Trout		As Acreknowe Reservoir.	Any legal method.
Wooden Loch	Eckford	Rainbow Trout	1 Apr. to 31 Oct.	Mr. Graham, Eckford Cottage, Eckford, Kelso. Tel: (01835) 850255.	1 boat. No bank fishing. Only rainbow trout after 30 Sep. Only 2 rods at any time. Advance booking necessary. No Sundays.

DUMFRIES and GALLOWAY RIVERS AND LOCHS

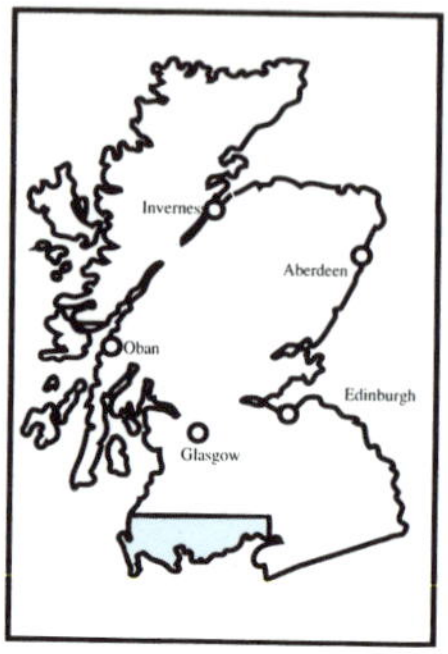

Area Tourist Board
Dumfries & Galloway Tourist Board
Director of Tourism,
Dumfries & Galloway Tourist Board,
Campbell House, Bankend Road,
Dumfries DG1 4TH.
Tel: (01387) 250434.

River Purification Board
Solway River Purification Board
River's House,
Irongray Road,
Dumfries DG2 OJE.
Tel: (01387) 720502.

RIVERS

Water	Location	Species	Season	Permit available from	Other information
Annan (Map IV D6)	Hoddom & Kinmount Estates Ecclefechan	Salmon Sea Trout Brown Trout	25 Feb. to 15 Nov.	Miss Marsh, 1 Bridge End Cottage, Hoddom, Lockerbie DG11 1BE. Tel: (01576) 300488.	No Sunday fishing. Fly water unless the spinning mark is covered.
	Halleaths Estate Lockerbie	Salmon Sea Trout	25 Feb. to 15 Nov.	Messrs. McJerrow & Stevenson (Solicitors), 55 High Street, Lockerbie. Tel: (01576) 202123.	Limited number of tickets.
	Kirkwood & Jardine Hall Beats	Salmon Sea Trout Brown Trout	25 Feb. to 15 Nov.	Mr. Anthony Steel, Kirkwood, Lockerbie. Tel: (01576) 510212/510200.	Kirkwood is mainly fly fishing (spinning and worming only in spate conditions). Jardine Hall – spinning and worming allowed.
	Royal Four Towns Water Lockerbie	Salmon Sea Trout Brown Trout	25 Feb. to 15 Nov.	Clerk to the Commissioners of Royal Four Towns Fishing Mrs. K. Ratcliffe, Clerk, 'Jay-Ar', Preston House Road, Hightae, Lockerbie. Tel: (01387) 510220. Castle Milk Estates Office, Norwood, Lockerbie. Tel: (01576) 810203.	No Sunday fishing.
	St. Mungo Parish	Salmon Sea Trout Brown Trout	25 Feb. to 15 Nov.	Castle Milk Estates Office, Norwood, Lockerbie. Tel: (01576) 510203.	Fly fishing only. No Sunday fishing.
	Warmanbie Estate	Salmon Sea Trout Brown Trout	25 Feb. to 15 Nov.	Warmanbie Hotel & Restaurant, Annan DG12 5LL. Tel: (01461) 204015.	Fly, spinning, worm all season. Access to many other stretches. For residents only.

Water	Location	Species	Season	Permit available from	Other information
Bladnoch (Map IV B6)	Newton Stewart	Salmon	1 Mar. to 31 Oct.	Newton Stewart A.A. Galloway Guns & Tackle, 36 Arthur Street, Newton Stewart. Tel: (01671) 403404. Palakona Guest House, Queen Street, Newton Stewart DG8 6JL. Tel: (01671) 402323. (For guests only.)	
Cairn	Dumfries	Brown Trout Salmon Sea Trout	15 Mar. to 6 Oct. 1 Apr. to end Oct.	Dumfries & Galloway A.A. Secretary: D. Byers, 4 Bloomfield, Edinburgh Road, Dumfries DG1 1SG. Tel: (01387) 253850.	Limited number of permits. No Sunday fishing. Restrictions depend on water level. Visitors Mon.–Fri. only.
Cree (and Pencill Burn) (Map IV B6)	Drumlamford Estate	Salmon Trout	Apr. to Oct.	The Keeper, The Kennels, Drumlamford Estate, Barrhill. Tel: (01465) 821256.	No Sunday fishing.
	Newton Stewart	Salmon Sea Trout	1 Mar. to 14 Oct.	Newton Stewart A.A. Galloway Guns & Tackle, 36 Arthur Street, Newton Stewart. Tel: (01671) 403404. Palakona Guest House, Queen Street, Newton Stewart DG8 6JL. Tel: (01671) 402323. (For guests only.)	No Sunday fishing. Rules printed on permits.
Black Water of Dee (Map IV C6)	Mossdale	Trout Pike Perch Salmon	15 Mar. to 30 Sep. 11 Feb. to 31 Oct.	Local hotels and shops.	
Esk (Map IV E5)	East Dumfriesshire	Salmon Sea Trout/ Herling Brown Trout	1 Feb. to 31. Oct. 1 May to 30 Sep. 15 Apr. to 30 Sep.	Esk & Liddle Fisheries R.J.B. Hill, Bank of Scotland Buildings, Langholm. Tel: (013873) 80428. George Graham, Hagg-on-Esk, Old School, Canonbie. Tel: (013873) 71416.	Spinning allowed until 14 Apr. and otherwise only when water is above markers at Skippers Bridge, Canonbie Bridge and Willow Pool.
Ken	New Galloway	Brown/ Rainbow Trout Perch Pike Roach Salmon	15 Mar. to 30 Sep.	Mr. Swain, Kenmure Arms Hotel, High Street, New Galloway. Tel: (01644) 420240/420360. Andrew & Ann Ramsay, Kenbridge Hotel, New Galloway. Tel: (01644) 420211/420744. Fax: (01644) 420485.	Boats available from hotel. Free fishing at hotel on River Ken.
Liddle	Newcastleton Ticket	Salmon Sea Trout Brown Trout	15 Apr. to 31 Oct. 1 May to 30 Sep. 15 Apr. to 30 Sep.	J.D. Ewart, Tackle Agent, Newcastleton. Tel: (01387) 375257. R.J.B. Hill, Bank of Scotland Buildings, Langholm. Tel: (01387) 380428.	Spinning allowed when water is above markers at Newcastleton and Kershopefoot Bridges. No Sunday fishing. Day tickets available.
Milk	Scroggs Bridge	Sea/ Brown Trout	1 Apr. to 30 Sep.	Mr. Anthony Steel, Kirkwood, Lockerbie. Tel: (01576) 510212/510200.	Mainly fly fishing. No Sunday fishing.
Minnoch	Newton Stewart	Salmon	1 Mar. to 30 Sep.	Galloway Guns & Tackle, 36 Arthur Street, Newton Stewart. Tel: (01671) 403404.	Fly, spin or worm.

Water	Location	Species	Season	Permit available from	Other information
Nith (Map IV D5)	Dumfries	Salmon Sea Trout Brown Trout	25 Feb. to 30 Nov. 15 Mar. to 6 Oct.	Dumfries & Galloway Council, Housing Services, 81-85 Irish St., Dumfreis. Tel: (01387) 259991.	No Sunday fishing. Advance booking.
				Dumfries & Galloway Angling Association, Secretary, D. Byers, 4 Bloomfield Edinburgh Road, Dumfries DG1 1SG. Tel: (01387) 253850.	Limited number of permits. Weekly permits from Mon. to Fri. Advance booking possible. Spinning restrictions.
	Thornhill	Salmon Sea Trout Brown Trout	25 Feb. to 30 Nov. 1 Apr. to 31 Sep.	The Drumlanrig Castle Fishings, The Buccleuch Estates Ltd., Drumlanrig Mains, Thornhill DG3 4AG. Tel: (01848) 600283.	Lower, Middle & Upper beats. Average weight of fish caught: Salmon 9lbs 8oz, Grilse 6 lbs, Sea Trout 2lbs, Brown Trout 8 oz, Grayling, 8 oz.Popular flies: Stoats Tail, General Practitioner, Silver Doctor, Flying C, Silver Toby. Spinning, worming (until 31 Aug.). Weekly and daily lets up to 3 rods/beat.
		Salmon Sea Trout Brown Trout	25 Feb. to 30 Nov. 1 Apr. to 30 Sep.	The Drumlanrig Castle Fishings, The Buccleuch Estates Ltd., Drumlanrig Mains, Thornhill DG3 4AG. Tel: (01848) 600283.	Lower, Middle & Upper beats. Average weight of fish caught: Salmon 9lbs 8oz, Grilse 6 lbs, Sea Trout 2lbs, Brown Trout 8 oz, Grayling, 8 oz. Weekly and daily lets up to 3 rods/beat.
		Salmon Sea Trout Brown Trout	25 Feb. to 30 Nov.	Mid Nithsdale A.A. Secretary: Mr. I.R. Milligan, 37 Drumlanrig Street, Thornhill DG3 5LS. Tel: (01848) 330555.	No day permits on Saturdays. Spinning and worming allowed only in flood conditions. Advisable to book for autumn fishing.
Nith (and tributaries Kello Crawick Euchan Mennock)	Sanquhar	Salmon Sea Trout Brown Trout Grayling	15 Mar. to 30 Nov. Jan., Feb.	Upper Nithsdale Angling Club, Pollock & McLean, Solicitors, 61 High Street, Sanquhar. Tel: (01659) 50241.	No Sunday fishing. Visitors and residents. Day tickets (Mon.–Fri.) – limit of 30 per day during months: Sep., Oct. & Nov. Week tickets – limit of 10 per week during season.
Tarf	Kirkcowan	Sea Trout Brown Trout	Easter to 30 Sep.	A. Brown, Three Lochs Holiday Park, Kirkcowan, Newton Stewart. Tel: (01671) 830304.	
Upper Tarf	Nr. Newton Stewart	Salmon Trout	1 Mar. to 14 Oct. 15 Mar. to 6 Oct.	Palakona Guest House, Queen Street, Newton Stewart DG8 6JL. Tel: (01670) 402323. (For guests only.) Galloway Country Sports. Tel: (01988) 840695 – all day tickets.	Fly, spin or worm.
Urr	Castle Douglas	Salmon Sea Trout Brown Trout	25 Feb. to 30 Nov. 15 Mar. to 6 Oct.	Castle Douglas & District A.A. Tommy's Sport Shop, 178 King Street, Castle Douglas. Tel: (01566) 502851. Dalbeattie A.A. Ticket Secretary: M. McCowan & Son, 43 High Street, Dalbeattie. Tel: (01556) 610270.	

Water	Location	Species	Season	Permit available from	Other information
Urr cont.	Dalbeattie	Salmon Sea Trout Brown Trout	25 Feb. to 30 Nov. 15 Mar. to 6 Oct.	Dalbeattie A.A. Ticket Secretary: M. McCowan & Son, 43 High Street, Dalbeattie. Tel: (01556) 610270.	
White Esk	Eskdalemuir	Salmon Sea Trout	15 Apr. to 30 Oct. 15 Apr. to 30 Sep.	Hart Manor Hotel, Eskdalemuir, by Langholm. Tel: (01387) 373217.	Fly and spinner and worm.

LOCHS & RESERVOIRS

Water	Location	Species	Season	Permit available from	Other information
Barend Loch	Sandyhills	Rainbow Trout Carp	Open all year	Barend Properties, Reception, Sandyhills, Dalbeattie. Tel: (01387) 780663.	
Barscobe Loch	Balmaclellan	Brown Trout	15 Mar. to 6 Oct.	Lady Wontner, Barscobe, Balmaclellan, Castle Douglas. Tel: (01644) 420245/420294.	Fly fishing only. Obtain permit first.
Black Loch	Newton Stewart	Stocked Brown Trout	15 Mar. to 30 Sep.	Forest Enterprise, Creebridge, Newton Stewart. Tel: (01671) 402420. Talnotry Campsite, Queens Way, Newton Stewart. Tel: (01671) 402170. Clatteringshaws Wildlife Visitors Centre, New Galloway. Tel: (01644) 420285.	Fly only until 1 July. Sunday fishing.
Black Loch	Nr. Kirkcowan	(Stocked) Brown Trout Pike	15 Mar. to 6 Oct. No close season.	Palakona Guest House, Queen Street, Newton Stewart. Tel: (01671) 402323. (Guests only.) Galloway Country Sports. Tel: (01988) 840695 – all day tickets.	Any legal method permitted.
Bruntis Loch	Newton Stewart	Brown/ Rainbow Trout	1 May to 30 Sep.	Newton Stewart A.A., Galloway Guns & Tackle, 36 Arthur Street, Newton Stewart. Tel: (01671) 403404.	Fly fishing only (fly and worm from 1 June). Bank fishing only. Sunday fishing.
Clattering-shaws Loch	6 miles west of New Galloway	Brown Trout Pike Perch	Open all year for coarse fish	Clatteringshaws Wildlife Visitors Centre, New Galloway. Tel: (01644) 420285. Galloway Guns & Tackle, 36 Arthur Street, Newton Stewart. Tel: (01671) 403404. Kenmure Arms Hotel, High Street, New Galloway. Tel: (01644) 420240.	Fly fishing, spinning or worm fishing permitted.
Dalbeattie Reservoir	Dalbeattie	Brown/ Rainbow Trout	1 Apr. to 30 Sep.	Dalbeattie A.A. Ticket Secretary: M. McCowan & Son, 43 High Street, Dalbeattie. Tel: (01556) 610270.	Bank fishing. Fly only. Boats for hire.
Loch Dee	Castle Douglas	Brown Trout	15 Mar. to 30 Sep.	Forest Enterprise, Creebridge, Newton Stewart. Tel: (01671) 402420. Talnotry Campsite, Queens Way, Newton Stewart. Tel: (01671) 402170. Clatteringshaws Wildlife Visitors Centre, New Galloway. Tel: (01644) 420285.	Fly fishing only, sunrise to sunset. Bank fishing only. Sunday fishing. Annual fly fishing competition in August.

Water	Location	Species	Season	Permit available from	Other information
Dindinnie Reservoir	Stranraer	Brown Trout	1 May to 30 Sep.	Stranraer & District A.A. The Sports Shop, 90 George Street, Stranraer. Tel: (01776) 702705. Local hotels.	Fly fishing only. Sunday fishing.
Loch Dornal	Drumlamford Estate	Coarse Stocked Trout	Apr. to Oct.	The Keeper, The Kennels, Drumlamford Estate, Barrhill. Tel: (01465) 821256.	Spinning allowed. Boats available. Fly fishing.
Loch Drumlam-ford	Drumlamford Estate	Stocked Trout	Apr. to Oct.	The Keeper, The Kennels, Drumlamford Estate, Barrhill. Tel: (01465) 821256.	Fly fishing only. Boats available.
Loch Dunskey (lower)	Portpatrick	Rainbow & Brown Trout	Apr. to Oct.	The Keeper, Dunsky Estate, Portpatrick. Tel: (01776) 810364/810848.	Max 4 rods. Boat available. 11 acres.
	Portpatrick	Rainbow & Brown Trout	Apr. to Oct.	The Keeper, Dunsky Estate, Portpatrick. Tel: (01776) 810364/810848.	Max 2 rods. Boat avaialbe. 5 acres.
Loch Ettrick	Closeburn	Rainbow Trout (stocked) Brown Trout	1 Apr. to 31 Oct.	John Crofts, Blawbare, Ettrick, Thornhill DG3 5HL. Tel: (01848) 330154. Closeburn Post Office. Tel: (01848) 331230.	Average weight of fish: 1 lb to 2 lbs. Popular flies: Nymphs. Fly fishing only. 4 boats availble.
Fynntalloch Loch	Newton Stewart	Brown/ Rainbow Trout	1 May to 6 Oct.	Newton Stewart A.A., Galloway Guns & Tackle, 36 Arthur Street, Newton Stewart. Tel: (01671) 403404.	Fly fishing only. Bank fishing only.
Glenkiln Reservoir	Dumfries	Brown Trout (stocked) Rainbow Trout	1 Apr. to 30 Sep.	District Manager, West of Scotland Water, Dumfries and Galloway District, Marchmount House, Dumfries DG1 1PW. Tel: (01387) 250000.	Enquiries to Mr. Ling at number opposite.
Jericho Loch	Dumfries	Brown/ Rainbow Trout Brook Trout	1 Apr. to 31 Oct.	McMillan's Tackle Shop, Friars Vennel, Dumfries. Pattie's Tackle Shop, Queensberry Street, Dumfries. Club bookings – contact Jimmy Younger. Tel: (01387) 750247. Day-tickets from Grove Service Station, Heath Hall Dumfries.	Bank fishing only. Fly fishing only. Popular flies: lures, nymphs, traditionals. Sunday fishing.
Loch Ken	West Bank Lochside Aird's (Viaduct)	Salmon Trout and coarse fish	Open all year for coarse fish	Andrew & Ann Ramsay, Kenbridge Hotel, New Galloway. Tel: (01644) 420211/420744. Fax: (01644) 420485.	Surcharged if permits bought form bailiffs.
	New Galloway	Brown Trout Salmon Pike Perch Roach	15 Mar. to 30 Sep. All year round	Kenmure Arms Hotel, High Street, New Galloway. Tel: (01644) 420240. Local shops.	Sunday fishing allowed except for salmon. Worm and spinning permitted. Boats available.
Kettleton Reservoir	Thornhill	Brown/ Rainbow Trout	1 Apr. to 30 Sep.	I.R. Milligan, 37 Drumlanrig Street, Thornhill. Tel: (01848) 330555.	Fly fishing only. Popular flies: Muddler, Black Pennel.

Water	Location	Species	Season	Permit available from	Other information
Kirriereoch Loch	Newton Stewart	Brown Trout (stocked)	1 May to 6 Oct.	Newton Stewart A.A. Galloway Guns & Tackle, 36 Arthur Street, Newton Stewart. Tel: (01671) 403404. Glentrool Holiday Park, Glentrool. Tel: (01671) 840280.	Fly fishing only (fly & worm after 1 June). Bank fishing only. Sunday fishing.
Knock-quassan Reservoir	Stranraer	Brown Trout	1 May to 30 Sep.	Stranraer & District A.A. The Sports Shop, 90 George Street, Stranraer. Tel: (01776) 702705. Local hotels.	Bank fishing only. Fly and spinning. Sunday fishing.
Laird-mannoch Loch	Twynholm	Wild Brown Trout	1 Apr. to 30 Sep.	G.M. Thomson & Co. Ltd., 27 King Street, Castle Douglas. Tel: (01556) 502701/502973.	Boat fishing only. Limited rods. Limited days. Self-catering accommodation available.
Lillies Loch	Castle Douglas	Brown Trout	15 Mar. to 30 Sep.	Forest Enterprise, Creebridge, Newton Stewart. Tel: (01671) 402420. Talnotry Campsite, Queens Way, Newton Stewart. Tel: (01671) 402170.	Bank fishing only. Any legal method. Sunday fishing.
Lochen-breck Loch	Lauriston	Brown/ Rainbow Trout	1 Apr. to 30 Sep.	Watson McKinnel, 15 St. Cuthbert Street, Kirkcudbright. Tel: (01557) 330693. M. & E. Brown, 52 High Street, Gatehouse of Fleet. Tel: (01557) 814222. (Shop hours: 6.30am–5pm.)	8.30am–10pm. Bank and fly fishing. Five boats. Sunday fishing.
Loch of the Lowes	Newton Stewart	Brown Trout (stocked)	15 Mar. to 30 Sep.	Forest Enterprise, Creebridge, Newton Stewart. Tel: (01671) 402420. Talnotry Campsite, Queens Way, Newton Stewart. Tel: (01671) 402170. Clatteringshaws Wildlife Visitors Centre, New Galloway. Tel: (01644) 420285.	Fly only. Sunday fishing.
Morton Castle Loch	Thornhill	Stocked Brown/ Rainbow Trout	1 Apr. to 30 Sep.	The Buccleuch Estates Ltd., Drumlanrig Mains, Thornhill DG3 4AG. Tel: (01848) 600283.	Average weight of fish: 2.25 lbs. Popular flies: Montana, Damsel, P/T Nymph, Ace of Spades, Coachman (dry). Fly fishing only. Bank and boat fishing. Let on a daily basis for up to 3 rods.
Mossdale Loch	Mossdale Nr. New Galloway	Stocked Rainbow Trout Wild Brown Trout	15 Mar. to 30 Sep.	The Mossdale Post Office, Mossdale, Castle Douglas DG7 2NF. Tel: (01644) 450281.	Fly fishing only from boat. Boats available from Post Office. Sunday fishing.
Loch Nahinie	Drumlamford Estate	Stocked Trout	Apr. to Oct.	The Keeper, The Kennels, Drumlamford Estate, Barrhill. Tel: (01465) 821256.	Fly fishing only. Boats available.
Ochiltree Loch	Newton Stewart	Brown/ Rainbow Trout	1 May to 6 Oct.	Newton Stewart A.A. Galloway Guns & Tackle, 36 Arthur Street, Newton Stewart. Tel: (01671) 403404	Fly fishing only. Bank fishing only. Sunday fishing.

Water	Location	Species	Season	Permit available from	Other information
Penwhirn Reservoir	Stranraer	Brown Trout	15 Mar. to 30 Sep.	Stranraer & District A.A. The Sports Shop, 90 George Street, Stranraer. Tel: (01776) 702705. Local hotels.	Fly fishing and spinning. Bank fishing. Sunday fishing.
Piltanton Burn	Dunragit	Brown/ Rainbow Trout Salmon	1 May to 31 Oct.	Mr J. Duffy, 2 Orchard Road, Dunragit, Stranraer. The Sports Shop, 90 George Street, Stranraer. Tel: (01671) 403403.	Spinning and worming allowed. Fly fishing.
Loch Roan	Castle Douglas	Brown/ Rainbow Trout	1 Apr. to 6 Oct.	Tommy's Sports Shop, 178 King Street, Castle Douglas. Tel: (01556) 502851.	Fly fishing only. Four boats.
Slatehouse Loch	Thronhill	Rainbow Trout	1 Apr. to 30 Sep.	Buccleuch Estates Ltd., Drumlanrig Mains, Thronhill, DG3 4AG. Tel: (01848) 600283.	Average weight 2.2lb. Popular flies include Montana, Damsel, Nymph. Ace of Spades. Fly fishing only. Bank fishing only, let on a daily basis for up to 3 rods. Tuition is available at an additional cost.
Solway Fishery	Nr. New Abbey	Brown/ American Brook/ Rainbow Trout	Feb. to Nov.	Solway Fishery. Tel: (01387) 850235.	Average weight of fish caught: 1.5 lbs. Popular flies: Nymphs, Buzzers and Damsels. No boats. Tackle for hire.
Soulseat Loch	Stranraer	Brown/ Rainbow Trout	15 Mar. to 30 Sep.	Stranraer & District A.A. The Sports Shop, 90 George Street, Stranraer. Tel: (01776) 702705. Local hotels.	Fly, spinning and bait. Bank fishing and two boats. Sunday fishing.
Spa-wood Loch	Nr. Newton Stewart	Wild Brown Trout	15 Mar. to 30 Sep.	Palakona Guest House, Queen Street, Newton Stewart DG8 6JL. Tel: (0671) 402323.	Guests only.
Starburn Loch	Thornhill	Wild Brown Trout	1 Apr. to 31 Aug.	The Buccleuch Estates Ltd., Drumlanrig Mains, Thornhill DG3 4AG. Tel: (01848) 600283.	Average weight of fish: 2.2 lbs. Popular flies: Montana, Damsel, P/T Nymph, Ace of Spades, Coachman (dry). Fly fishing only. Bank and boat fishing available. Let on a daily basis for up to 3 rods.
Stroan Loch	Mossdale	Brown Trout Pike Perch	1 Apr. to 30 Sep.	Forest Enterprise, 21 King Street, Castle Douglas. Tel: (01556) 503626. Kenmure Arms Hotel, High Street, New Galloway. Tel: (01644) 420240.	On Raiders Road Forest Drive.
Loch Whinyeon	Gatehouse of Fleet	Brown Trout	1 Apr. to 30 Sep.	M. & E. Brown, 52 High Street, Gatehouse of Fleet. Tel: (01557) 814222. Watson McKinnel, 15 St. Cuthbert Street, Kirkcudbright. Tel: (01557) 330693.	8am to 10pm. Bank and boat fishing. 2 boats available. Fly fishing only.

STRATHCLYDE (SOUTH)

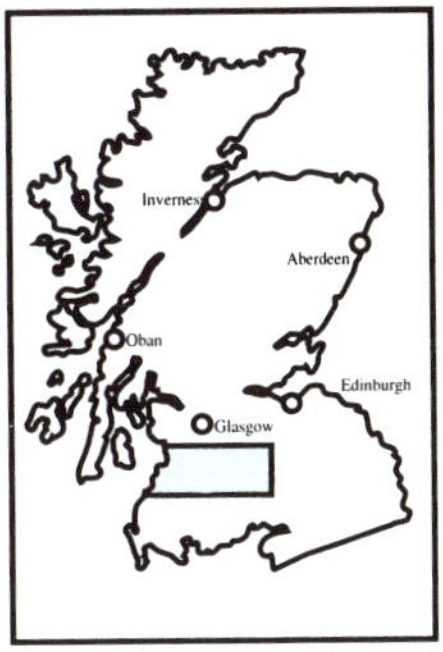

Constituent Area Tourist Boards
Ayrshire Tourist Board
Director of Tourism, Tourist Information Centre, Burns House, Park House Street, Ayr.
Tel: (01292) 284196.

Clyde Valley Tourist Board
Tourism Officer,
Tourist Information Centre,
Horsemarket, Ladyacre Road,
Lanark ML11 7LQ.
Tel: (01555) 661661.

Tourist Information Centre
Tourism Officer,
Promenade, Largs,
Ayrshire KA30 8BG.
Tel: (01475) 673765.

Isle of Arran Tourist Board
Area Tourist Officer,
Information Centre, The Pier,
Brodick, Isle of Arran KA27 8AU
Tel: (01770) 302140.

Greater Glasgow Tourist Board,
Chief Executive, Greater Glasgow Tourist Board,
35 St. Vincent Place,
Glasgow G1 2ER.
Tel: 0141-204 4400.

River Purification Board
Clyde River Purification Board
River House,
Murray Road,
East Kilbride.

RIVERS

Water	Location	Species	Season	Permit available from	Other information
Annick	Irvine	Salmon Sea Trout Brown Trout	15 Mar.to 31 Oct. 15 Mar. to 6 Oct.	Mr R.W. Gillespie, 16 Marble Avenue, Dreghorn.	
Annick (and Glazert)	Kilmaurs	Salmon Sea Trout Brown Trout	15 Mar. to 31Oct. 15 Mar. to 6 Oct.	Kilmaurs A.C., T.C McCabe, 8 East Park Crescent, Kilmaurs. Mr. D. Dunn, 22 Habbieauld Road, Kilmaurs. Tel: (01563) 523846. Pages etc., Main Street, Kilmaurs. Tel: (01563) 538570.	
Avon	Strathaven	Brown Trout Grayling	15 Mar. to 6 Oct. No close season	Country Lines, 29 Main Street, The Village, East Kilbride. Tel: (01355) 228952. Sports Emporium, Hamilton. Tel: (01698) 283903. P. & R. Torbet, 15 Strand Street, Kilmarnock. Tel: (01563) 541734.	Any legal method.
Ayr	Failford	Salmon Sea Trout Trout	10 Feb. to 31 Oct.	Gamesport of Ayr, 60 Sandgate, Ayr. Tel: (01292) 263822.	No Saturday or Sunday visitor permits.
	Mauchline	Salmon Sea Trout Brown Trout	15 Mar. to 31 Oct. 15 Mar.to15 Sep.	Linwood & Johnstone, Newsagent, The Cross, Mauchline. Tel: (01290) 550219.	

Water	Location	Species	Season	Permit available from	Other information
Ayr (Cessnock Lugar)	Mauchline	Salmon Sea Trout Brown Trout	11 Feb. to 31 Oct. 15 May to 6 Oct.	Linwood & Johnstone, Newsagents, The Cross, Mauchline. Tel: (01290) 550219.	
Ayr (Lugar)	Mauchline	Salmon Sea Trout Brown Trout	15 Mar. to 30 Oct. 15 Mar. to 15 Sep.	Linwood & Johnstone, Newsagents, The Cross, Mauchline. Tel: (01290) 550219.	
Cart	Busby	Brown Trout	15 Mar. to 6 Oct.	Tackle & Guns, 920 Pollokshaws Road, Glasgow G41 2ET. Tel: 0141-632 2005.	Average weight of fish caught: 8–10 oz. Popular flies: small spider flies. Bait fishing allowed, no spinning.
Cessnock	Mauchline	Brown Trout	15 Mar. to 15 Sep.	Linwood & Johnstone, Newsagents, The Cross, Mauchline. Tel: (01290) 550219.	
Clyde (Map IV C4)	Thankerton and Roberton	Brown Trout Grayling	15 Mar. to 5 Oct. 7 Oct. to 14 Mar.	B.F. Dexter, Secretary, 18 Boghall Park, Biggar. H. Bryden, Newsagent, 153 High Street, Biggar. J & A O'Hara, Grocers, Mill Rd., Thankerton. Anglers Attic, 44 Kirk Rd., Wishaw. Wyndales Hotel, Symington.	Protection order in force, permits to be obtained before going to river.Spinning with legal lures allowed from 1 May. Fly fishing at all times. Flies in normal use size 14. Ground baiting and keep nets are not allowed. No Sunday fishing.
Douglas (and Clyde)	Douglas Water	Brown Trout Grayling	15 Mar. to 30 Sep. All year.		Permits widely available in tackle shops in Glasgow and Lanarkshire.
Garnock	Kilbirnie	Brown Trout Salmon Sea Trout	15 Mar. to 6 Oct. 15 Mar. to 31 Oct.	Kilbirnie A.C., I. Johnstone, 12 Grahamston Avenue, Glengarnock KA14 3AF. Tel: (01505) 682154. R.T. Cycles, Glengarnock. Tel: (01505) 682191.	No Sunday fishing after 1 July.
Garnock (and Lugton)	Kilwinning	Salmon Sea Trout Brown Trout	15 Mar. to 31 Oct. 15 Mar. to 6 Oct.	Jamieson Hardware, 130 Main Street, Kilwinning. Tel: (01294) 551470.	Day permits.
Gryfe	Bridge of Weir	Brown Trout	15 Mar. to 6 Oct. 15 Mar. to 31 Oct.	M. Duncan, Newsagent, Main Street, Bridge of Weir. Tel: (01505) 612477.	No Saturday or Sunday fishing.
Iorsa	Isle of Arran	Salmon Sea Trout	Jun. to Oct.	The Estate Office, Dougarie, Isle of Arran. Tel: (01770) 840259.	
Irvine (Map IV B4)	Hurlford and Crookedholm	Salmon Sea Trout	15 Mar. to 31 Oct. 15 Mar. to 6 Oct.	P. & R. Torbet, 15 Strand Street, Kilmarnock. Tel: (01563) 541734.	
	Kilmarnock	Salmon Sea Trout Brown Trout	15 Mar. to 31 Oct. 15 Mar. to 6 Oct.	McCririck & Sons, 38 John Finnie Street, Kilmarnock. Tel: (01563) 525577.	No Sunday fishing after 31 July.

Water	Location	Species	Season	Permit available from	Other information
Irvine (and Annick)	Dreghorn	Salmon Sea Trout Brown Trout	31 Oct. 15 Mar. to 6 Oct.	Mr R.W. Gillespie, 16 Marble Avenue, Dreghorn.	River Irvine only, extension of season for salmon and sea trout – 1 to 15 November. Fly only.
Irvine (and Cessnock)	Galston	Salmon Sea Trout Brown Trout	15 Mar. to 30 Nov. 15 Mar. to 6 Oct.	P. & R. Torbet, 15 Strand Street, Kilmarnock. Tel: (01563) 541734.	
Kelvin	Glasgow–Strathkelvin	Salmon Sea Trout	11 Feb. to 31 Oct.	Tackle & Guns Ltd., 920 Pollokshaws Road, Glasgow G41 2ET. Tel: 0141-632 2005.	Any legal bait permitted.
Machrie	Arran	Salmon Sea Trout	Jun. to Oct.	Margo M. Wilson, Boltachan House, Aberfeldy PH15 2LA. Tel: (01887) 820496.	No Sunday fishing. Booking: Nov.–Oct.
Rotten Calder	East Kilbride	Brown Trout	15 Mar. to 6 Oct.	Country Lines, 29 Main Street, The Village, East Kilbride. Tel: (013552) 28952.	Any legal method.
Stinchar (Map IV B5)	Bardrochart Beat	Salmon Sea Trout	25 Oct. to 31 Oct.	Bardrochart Estate, Oaknowe, Colmonell, Ayrshire KA26 0SG. Tel: (01465) 88202.	Fly only. Fishing restricted to left bank.
	Dalreoch Estate	Salmon Sea Trout	25 Feb. to 31 Oct.	D. Overend, Dalreoch Lodge, Colmonell, Ayrshire KA26 0SQ. Tel: (01465) 881214.	Fly only, except in high water when spinning is allowed. Double bank fishing.

LOCHS & RESERVOIRS

Water	Location	Species	Season	Permit available from	Other information
Ardgowan Loch	Greenock	Brown/ Rainbow Trout	All year	At Ardgowan Loch. Tel: (01475) 522492.	Average weight of fish caught: from 1 lb 4 oz. Popular flies: Buzzers, Muddlers, traditional wet and drys. Lures in winter. Fly fishing only on 32 acres. Bait allowed on 5 acres. 6 boats available. Bank fishing. Stocked weekly.
Loch Arklet	Stirling & Trossachs	Brown Trout	30 Mar. to 28 Sep.	West of Scotland Water, 419 Balmore Road, Glasgow. Tel: 0141-355 5333. Or on location.	Fly fishing by rowing boat only. No live bait/spinning. Rowing boats supplied. 7 days fishing.
Loch Belston	Sinclairston	Brown Trout Rainbow Trout	15 Mar. to 15 Sep.	Bailiffs at loch.	Boats available.
		Rainbow Trout	No close season	Gamesport of Ayr, 60 Sandgate, Ayr. Tel: (01292) 263822.	
Loch Bradan	Straiton	Brown Trout (stocked)	15 Mar. to 30 Sep.	Forest Enterprise, Straiton. Tel: (01655) 770637. Mr. R. Heaney, Tallaminnoch, Straiton. Tel: (01655) 770617.	Five boats. Sunday fishing.

Water	Location	Species	Season	Permit available from	Other information
Loch Brecbowie	Straiton	Brown Trout	15 Mar. to 30 Sep.	Forest Enterprise, Straiton. Tel: (01655) 770637.	Fly fishing advised. Sunday fishing.
Burnfoot Reservoir	Nr. Fenwick	Brown/ Rainbow Trout	15 Mar. to 6 Oct.	Kilmaurs A.C., Mr. T.C. McCabe, 8 East Park Crescent, Kilmaurs. Mr. D. Dunn, 22 Habbieauld Road, Kilmaurs. Tel: (01563) 523846. J. L. McGarrity, 18, Main Street, Kilmaurs. Tel: (01563) 538287.	Average weight of fish caught: 1 lb–5 lbs. Popular flies: Butcher, Montana, Nymph, Viva, Soldier Palmer. Any legal method – no swim feeders or floats.
Busbie Muir Reservoir	Ardrossan	Brown Trout	1 Apr. to 6 Oct.	Ardrossan Eglinton A.C.Alpine Stores, Dalry Road, Ardrossan. Tel: (01294) 467979.	Obtain permits before fishing. Average weight of fish caught: 8–12 oz. Two boats, keys available from Alpine Store.
Camphill Reservoir	Kilbirnie	Brown Trout	1 Apr. to 6 Oct.	Kilbirnie A.C., I. Johnstone, 12 Grahamstone Avenue, Glengarnock KA14 3AF. Tel: (01505) 682154. R.T. Cycles, Glengarnock. Tel: (01505) 682191.	Fly only. Boat only.
Dhu Loch	Straiton	Brown Trout	15 Mar. to 30 Sep.	Mr. R. Heaney, Tallaminnoch, Straiton. Tel: (01655) 770617.	Fly only.
Glen Finglas	Stirling & Trossachs	Brown Trout	30 Mar. to 28 Sep.	West of Scotland Water, 419 Balmore Road, Glasgow. Tel: 0141-336 5333.Or on location.	Fly fishing by rowing boat only. No live bait/spinning. Rowing boats supplied. 7 days fishing.
Loch Goin (between orange markers)	Nr. Eaglesham	Brown Trout	15 Mar. to 6 Oct.	Kilmaurs A.C., Mr T.C. McCabe, 8 East Park Crescent, Kilmaurs. Mr. D. Dunn, 22 Habbieauld Road, Kilmaurs. Tel: (01563) 523846.	Average weight of fish caught: 8 oz to 3 lbs. No other baits – fly only.
Craigendunton Reservoir	Nr. Kilmarnock	Rainbow/ Brown Trout	15 Mar. to 6 Oct.	Kilmarnock A.C.McCririck & Sons, 38 John Finnie Street, Kilmarnock. Tel: (01563) 525577.	Average weight of fish caught: Rainbow 1 lb 8 oz, Brown Trout 12 oz. Fly and spinning only; no live bait.
Harelaw Dam	Neilston	Brown Trout	15 Mar. to 6 Oct.	Tackle & Guns, 920 Pollokshaws Road, Glasgow. Tel: 0141-632 2005.	Average weight of fish caught: 1 lb 2 oz.. For boats day or evening contact: Dougie Brown, 10 Garrioch Drive, Glasgow. Tel: 0141-946 6060.
Headshaw Loch	Nr. Ashkirk Village	Brown/ Rainbow Trout	Apr. to Nov.	Manager at Headshaw Loch. Tel: (0374) 287762, or Headshaw Farm Tel: (01750) 32233.	Average weight of fish caught: 2–4 lbs. Fly only. 7 boats, bank fishing. Bag limit 3 fish.
Hillend Reservoir	Nr. Caldercruix	Brown Trout Pike Perch	15 Mar. to 6 Oct.	Bailiff at Reservoir.Tel: (0831) 757432. Cafaro Bros., 140 Renfield Street, Glasgow. Tel: 0141-332 6224. PD Tackle, 69 Main Street Village, Cumbernauld. Tel: (01236) 735527. Grant's of Airdrie, 120 Stirling Street, Airdrie. Tel: (01236) 755532.	Average weight of fish caught: 1 lb 4 oz – 3.5 lbs. No ground baitingor swim feeders or illegal substances.10 boats available. Bank fishing. For further details: Mt. Potter, Secretary, 12 Sharp Avenue, Kirkwood, Coatbridge ML5 5RT. Hut number: (01236) 843611.

Water	Location	Species	Season	Permit available from	Other information
Howwood Fishery (Bowfield Dam)	Nr. Howwood	Brown/ Rainbow/ Brook/ Golden Trout	All year	Armadale Sports, Armadale. Bailiff. Tel: (01505) 702688.	Average weight of fish caught: 1.5 lbs +. Fly only. 3 boats available. Bank fishing. Refreshments sold. Resident qualified instructor.
Loch Katrine	Stirling & Trossachs	Brown Trout	30 Mar. to 28 Sep.	West of Scotland Water, 419 Balmore Road, Glasgow. Tel: 0141-336 5333. Or on location.	Fly fishing by rowing boat only. No live bait/spinning. Rowing boats supplied. 7 days fishing.
Kilbirnie Loch	Kilbirnie	Brown/ Rainbow Trout	15 Mar. to 6 Oct.	Kilbirnie A.C., I. Johnstone, 12 Grahamston Avenue, Glengarnock KA14 3AF. Tel: (01505) 682154. R.T. Cycles, Glengarnock. Tel: (01505) 682191.	All legal methods. Boats available.
Maich Water	Lochwinnoch	Brown/ Rainbow Trout	All year	From Maich Water Fishery. Tel: (01505) 842341. Average weight of fish caught: 1.5 lbs.	Popular flies: Damsels, Buzzers, Nymphs & Sedges. Fly and bait. 1 boat and bank fishing. Stocked 3 times weekly. Amenities for disabled. Clubhouse serving refreshments.
Mill Glen Reservoir	Ardrossan	Brown Trout	15 Mar. to 6 Oct.	Ardrossan Eglinton A.C. Alpine Stores, Dalry Road, Ardrossan. Tel: (01294) 467979.	Obtain permits before fishing. Average weight of fish caught: 8–12 oz. Popular flies: Wickhams, Kate McLaren, Soldier Palmer, Grouse & Claret, Invicta, Blae & Black. Fly fishing only.
Newmills (6 lochs)	Cleghorn	Rainbow Trout	All year	At Newmills. Tel: (01555) 870730.	Average weight of fish caught: 1 lb 2 oz. Popular flies: Lures, Cats Whiskers, Ace of Spades, Vivas. 2 boats (1 for disabled). Bank fishing. Tackle for sale/hire.
North Craig Reservoir	Kilmaurs	Rainbow Trout	Open all year	Kilmaurs A.C., T.C. McCabe, 8 East Park Crescent, Kilmaurs. Mr. D. Dunn, 22 Habbieauld Road, Kilmaurs. Tel: (01563) 523846. Pages etc., Main Street, Kilmaurs. Tel: (01563) 538570.	Average weight of fish caught: 1–5 lbs. Popular flies: Butcher, Soldier Palmer, Blue Zulu, Baby Doll, Viva. Any legal method.
Pen-whapple Reservoir	Nr. Girvan	Stocked Brown Trout	1 Apr. to 15 Sep.	Mrs. Stewart, Lanes Farm, nr. Girvan (1/4 mile from reservoir).	Fly fishing only (Mon.–Sat.). No Sunday fishing. Average weight of fish caught: 1 lb. Popular flies: Kate McLaren, Zulu, Invicta; traditional patterns. 4 boats available.
Port-na-Lochan	Black-waterfoot	Rainbow Trout	All year	Kinloch Hotel, Blackwaterfoot, Isle of Arran. Tel: (01770) 860444.	Average weight of fish caught: 1.25 lbs to 1.75 lbs. Fly fishing only. Popular flies: Viva, Alexandria, Montana Nymph, Peter Ross. Bait fishing at specific times only. Bank fishing only.

Water	Location	Species	Season	Permit available from	Other information
Raith & Prestwick Reservoir	Monkton	Rainbow Trout	15 Mar. to 15 Nov.	Gamesport of Ayr, 60 Sandgate, Ayr. Tel: (01292) 263822. Newhall's Newsagent, Monkton. Wheatsheaf Inn, Monkton.	Average weight of fish caught: 1–4 lbs. Popular flies: Butcher, Greenwell Glory. Worm fishing. No Sunday fishing. Weekdays 8am - 6pm.
Spring-water Loch	Nr. Dalrymple	Rainbow/ Brown/ Brook Trout	All year	At Springwater Loch. Tel: (01292) 560343.	Average weight of fish caught: 3–4 lbs. Popular flies: Buzzers, Hoppers, Damsels, Nymphs, Cats Whiskers and Vivas. Fly only (bait loch 2 acres) available. Stocked every day. Tackle for hire.
Strath-clyde Country Park Loch	Motherwell	Bream Tench Roach Carp Perch	All year	Booking Office, Strathclyde Country Park, 366 Hamilton Road, Motherwell. Tel: (01698) 266155.	

STRATHCLYDE (NORTH)

ARGYLL AND BUTE RIVERS AND LOCHS

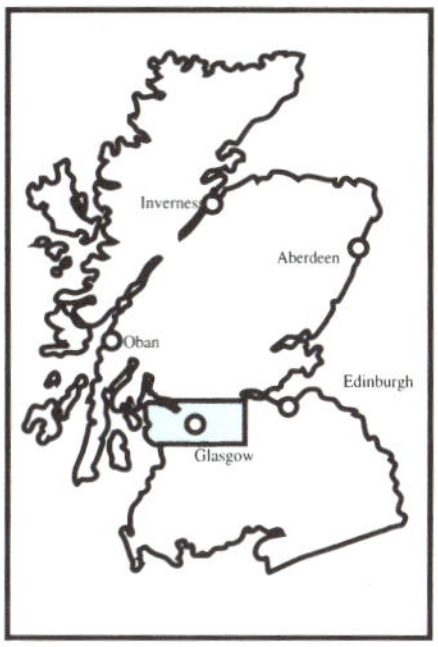

Constituent Area Tourist Boards
Bute and Cowal Tourist Board
Area Tourist Officer,
Information Centre,
7 Alexandra Parade,
Dunoon, Argyll PA23 8AB.
Tel: (01369) 703785.

Area Tourist Officer,
Tourist Information Centre,
15 Victoria Street,
Rothesay,
Isle of Bute PA20 0A
Tel: (01700) 502151

West
Highlands & Islands of Argyll Tourist Board
Area Tourist Officer,
Tourist Information Centre,
Argyll Square, Oban,
Argyll PA34 4AR.
Tel: (01631) 563122.

River Purification Board
Clyde River Purification Board
River House,
Murray Road,
East Kilbride G75 0LA.

RIVERS

Water	Location	Species	Season	Permit available from	Other information
Aros	Mull	Salmon Sea Trout	End Jun. to mid-Oct.	Tackle & Books, Main Street, Tobermory, Isle of Mull. Tel: (01688) 302336.	No Sunday fishing.
Awe (Map III B6)	Inverawe Taynuilt	Salmon Sea Trout	May to Oct.	Inverawe Fisheries, Taynuilt, Argyll. Tel: (01866) 822446.	Fly fishing only.
Bellart	Mull	Sea Trout Salmon	Jun. to end Oct.	Tackle & Books, Main Street, Tobermory, Isle of Mull. Tel: (01688) 302336.	No Sunday fishing.
Cur	13 miles from Dunoon	Salmon Sea Trout Brown Trout	1 Apr. to 15 Oct.	Dunoon & District A.C. Purdies of Argyll, 112 Argyll Street, Dunoon. Tel: (01369) 703232.	Fishing all legal methods. Bookings: Hon. Sec. A.H. Young, 'Ashgrove', 28 Royal Crescent, Dunoon PA23 7AH. Tel: (01369) 705732.
Douglas	Inveraray	Salmon Sea Trout	May to mid-Oct.	Argyll Caravan Park, Inveraray, Argyll. Tel: (01499) 302285.	No Sunday fishing. Fly fishing only.
Euchar	Kilninver	Salmon Sea Trout Brown Trout	1 Jun. to 15 Oct.	Mrs. Mary McCorkindale, Glenann, Kilninver, by Oban, Argyll. Tel: (01852) 316282.	No Sunday fishing.
		Salmon Sea Trout	Mid-Jul. to mid-Oct.	J.T.P. Mellor, Barncromin Farm, Knipoch, by Oban, Argyll. Tel: (01852) 316273.	(Tues., Wed. & Thurs.)
Finnart	12 miles from Dunoon	Occ. Salmon Sea Trout Brown Trout	1 Apr. to 15 Oct.	Dunoon & District A.C. Purdie's of Argyll, 112 Argyll Street, Dunoon. Tel: (01369) 703232.	Fishing all legal methods. Advanced bookings: Hon. Sec. A.H. Young, 'Ashgrove', 28 Royal Crescent, Dunoon PA23 7AH.Tel: (01369) 705732.
Goil	Lochgoilhe ad	Salmon Sea Trout	May to end Oct.	River Goil A.C. J. Lamont, Shore House Inn, Lochgoilhead. Tel: (01301) 703340.	Fly and worm. No spinning. No sea baits. No Sundays.

Water	Location	Species	Season	Permit available from	Other information
Grey	Islay	Salmon Sea Trout	Jul. to Oct.	Brian Wiles, Head Gamekeeper's House, Islay House Square, Bridgend. Tel: (01496) 810293.	Fly only. No night fishing.
Laggan	Islay	Salmon Sea Trout	Jul. to Oct.	Brian Wiles, Head Gamekeeper's House, Islay House Square, Bridgend. Tel: (01496) 810293.	Fly fishing only. No night fishing.
Massan	6 miles from Dunoon	Salmon Sea Trout Brown Trout	1 Apr. to 15 Oct.	Dunoon & District A.C. Purdie's of Argyll, 112 Argyll Street, Dunoon. Tel: (01369) 703232.	All legal methods. Advanced bookings: Hon. Sec. A.H. Young, 'Ashgrove', 28 Royal Crescent, Dunoon PA23 7AH. Tel: (01369) 705732.
Orchy (Map III B6)	Dalmally	Salmon	11 Feb. to 15 Oct.	W.A. Church, Croggan Crafts, Dalmally, Argyll. Tel: (01838) 200201.	
Ruel (Map IV B3)	Glendaruel	Salmon Sea Trout	16 Feb. to 31 Oct.	Glendaruel Hotel, Clachan of Glendaruel, Argyll PA22 3AA. Tel: (01369) 820274. Dunoon & District A.C. Purdie's of Argyll, 112 Argyll Street, Dunoon. Tel: (01369) 703232.	No Sunday fishing. All legal methods. Advanced booking: Hon. Sec. A.H. Young, 'Ashgrove', 28 Royal Crescent, Dunoon PA23 7AH. Tel: (01369) 705732.
Sorn	Islay	Salmon Sea Trout	October	Brian Wiles, Head Gamekeeper's House, Islay House Square, Bridgend. Tel: (01496) 810293.	Fly fishing only. No night fishing.

LOCHS & RESERVOIRS

Water	Location	Species	Season	Permit available from	Other information
Loch a'Bharrain	Nr. Oban	Brown Trout	15 Mar. to 6 Oct.	D. Graham, Combie Street, Oban. Sports Centre, Oban. Anglers' Corner, 2 John Street, Oban. Tel: (01631) 566374. Post Office, Kilmelford. Mr. Morrison, Ledaig Leisure, Benderloch.	Standard trout flies wet or dry (12 & 14). Peaty loch with small fish.
Loch a'Chaor-ainn	Nr. Kilmelford	Brown Trout	15 Mar. to 6 Oct.	D. Graham, 11-15 Combie Street, Oban. Tel: (01631) 562069. Oban Sports Centre, 4 Craigard Road, Oban PA34 5NP. Tel: (01631) 563845. Anglers' Corner, 2 John Street, Oban. Tel: (01631) 566374. Post Office, Kilmelford. Mr. Morrison, Ledaig Leisure, Benderloch.	Popular flies: imitations of natural flies. The loch contains trout up to 2 lbs.
Loch a'Cheigin	Nr. Kilmelford	Brown Trout	15 Mar. to 6 Oct.	D. Graham, Combie Street, Oban. Oban Sports Centre, 4 Craigard Road, Oban PA34 5NP. Tel: (01631) 563845. Anglers' Corner, 2 John Street, Oban. Tel: (01631) 566374. Post Office, Kilmelford. Mr. Morrison, Ledaig Leisure, Benderloch.	Popular flies: standard trout patterns, size 14.

Water	Location	Species	Season	Permit available from	Other information
Loch a'Chlachain	Nr. Kilmelford	Brown Trout	15 Mar. to 6 Oct.	D. Graham, Combie Street, Oban. Oban Sports Centre, 4 Craigard Road, Oban PA34 5NP. Tel: (01631) 563845. Anglers' Corner, 2 John Street, Oban. Tel: (01631) 566374. Post Office, Kilmelford. Mr. Morrison, Ledaig Leisure, Benderloch.	Popular flies: standard trout flies, wet or dry (12 & 14).
Loch a' Chrea-chain	Nr. Kilmelford	Brown Trout	15 Mar. to 6 Oct.	D. Graham, Combie Street, Oban. Sports Centre, Oban. Anglers' Corner, 2 John Street, Oban. Tel: (01631) 566374. Post Office, Kilmelford. Mr. Morrison, Ledaig Leisure, Benderloch.	Popular flies: standard pattern trout flies sizes 12 & 14, also big lure type flies for the bigger trout.
Loch a'Cruaiche	Nr. Kilmelford	Brown Trout	15 Mar. to 6 Oct.	D. Graham, Combie Street, Oban. Sports Centre, Oban. Anglers' Corner, 2 John Street, Oban. Tel: (01631) 566374. Post Office, Kilmelford. Mr. Morrison, Ledaig Leisure, Benderloch.	Small weedy loch with small trout.
Loch a'Mhinn	Nr. Kilmelford	Brown Trout	15 Mar. to 6 Oct.	D. Graham, Combie Street, Oban. Sports Centre, Oban. Anglers' Corner, 2 John Street, Oban. Tel: (01631) 566374. Post Office, Kilmelford. Mr. Morrison, Ledaig Leisure, Benderloch.	Popular flies: standard trout flies, wet or dry (12 & 14). The loch contains small fat trout, frequently difficult to catch.
Loch a'Phearsain	Nr. Kilmelford	Brown Trout	15 Mar. to 6 Oct.	D. Graham, Combie Street, Oban. Sports Centre, Oban. Anglers' Corner, 2 John Street, Oban. Tel: (01631) 566374. Post Office, Kilmelford. Mr. Morrison, Ledaig Leisure, Benderloch.	Average weight of fish: 8 oz to 1 lb. Popular flies: standard patterns, sizes 12 & 14.
Loch an Daimh	Nr. Kilmelford	Brown Trout	15 Mar. to 6 Oct.	D. Graham, Combie Street, Oban. Sports Centre, Oban. Anglers' Corner, 2 John Street, Oban. Tel: (01631) 566374. Post Office, Kilmelford. Mr. Morrison, Ledaig Leisure, Benderloch.	The loch contains trout up to 6 oz, but they are difficult to catch. Popular flies: standard trout flies, wet or dry (10 & 14).
Loch an Losgainn Beag	Nr. Kilmelford	Brown Trout	15 Mar. to 6 Oct.	D. Graham, Combie Street, Oban. Sports Centre, Oban. Anglers' Corner, 2 John Street, Oban. Tel: (01631) 566374. Post Office, Kilmelford. Mr. Morrison, Ledaig Leisure, Benderloch.	Popular flies: standard trout flies, wet or dry (10 to 14). The loch contains very large trout that are difficult to catch. Reputed to fish best in the evening during June.
Loch an Losgainn Mor	Nr. Kilmelford	Brown Trout	15 Mar. to 6 Oct.	D. Graham, Combie Street, Oban. Sports Centre, Oban. Anglers' Corner, 2 John Street, Oban. Tel: (01631) 566374. Post Office, Kilmelford. Mr. Morrison, Ledaig Leisure, Benderloch.	Popular flies: standard trout flies, wet or dry (10 to 14). The loch contains trout of 6 oz but they are difficult to catch.

Water	Location	Species	Season	Permit available from	Other information
Loch Airigh-Shamhraidh	Musdale	Brown Trout	15 Mar. to 6 Oct.	D. Graham, Combie Street, Oban. Sports Centre, Oban. Anglers' Corner, 2 John Street, Oban. Tel: (01631) 566374. Post Office, Kilmelford. Mr. Morrison, Ledaig Leisure, Benderloch.	Popular flies: standard trout flies wet or dry (12 & 14). Loch is full of easily caught trout.
Aros Lake	Mull	Rainbow Trout	All year	Tobermory AA., c/o Browns Shop, Tobermory. Tel: (01688) 302020.	Bank fishing only. Spinning permitted. Bag limit 5 fish.
Loch Ascog	Argyll	Brown/ Rainbow Trout	15 Mar. to 5 Oct.	Kyles of Bute A.C. A.H. Richardson, Allt Beag, Tighnabruaich PA21 2BE. Tel: (01700) 811486.	Fly only.
Loch Assopol	Mull	Salmon Sea Trout Brown Trout	Apr. to start Oct.	Argyll Arms Hotel, Bunessan, Isle of Mull. Tel: (01681) 700240.	Fly and spinner only. No Sunday fishing.
Glen Astil Lochs (2)	Isle of Islay	Brown Trout	15 Mar. to 30 Sep.	I.G. Laurie, Newsagent, 19 Charlotte Street, Port Ellen, Isle of Islay. Tel: (01496) 302264.	Fly only. No Sunday fishing. No catch limit. Permit covers all 5 lochs of Port Ellen Angling Club (see Loch Kinnabus). Boat available.
Loch Avich	Taynuilt	Brown Trout Rainbow Trout	15 Mar. to 6 Oct.	Mr. N.D. Clark, 11 Dalavich, by Taynuilt, Argyll PA35 1HN. Tel: (01866) 844209. W.A. Church, Croggan Crafts, Dalmally, Argyll. Tel: (01838) 200201.	5 boats available.
	Nr. Kilmelford	Brown Trout	15 Mar. to 6 Oct.	D. Graham, Combie Street, Oban. Sports Centre, Oban. Anglers' Corner, 2 John Street, Oban. Tel: (01631) 566374. Post Office, Kilmelford. Mr. Morrison, Ledaig Leisure, Benderloch.	Popular flies: standard patterns sizes 12 & 14.
Loch Awe	South Lochaweside by Dalmally	Salmon Sea Trout Brown Trout Rainbow Trout Perch Char Pike	11 Feb. to 15 Oct. 15 Mar. to 6 Oct. All year	Ardbrecknish House, by Dalmally, Argyll. Tel: (01866) 833223/833256.	Boats, tackle and permits available. Clubs welcome.
		Salmon Sea Trout Brown Trout Rainbow Trout Perch Char Pike	15 Mar. to 15 Oct. 15 Mar. to 6 Oct. All year	The Portsonachan Hotel, nr. Dalmally PA33 1BL. Tel: (01866) 833224.	
		Brown/ Rainbow Trout	15 Mar. to 15 Oct.	Ford Hotel, Ford. Tel: (01546) 810273.	

Water	Location	Species	Season	Permit available from	Other information
Loch Awe cont.	Taynuilt	Salmon Sea Trout Brown Trout Rainbow Trout	12 Feb. to 15 Oct. 15 Mar. to 6 Oct.	Mr. D.N. Clark, 11 Dalavich, by Taynuilt PA35 1HN. Tel: (01866) 844209. Sports Centre, Oban. Anglers' Corner, 2 John Street, Oban. Tel: (01631) 566374.	Boats available.
	Argyll	Brown/ Rainbow Trout	15 Mar. to 6 Oct.	Oban Tourist Office, Boswell House, Argyll Square, Oban. Tel: (01631) 563122. W.A. Church, Croggan Crafts, Dalmally, Argyll. Tel: (01838) 200201.	Permits also available for pike fishing (no close season).
Ballygrant Loch	Ballygrant	Brown Trout	15 Mar. to 6 Oct.	Port Askaig Stores, Port Askaig, Isle of Islay. Tel: (01496) 840245.	Average weight of fish caught: 8–16 oz. Boats are available.
Loch Bealach Ghearran	Nr. Minard village	Brown Trout	15 Mar. to 6 Oct.	Intersport, Lochnell Street, Lochgilphead, Argyll. Forest District Office, Whitegates, Lochgilphead.	Average weight of fish caught: 8 oz. Popular flies: most dark flies.
Big Feinn	Nr. Kilmelford	Brown Trout	15 Mar. to 6 Oct.	D. Graham, Combie Street, Oban. Sports Centre, Oban. Anglers' Corner, 2 John Street, Oban. Tel: (01631) 566374. Post Office, Kilmelford. Mr. Morrison, Ledaig Leisure, Benderloch.	The loch contains very large trout which are very difficult to catch. It fishes best at the beginning of the season in windy conditions. Popular flies: large salmon flies – Demons or Terrors.
Blackmill Loch	Nr. Minard village	Brown Trout	15 Mar. to 6 Oct.	Intersport, Lochnell Street, Lochgilphead, Argyll. Forest District Office, Whitegates, Lochgilphead.	Average weight of fish caught: 8 oz. Popular flies: most dark flies.
Cam Loch	Nr. Ford	Brown Trout	15 Mar. to 6 Oct.	Ford Hotel, Ford. Tel: (01546) 810273.	Average weight of fish caught: 8 oz. Popular flies: most dark flies.
Loch Crauch Maolachy	Nr. Kilmelford	Brown Trout	15 Mar. to 6 Oct.	D. Graham, Combie Street, Oban. Sports Centre, Oban. Anglers' Corner, 2 John Street, Oban. Tel: (01631) 566374. Post Office, Kilmelford. Mr. Morrison, Ledaig Leisure, Benderloch.	Stocked trout reach 2 lbs or more. Standard patterns, sizes 12 & 14.
Dubh Loch	Kilninver	Loch Leven Trout Brown Trout	Apr. to mid-Oct.	J.T.P. Mellor, Barndromin Farm, Knipoch, by Oban. Tel: (01852) 316273.	Boat on loch.
Loch Dubh-Bheag	Nr. Kilmelford	Brown Trout	15 Mar. to 6 Oct.	D. Graham, Combie Street, Oban. Sports Centre, Oban. Post Office, Kilmelford. Mr. Morrison, Ledaig Leisure, Benderloch.	Popular flies: standard trout patterns, sizes 12 & 14.
Loch Dubh-Mor	Nr. Kilmelford	Brown Trout	15 Mar. to 6 Oct.	D. Graham, Combie Street, Oban. Sports Centre, Oban. Anglers' Corner, 2 John Street, Oban. Tel: (01631) 566374. Post Office, Kilmelford. Mr. Morrison, Ledaig Leisure, Benderloch.	Average weight of fish caught: 4 oz. Popular flies: standard patterns, 10 & 12.

Water	Location	Species	Season	Permit available from	Other information
Dunoon Reservoir	Dunoon	Rainbow & Brook Trout	1 Mar. to 30 Nov.	Dunoon & District A.C. Purdie's of Argyll, 112 Argyll Street, Dunoon. Tel: (01369) 703232.	Fly fishing only. Regularly stocked with rainbow trout up to 4 lbs.
Ederline Lochs (18 hill lochs)	Ford	Wild Brown Trout	May to 6 Oct.	The Keeper, Keepers Cottage, Ederline, Ford, Lochgilphead. Tel: (01546) 810215.	Average weight of fish caught: 8 oz. Fly only. Boats available on 5 lochs.
Loch Ederline (& 3 smaller lochs)	Ford	Pike Perch	No close season	The Keeper, Keepers Cottage, Ederline, Ford, Lochgilphead. Tel: (01546) 810215.	All baits allowed. 3 boats available.
Loch Fad	Bute	Brown/ Rainbow Trout	15 Mar. to 6 Oct.	Bailiff at Loch. Tel: (01700) 504871. Isle of Bute Trout Co. Ltd., Ardmaleish, Isle of Bute PA20 0QJ. Tel: (01700) 502451.	23 boats available. Bank fishing. Whole day and evening tickets. No night fishing.
		Rainbow Trout Brown Trout	Mar. to Oct.	Carleol Enterprises Angling Holidays, 3 Alma Terrace, Rothesay. Tel: (01700) 503716.	Accommodation specifically for anglers. Permits arranged.
Loch Fada	Isle of Colonsay	Brown Trout	15 Mar. to 30 Sep.	The Hotel, Isle of Colonsay, Argyll PA61 7YP. Tel: (01951) 200316.	Fly fishing only.
Loch Finlaggan	Islay	Brown Trout	15 Mar. to 30 Sep.	Brian Wiles, Islay House Square, Bridgend, Isle of Islay, Argyll PA44 7NZ. Tel: (01496) 810293.	Two boats.
Forestry Hill Lochs	Ford	Brown Trout	15 Mar. to 6 Oct.	Ford Hotel, Ford, Argyll. Tel: (01546) 810723.	
Loch Frisa	Mull	Brown Trout Sea Trout	Apr. to Oct.	Tobermory AA., c/o Browns Shop, Tobermory. Tel: (01688) 302020.	Bank fishing. Spinning best.
Loch Glashan	Nr. Lochgair village	Brown Trout	15 Mar. to 6 Oct.	Intersport, Lochnell Street, Lochgilphead, Argyll. Forest District Office, Whitegates, Lochgilphead.	Average weight of fish caught: 12 oz. Popular flies: most dark flies. One boat is available.
Loch Gleann A' Bhearraidh	Lerags by Oban	Brown Trout	15 Mar. to 6 Oct.	Cologin Homes Ltd., Lerags, by Oban, Argyll. Tel: (01631) 564501. The Barn Bar, Cologin, Lerags, by Oban. Forest Enterprise, Millpark Road, Oban Tel: (01631) 566155.	One boat available.
Loch Gully	Nr. Kilmelford	Brown Trout	15 Mar. to 6 Oct.	D. Graham, Combie Street, Oban. Sports Centre, Oban. Anglers' Corner, 2 John Street, Oban. Tel: (01631) 566374. Post Office, Kilmelford. Mr. Morrison, Ledaig Leisure, Benderloch.	The loch contains some good fat trout. Popular flies: standard patterns, 12 & 14.
Iasg Loch	Nr. Kilmelford	Brown Trout	15 Mar. to 6 Oct.	D. Graham, Combie Street, Oban. Sports Centre, Oban. Anglers' Corner, 2 John Street, Oban. Tel: (01631) 566374. Post Office, Kilmelford. Mr. Morrison, Ledaig Leisure, Benderloch. Tel: (01631) 720393.	Popular flies: standard patterns, 10 & 12.

Water	Location	Species	Season	Permit available from	Other information
Inverawe	Taynuilt	Rainbow Trout	Mar. to Dec.	Inverawe Fisheries, Taynuilt, Argyll. Tel: (01866) 822446.	3 lochs and beginners loch. Fly fishing only. Fishing lessons available.
Kinnabus Lochs (3)	Islay	Brown Trout Arctic Char	15 Mar. to 30 Sep.	I. G. Laurie, Newsagent, 19 Charlotte Street, Port Ellen, Isle of Islay. Tel: (01496) 302264.	Boat available. Fly only. No Sunday fishing. No catch limit. Ticket covers all five lochs (see Glen Astil).
Lochgilp-head Lochs	Lochgilphead	Brown Trout	15 Mar. to 6 Oct.	Lochgilphead and District A.C., c/o The Sports Shop, 31 Lochnell Street, Lochgilphead PA31 8JL. Tel: (01546) 602390.	10 lochs. Fly only. No Sunday fishing.
Loch Loskin	1 mile from Dunoon	Brown/ Sea Trout	1 Apr. to 30 Sep.	Dunoon & District A.C. Purdie's of Argyll, 112 Argyll Street, Dunoon. Tel: (01369) 703232.	Fly only. Boat only.
Loch Lossit	Ballygrant	Brown Trout	15 Mar. to 6 Oct.	Port Askaig Stores, Port Askaig, Isle of Islay. Tel: (01496) 840245.	Average weight of fish caught: 8–16 oz. Boats available.
Loch Lussa	Campbeltown	Brown Trout	15 Mar. to 6 Oct.	A.P. MacGrory & Co., 16/20 Main Street, Campbeltown. Tel: (01586) 552132.	
Mishnish	Mull	Brown Trout	1 Apr. to 30 Sep.	Tobermory A.A., c/o Browns Shop, Tobermory. Tel: (01688) 302020.	Average weight of fish caught: 12 oz. Standard trout flies. 3 boats available. No Sunday fishing. Bag limit 5 fish.
MacKays Loch	Oban	Brown Trout Rainbow Trout	All Year	The Angler's Cornor, 2 John Street, Oban PA34 5NS. Tel: (01631) 566374.	3 boats available. Fly only. Day and half day permits.
Loch na Curraigh	Nr. Kilmelford	Brown Trout	15 Mar. to 6 Oct.	D. Graham, Combie Street, Oban. Sports Centre, Oban. Anglers' Corner, 2 John Street, Oban. Tel: (01631) 566374. Post Office, Kilmelford. Mr. Morrison, Ledaig Leisure, Benderloch.	The loch has some fat 8 oz–1lb trout that sometimes rise freely. The south end is floating bog and fishing from this bank is not advised. Popular flies: standard trout flies, wet or dry (12 & 14).
Loch nam Ban	Nr. Kilmelford	Brown Trout	15 Mar. to 6 Oct.	D. Graham, Combie Street, Oban. Sports Centre, Oban. Anglers' Corner, 2 John Street, Oban. Tel: (01631) 566374. Post Office, Kilmelford. Mr. Morrison, Ledaig Leisure, Benderloch.	Fish up to 2 lbs have been caught on occasion. Popular flies: standard trout flies, wet or dry (12 & 14).
Loch na Sailm	Nr . Kilmelford	Brown Trout	15 Mar. to 6 Oct.	D. Graham, Combie Street, Oban. Sports Centre, Oban. Anglers' Corner, 2 John Street, Oban. Tel: (01631) 566374. Post Office, Kilmelford. Mr. Morrison, Ledaig Leisure, Benderloch.	The loch has been dammed to improve fishing. Popular flies: standard trout pattern, sizes 12 & 14.

Water	Location	Species	Season	Permit available from	Other information
Loch Nell	Nr. Oban	Salmon Sea Trout Brown Trout Char	15 Mar. to 6 Oct. (Brown Trout)	D. Graham, Combie Street, Oban. Sports Centre, Oban. Anglers' Corner, 2 John Street, Oban. Tel: (01631) 566374. Post Office, Kilmelford. Mr. Morrison, Ledaig Leisure, Benderloch.	Popular flies: standard patterns, salmon and sea trout flies (8 & 10). Fly, spinning and bubble & fly are permitted. Boat available.
Oude Reservoir	14 miles from Oban	Brown Trout	15 Mar. to 6 Oct.	D. Graham, Combie Street, Oban. Sports Centre, Oban. Anglers' Corner, 2 John Street, Oban. Tel: (01631) 566374. Post Office, Kilmelford. Mr. Morrison, Ledaig Leisure, Benderloch.	Bank fishing can be difficult because of the fluctuating water level. Popular flies: standard trout flies, wet or dry (12 & 14). A boat is often located on this loch for periods.
Powder-works Dam	Argyll	Brown/ Rainbow Trout	15 Mar. to 5 Oct.	Kyles of Bute A.C., c/o Kames Hotel. Tel: (01700) 811489. Several shops in Kames and Tighnabruaich.	Fly and bait only, no spinning.
Loch Scamma-dale	Kilninver	Salmon Sea Trout Brown Trout	1 Jun. to 15 Oct. 15 Mar. to 6 Oct.	Mrs. McCorkindale, 'Glenann', Kilninver, by Oban, Argyll. Tel: (01852) 316282.	No Sunday fishing.
Loch Seil	Kilninver	Sea Trout Brown Trout	Apr. to mid-Oct.	J.T.P. Mellor, Barndromin Farm, Knipoch, by Oban, Argyll. Tel: (01852) 316273.	Boat on loch.
Sior Lochs	Nr. Oban	Brown Trout	15 Mar. to 6 Oct.	D. Graham, Combie Street, Oban. Sports Centre, Oban. Anglers' Corner, 2 John Street, Oban. Tel: (01631) 566374. Post Office, Kilmelford. Mr. Morrison, Ledaig Leisure, Benderloch.	Popular flies: standard trout flies, wet or dry (12 & 14). The lochs fish best in April and May.
Loch Squabain	Mull	Salmon Sea Trout Brown Trout		Tackle & Books, Main Street, Tobermory, Mull. Tel: (01688) 302336.	Boat fishing only. Weedy.
Loch Tarsan	8 miles from Dunoon	Brown Trout	1 Apr. to 30 Sep.	Dunoon & District A.C. Purdie's of Argyll, 112 Argyll Street, Dunoon. Tel: (01369) 703232.	Fly only. Boats available.
Tighna-bruaich Reservoir (2 other lochs)	Tighnabruaich	Brown/ Rainbow Trout	15 Mar. to 5 Oct.	Kyles of Bute A.C. Sec. A.H. Richardson, Allt Beag, Tighnabruaich PA21 2BE. Tel: (01700) 811486.	Fly and bait only. No spinning.
Torr Loch	North end of Mull	Wild Brown Trout Sea Trout	Apr. to Oct.	Tackle & Books, Main Street, Tobermory, Mull. Tel: (01688) 302336.	No Sunday fishing. 1 boat. Banks clear. Fly only.
Loch Tralaig	Nr. Kilmelford	Brown Trout	15 Mar. to 30 Sep.	Mrs. E. Mellor, Barndromin Farm, Knipoch, by Oban. Tel: (01852) 316273.	Fishing from bank only.

Water	Location	Species	Season	Permit available from	Other information
Loch Turamin	Isle of Colonsay	Brown Trout	15 Mar. to 30 Sep.	The Hotel, Isle of Colonsay, Argyll.	Fly fishing only. Boas are available.
Wee Feinn Loch	Nr. Kilmelford	Brown Trout	15 Mar. to 6 Oct.	D. Graham, Combie Street, Oban. Sports Centre, Oban. Anglers' Corner, 2 John Street, Oban. Tel: (01631) 566374. Post Office, Kilmelford. Mr. Morrison, Ledaig Leisure, Benderloch.	A small loch that contains trout up to 2lbs. Popular flies: standard trout patterns sizes 10 & 12.

FORTH and LOMOND

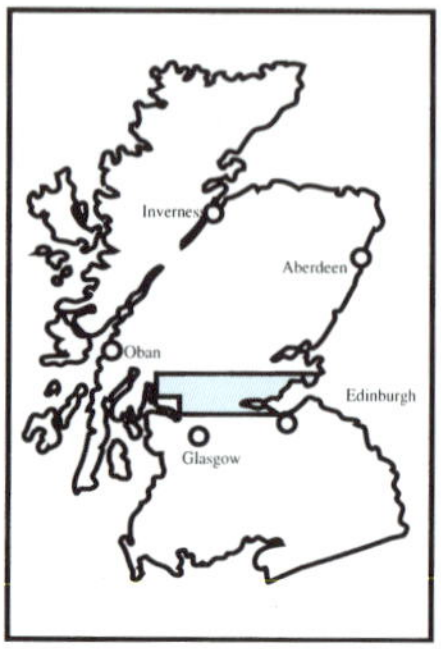

Constituent Area Tourist Boards

Edinburgh Tourist Board
Waverley Market,
3 Princes Street,
Edinburgh EH2 2QP.
Tel: 0131-557 2727.

Forth Valley Tourist Board
Tourist Officer,
Tourist Information Centre,
Burgh Hall, The Cross,
Linlithgow,
West Lothian EH49 7AH.
Tel: (01506) 844600.

Loch Lomond, Stirling and Trossachs Tourist Board
Tourism Officer,
Loch Lomond, Stirling and Trossachs Tourist Board,
41 Dumbarton Road,
Stirling FK8 2LQ.
Tel: (01786) 475019.

St. Andrews and North East Fife Tourist Board
Tourism Manager,
St. Andrews and North East Fife Tourist Board,
70 Market Street, St. Andrews,
Fife KY16 9NU.
Tel: (01334) 474609.

Kirkcaldy District Council
Tourist Officer,
Kirkcaldy District Council, Information Centre,
Durie Street,
Leven, Fife.
Tel: (01333) 429464.

East Lothian Tourist Board
Tourism Director,
East Lothian Tourist Board,
Brunton Hall,
Musselburgh EH21 6AE.
Tel: 0131-665 3711.

Other Tourist Organisations
MIDLOTHIAN

River Purification Board
Forth River Purification Board
Clearwater House,
Heriot Watt Research Park,
Avenue North,
Edinburgh EH14 4AP.
Tel: 0131-449 7296

RIVERS

Water	Location	Species	Season	Permit available from	Other information
Allan (Map IV C3)	Bridge of Allan	Salmon Sea Trout Brown Trout	15 Mar. to 31 Oct. 15 Mar. to 6 Oct.	Country Pursuits, 46 Henderson Street, Bridge of Allan. Tel: (01786) 834495.	
Almond	Cramond	Salmon Sea Trout Brown Trout	1 Feb. to 31 Oct. 15 Mar. to 6 Oct.	Country Life, Balgreen Road, Edinburgh. Tel: 0131-337 6230. Davidsons Mains P.O., 49 Corbiehill Rd., Edinburgh. Tel: 0131-336 5346.	Mouth to Old Cramond Brig. East bank only.
	West Lothian	Salmon Sea Trout Brown Trout	1 Feb. to 31 Oct. 15 Mar. to 6 Oct.	City Sports, 18 Almondvale South, Livingston. Tel: (01506) 434822. Country Life, Balgreen Road, Edinburgh. Tel: 0131-337 6230.	20 miles of river.

Water	Location	Species	Season	Permit available from	Other information
Devon	Dollar	Salmon Sea Trout Brown Trout	15 Mar. to 30 Oct. 15 Mar. to 5 Oct.	Devon Angling Assoc., R Breingan, 33 Redwell Place, Alloa. Tel: (01259) 215185. Scobbie Sports, 2/4 Primrose Street, Alloa. Tel: (01259) 722661. D.W. Black, The Hobby & Model Shop, 10–12 New Row, Dunfermline. Tel: (01383) 722582. D. Crockart & Son, 47 King Street, Stirling. Tel: (01786) 473443.	No Sunday fishing. Devonside Bridge upstream with excluded stretches. Fly fishing only from 15 Mar. to 12 Apr.
	Hillfoots	Salmon Sea Trout Brown Trout	15 Mar. to 31 Oct. 15 Mar. to 6 Oct.	Country Pursuits, 46 Henderson Street, Bridge of Allan. Tel: (01786) 834495.	No Sunday fishing.
Eden	Cupar area	Brown Trout Sea Trout Salmon	15 Mar. to 5 Oct. 15 Feb. to 31 Oct.	J. & R. Caldwell, Foodstore & Fishing Tackle, Main Street, Methilhill, Fife. Tel: (01592) 712215.	All legal methods permitted.
Endrick	Drymen	Salmon Sea Trout Brown Trout	11 Feb. to 31 Oct. 15 Mar. to 6 Oct.	Loch Lomond Angling Improvement Assoc., C. McCrory, P.O. Box 3559, Uddingston G71 7SJ. Tel: (01506) 655063.	Members only. No Sunday fishing. No worm fishing. Spinning restricted.
		Dace Chub Roach Eels	Open all year	The Bridge House, Drymen G63 0EY. Tel: (01360) 660355.	Fishes Spring to Autumn. Good dace shoals.
Esk	Musselburgh (Estuary to Buccleuch Estate both banks)	Salmon Sea Trout Brown Trout	15 Mar. to 31 Oct. 15 Mar. to 6 Oct.	Country Life, Balgreen Road, Edinburgh. Tel: 0131-337 6230.	No Sunday fishing. A max. of 6 fish per day. Spinning reels are prohibited. Further regulations on permit.
Esk (North and South)	Midlothian	Brown/ Rainbow Trout Grayling	15 Mar. to 6 Oct. 7 Oct. to 14 Mar. Special winter permit	F. & D. Simpson, 28/30 West Preston Street, Edinburgh EH8 9PZ. Tel: 0131 667 3058. Country Life, Balgreen Road, Edinburgh. Tel: 0131-337 6230. Laird & Dog Hotel, High Street, Lasswade. Bailiffs at water.	Fly rod and reel only to be used. Stocked at beginning of every month. Reductions for disabled, children and OAPs. Platform at Lasswade for disabled. Regulations on permit. Sunday fishing.
Forth (Map IV C3)	Stirling	Salmon Sea Trout Brown Trout	1 Feb. to 31 Oct. 15 Mar. to 6 Oct.	D. Crockart & Son, 47 King Street, Stirling. Tel: (01786) 473443. Mitchell's Tackle, 13 Bannockburn Road, Stirling. Tel: (01786) 445587. Country Pursuits, 46 Henderson Street, Bridge of Allan. Tel: (01786) 834495.	Information leaflet with maps, prices, rules. No bait fishing before 1 May or after 31 Aug.
Fruin	Helensburgh	Salmon Sea Trout Brown Trout	11 Feb. to 31 Oct. 1 Mar. to 6 Oct.	Loch Lomond Angling Improvement Assoc., C. McCrory, P.O. Box 3559, Uddingston G71 7SJ. Tel: (01506) 655063.	Members only. Fly fishing only.

Water	Location	Species	Season	Permit available from	Other information
Water of Leith	Edinburgh	Brown Trout	1 Apr. to 30 Sep.	The City of Edinburgh Council, Recreation Dept., 17 Waterloo Place, Edinburgh EH1 3BG. 0131-529 7844. Ext. 3286. Post Office, 36 Main Street, Balerno. Tel: 0131-449 3077. Post Office, Bridge Road, Colinton, Edinburgh. Tel: 0131-441 1003. Country Life, Balgreen Road, Edinburgh. Tel: 0131-337 6230.	Fly fishing above Slateford Road Bridge. No spinning. Regulations on permit.
Leven	Dumbarton	Salmon Sea Trout Brown Trout	11 Feb. to 31 Oct. 15 Mar. to 6 Oct.	Loch Lomond Angling Improvement Assoc., C. McCrory, P.O. Box 3559, Uddingston G71 7SJ. Tel: (01506) 655063. Tackle & Guns, 920 Pollokshaws Road, Glasgow. Tel: 0141-632 2005.	Members may fish all Association waters. No Sunday fishing. Day tickets available.
Leven (Fife)	Markinch to Leven	Brown Trout Salmon Sea Trout	15 Mar. to 30 Sep. 11 Feb. to 15 Oct.	J. Caldwell, Newsagent & Fishing Tackle, Main Street, Methilhill, Fife. Tel: (01592) 712215.	All legal methods. No shrimp or prawn.
Teith (Map IV C3)	Callander	Salmon Sea Trout Brown Trout	1 Feb. to 31 Oct.	J. Bayne, Main Street, Callander. Tel: (01877) 330218. (Season permits only.) Country Pursuits, 46 Henderson Street, Bridge of Allan. Tel: (01786) 834495.	Information leaflet with maps, prices, rules. No Sunday fishing.
	Gart Farm by Callander	Salmon Sea Trout	1 Feb. to 31 Oct.	Country Pursuits, 46 Henderson Street, Bridge of Allan. Tel: (01786) 834495.	Season permits only.
Tyne	Haddington	Brown Trout Rainbow Trout Sea Trout	15 Mar. to 6 Oct.	East Lothian Angling Association, J.S. Main, Saddlers, 87 High Street, Haddington. Tel: (01620) 822148. John Dickson & Son Ltd., 21 Frederick Street, Edinburgh EH2 2NE. Tel: 0131-225 4218. Country Life, Balgreen Road, Edinburgh. Tel: 0131-337 6230.	Twenty miles of river. No Sunday fishing. No threadlines. No spinning.

LOCHS & RESERVOIRS

Loch Achray	By Callander	Brown Trout Perch Pike	15 Mar. to 6 Oct.	Forest Enterprise, Queen Elizabeth Forest Park Visitor Centre, Aberfoyle. Tel: (01877) 382383. Loch Achray Hotel, Trossachs. Tel: (01877) 376229/376240. Bayne's Fishing Tackle Shop, Callander.	Bank fishing only.
Allandale Tarn Fisheries	West Calder	Rainbow/ Brown Trout Landlock Salmon	All year	At Allandale Tarn Fishery. Tel: (01506) 873073.	Average weight of fish caught: 2 lbs 4 oz. Fly fishing only on lochan. Separate bait pond. Bank only. Members A.S.S.F. Trout Master Water & Premier Trout Fishery. Rods/tackle for hire. Snack bar. Smokery available.

Water	Location	Species	Season	Permit available from	Other information
Loch Ard	Kinlochard	Brown Trout	15 Mar. to 6 Oct.	Altskeith Hotel, Kinlochard FK8 3TL. Tel: (01877) 387266.	Average weight of fish caught:12 oz. Popular flies: Silver Butcher, Kate McLaren, Alexandra. Fly fishing only. Boats are available.
Loch Arklet	By Inversnaid	Brown Trout	15 Mar. to 27 Sep.	West of Scotland Water, 419 Balmore Road, Glasgow G22 6NU, or at Loch Arklet.	Average weight of fish caught:8 to 12 oz. Popular flies: Silver Butcher, Grouse & Claret, Black Pennel, Greenwell's Glory. No live bait allowed. Rowing boats only are available.
Beecraigs Loch	Linlithgow	Brown Trout Rainbow Trout Brook Trout	1 Mar. to 31 Oct.	Beecraigs Country Park, The Park Centre, nr. Linlithgow. Tel: (01506) 844516.	Fly fishing only. Boat fishing only. Night fishing 11pm to 7am. May to August. Advance booking essential.
Bonaly Reservoir	Edinburgh	Brown/ Rainbow Trout	1 Apr. to 30 Sep.	None required.	
Bowden Springs	Linlithgow	Rainbow/ Brown Trout	3 Jan. to 23 Dec.	Grant Laidlaw, Bowden Springs Fishery, Carriber, Linlithgow. Tel: (01506) 847269.	Bank and boat fishing. Fly fishing only. Fish average 2lbs. Heaviest 19lbs. Float tubes for hire/sale. Corporate entertainment a speciality.
Cameron Reservoir	St. Andrews	Brown Trout	Mid-Apr. to end Sep.	St. Andrews Angling Club, Secretary, Mr. P. Malcolm, 54 St. Nicholas Street, St. Andrews. Tel: (01334) 476347. The bailiff at the fishing hut on Cameron Reservoir. During season. Tel: (01334) 840236.	Average weight of fish caught: 1 lb. Fly fishing only. 6 boats are available. Sunday fishing available.
Upper Carriston Reservoir	Nr. Markinch	Brown Trout	1 Apr. to 30 Sep.	J. & R. Caldwell, Foodstore & Fishing Tackle, Main Street, Methilhill, Fife. Tel: (01592) 712215.	Average weight of fish caught: 1 lb to 1 lb 8 oz. Fly fishing only. Bank fishing only – maximum 20 anglers. Day session: 10am–5pm. Evening session: 6pm–11pm.
Carron Valley Reservoir	Denny	Brown Trout	13 Apr. to 19 Sep.	Director of Finance, Central Regional Council, Viewforth, Stirling. Tel: (01786) 443000.	Boat fishing only.
Clubbie-dean Reservoir	Edinburgh	Brown/ Rainbow Trout	1 Apr. to 30 Sep.	East of Scotland Water, Fishing Desk, 55 Buckstone Terr., Edinburgh EH10 6XH. Tel: 0131-445 4141.	3 boats. Bag limit 6 trout. Fly fishing only. Sessions: May to August.
Cocksburn Loch	Bridge of Allan	Brown Trout	1 Apr. to 6 Oct.	Country Pursuits, 46 Henderson Street, Bridge of Allan. Tel: (01786) 834495.	Average weight of fish caught: 8–12 oz.
Crosswood Reservoir	West Calder	Brown Trout Brook Trout Rainbow Trout	1 Apr. to 30 Sep.	East of Scotland Water, Fishing Desk, 55 Buckstone Terr., Edinburgh EH10 6XH. Tel: 0131-445 4141.	Three boats available. 1 boat Edinburgh. 2 boats available – Livingston.

Water	Location	Species	Season	Permit available from	Other information
Loch Drunkie	Aberfoyle	Brown Trout	15 Mar. to 6 Oct.	Forest Enterprize, Queen Elizabeth Forest Park Visitor Centre, Aberfoyle.	Bank fishing only.
Loch Fitty	Kingseat Dunfermline	Salmon Brown/ Rainbow Trout	1 Mar. to Xmas	The Fishing Lodge, Loch Fitty, Dunfermline, Fife. Tel: (01383) 620666.	Boat and bank fly fishing. Day – 10am–5pm. Evenings – 5.30pm–dark. Reductions for single anglers, father & schoolboy son, husband and wife. Boats.
Gartmorn Dam Fishery	Nr. Alloa	Brown Trout	1 Apr. to 30 Sep.	Sep.–Apr.: Speirs Centre, 29 Primrose Street, Alloa FK10 1JJ. Tel: (01259) 213131. Apr.–Sep.: Visitor Centre, Gartmorn Dam Country Park, by Sauchie FK10 3AZ. Tel: (01259) 214319.	Average weight of fish caught: 1 lb 4 oz. Popular flies: Nymphs, Buzzers, Olives, Wickhams, 9 boats available. Disables anglers' wheelyboat. 2 sessions: 9am–5pm & 5pm–dusk.
Gladhouse Reservoir	Midlothian	Brown Trout	1 Apr. to 30 Sep.	East of Scotland Water, 55 Buckstone Terrace, Edinburgh EH10 6XH. Tel: 0131-445 6462.	Average weight of fish caught: 1 to 2 lbs. Local Nature Reserve. Double sessions: May–August. Day: 8am–4.30pm. Evening: 5pm–Sunset, plus 1 hour. Sunday fishing. Fly fishing only.
Glencorse Reservoir	Penicuik	Brown Trout Brook Trout Rainbow Trout	1 Apr. to 30 Sep.	East of Scotland Water, 55 Buckstone Terrace, Edinburgh EH10 6XH. Tel: 0131-445 6462.	Fly fishing only. 4 boats. Sessions: May to Aug.
Glen Finglas Reservoir	By Callander	Brown Trout	15 Mar. to 27 Sep.	West of Scotland Water, 419 Balmore Road, Glasgow G22 6NU, or at Glen Finglas.	Average weight of fish caught: 8 to 12 oz. Popular flies: Silver Butcher, Grouse & Claret, Black Pennel, Greenwell's Glory. No live bait allowed. Rowing boat available.
Loch Glow	Cleish Hills, nr. Kelty.	Brown Trout	15 Mar. to 6 Oct.	Tackle shops in Dunfermline, Cowdenbeath, Kelty and Kinross.	Fly, bait & Spinning. Regularly stocked with brown trout: some tagged fish. Further information: Mr. J. W. Mill. Tel: (01383) 722128.
Harlaw Reservoir	Balerno	Brown/ Rainbow Trout	1 Apr. to 30 Sep.	Day tickets: Fleming's Grocery Shop, 42 Main Street, Balerno. Tel: 0131-449 3833. Season Permits: Dalmeny Estate Office, South Queensferry, West Lothian.	Average weight of fish caught: 1–2 lbs. Fly fishing only. Bank fishing only. Season tickets issued by ballot – applications must be in by 1 March.
Harperrig Reservoir	West Calder	Brown Trout	1 Apr. to 30 Sep.	.Bank fishing only. Permits from machine at reservoir.	Correct coins required for machine: £1, 50p, 20p, 10p, 5p denominations. Four boats and bank fishing. No Sunday fishing. Fly fishing only.

Water	Location	Species	Season	Permit available from	Other information
Hopes Reservoir	Gifford	Brown Trout	1 Apr. to 30 Sep.	East of Scotland Water, Alderston House, Haddington EH41 3SY. Tel: (01620) 826422.	2 boats.
Hopetoun Quarry Pond	Nr. Winchburgh	Rainbow Trout	All year (at all times)	At Hopetoun Quarry Pond. Tel: 0131- 331 5312.	Average weight of fish caught: 1.5 lbs. Bait fishing only. Stocked bait/tackle for hire or sale.
Loch Katrine	Stronach-lachar	Brown Trout	15 Mar. to 27 Sep.	West of Scotland Water, 419 Balmore Road, Glasgow G22 6NU, or at Stronachlachar	Average weight of fish caught: 8 to 12 oz. Popular flies: Silver Butcher, Grouse & Claret, Black Pennel, Greenwell's Glory. No live bait allowed. Rowing boats only are available.
Lake of Menteith	Port of Menteith	Rainbow Trout	2 Apr. to 29 Oct.	Lake of Menteith Fisheries Ltd., Port of Menteith, Perthshire. Tel: (01877) 385664.	28 boats are available. No bank fishing.
Lindores Loch	Newburgh	Brown/ Rainbow Trout	Mar. to 30 Nov.	F.G.A. Hamilton, The Byre, Kindrochet, St. Fillans PH6 2JZ. Tel: (01764) 685337.	Two sessions: 9am–5pm. 5pm–10pm.
Linlithgow Loch	Linlithgow	Brown/ Rainbow Trout	15 Mar. to 6 Oct.	Tel: (0831) 288291.	Average weight of fish caught: 1 lb 8 oz. Popular flies: black lures, Green Peter, Grouse & Claret, Buzzers. Fly fishing only. 12 boats are available.
Lochore	Ballingry	Brown/ Rainbow Trout	1 Mar. to 30 Nov.	Lochore Meadows Country Park, Crosshill, Lochgelly, Fife KY5 8BA. Tel: (01592) 414312.	Sessions: any 8 hours till dusk, bank. Boats: Day 9am–4.30pm. Evening 5pm–dusk. Spinning and bait fishing from bank from 1 June.
Loganlea Trout Fishery	Nr. Penicuik	Wild Brown Trout Rainbow Trout	All year	Loganlea Trout Fishery, Milton Bridge, nr. Penicuik EH26 0PP. Tel: (01968) 679899.	Average weight of fish caught: 2 lbs. Fly fishing only. Stocked twice weekly with rainbows. Boats are available. Refreshments and tackle for sale.
Loch Lomond	Balloch to Ardlui	Salmon Sea Trout Brown Trout Pike Roach Perch	11 Feb. to 31 Oct. 15 Mar. to 6 Oct. No close season	Loch Lomond Angling Improvement Assoc., C. McCrory, P.O. Box 3559, Uddingston G71 7SJ. Tel: (01506) 655063.	Boats for hire locally. No Sunday fishing. Day permits available.
	Ardlui	Salmon Sea Trout Brown Trout Pike	11 Feb. to 31 Oct. 15 Mar. to 6 Oct.	Ardlui Hotel, Loch Lomond. Tel: (01301) 704243.	Popular flies: Silver Victor, Mallard, Claret. Other baits: Toby, Rapala, Sprat. Boats are available.
	Balmaha	Salmon Sea Trout Pike	Mar. to Oct. All year	MacFarlane & Son, The Boatyard, Balmaha. Tel: (01360) 870214.	Boats and outboard motors are available. Rods available. Permits sold.

Water	Location	Species	Season	Permit available from	Other information
	Rowardennan by Drymen	Salmon Sea Trout Brown Trout Pike	11 Feb. to 31 Oct. 15 Mar. to 6 Oct. All year	Rowardennan Hotel, Rowardennan. Tel: (01360) 870273.	Average weight of fish caught: Salmon 9 lbs; Sea Trout 3 lbs; Brown Trout 1 lb 12 oz. Other baits: Toby for trawling.
	Inverbeg	Salmon Sea Trout Brown Trout Pike Perch	11 Feb. to 31 Oct. 15 Mar. to 6 Oct. All year	Inverbeg Caravan Park, Inverbeg. Tel: (01436) 860267.	Popular flies: March Brown, Peter Ross. Live bait allowed.
Maltings Fishery	West Barns, Dunbar EH42 1RG	Brown/ Rainbow Trout	All year for Rainbow	Dunbar Trout Farm. Tel: (01368) 863244. Or at the fishery.	Fly only. Maximum fly size no. 10 long shank.
Markle Loch (5.5 acres)	nr. East Linton	Rainbow/ Brown Trout	All year	The Lodge, Markle Fisheries, Markle, East Linton EH40 3EB. Tel: (01620) 861213.	Average weight of fish caught: 2 lbs 4 oz. Popular flies: Damsel Nymphs, Buzzers, Hares Lug, mini lures, Dunkeld and dark traditional wets. Bank fishing only – no wading. Brown trout to be returned out of
Millhall Reservoir	Polmont	Brown/ Rainbow Trout	Mar. to Oct.	Avonbank Fishing Club, c/o Mr. Ian Geran, Polmont. Tel: (01324) 714190.	Average weight of fish caught: 1.5 lbs. Fly fishing only. 2 boats are available.
Monastery Loch (2.5 acres)	Nr. East Linton	Rainbow/ Brown Trout	All year	The Lodge, Markle Fisheries, Markle, East Linton EH40 3EB. Tel: (01620) 861213.	Average weight of fish caught: 2 lbs 4 oz. Popular flies: Damsel Nymphs, Buzzers, Hares Lug, mini lures, Dunkeld and dark traditional wets. Bank fishing only – no wading. Brown trout to be returned out of season.
Morton Fishery	Mid Calder	Rainbow Trout	11 Mar. to 29 Oct.	Morton Fishery, Morton Reservoir, Mid Calder, W. Lothian. Tel: (01506) 882293.	Fly fishing only. Advance bookings. Double sessions May–Aug., 9am–5pm, 5pm–dusk. Bag limits 3–6 fish per rod.
North Third	By Cambus-barron	Rainbow/ Brown Trout	15 Mar. to 31 Oct.	North Third Trout Fishery, 'Greathill', Cambusbarron, Stirling. Tel: (01786) 471967.	Fly fishing only. Boat and bank. Day permits only. Advance bookings advisable. Fishery record for rainbow trout 19 lbs 2 oz. Loch stocked in 1992 with American brook trout.
Parkley Fishery	Linlithgow	Brown/ Rainbow Trout	All year	Parkley Fishery, Edinburgh Road, Linlithgow. Tel: (01506) 842027. Mobile: (0836) 348037.	Bait and fly fishing permitted. Bank fishing only.
Raith Lake	Kirkcaldy (B925)	Wild Brown Trout Rainbow Trout American Brook Trout	All year	At Raith Lake. Tel (01592) 646466. Mobile: (0850) 532434.	Average weight of fish caught: 2 lbs. Fly fishing only. Stocked weekly. 13 boats are available.

Water	Location	Species	Season	Permit available from	Other information
Lochan Reoidhe	Aberfoyle	Brown Trout	15 Mar. to 6 Oct.	Forest Enterprise, Queen Elizabeth Forest Park Visitor Centre, Aberfoyle.	Fly fishing only. Limited rods. Advance bookings accepted.
Rosslynlee Reservoir	Nr. Penicuik	Brown/ Rainbow/ Brook Trout Salmon	All year	At Rosslynlee Reservoir. Tel: (01968) 679606.	Average weight of fish caught: 2 lbs. Fly fishing only. 1 boat available. Bank fishing. Rods for hire. Stocked weekly.
Selm Muir Loch	Mid Calder	Rainbow Trout	All year	Selm Muir Loch. George Gowland Tel: (01506) 884550.	Average weight of fish caught: 1 lb 4 oz. No spinning.
Swans-water Fishery	Stirling	Rainbow/ Brown Trout	All year for Rainbow	Swanswater Fishery.	Average weight of fish caught: 1 lb 12 oz. Popular flies: Viva, Black Pennel. Fly fishing only. 3 boats are available. Smokehouse and farm shop.
Threipmuir Reservoir	Balerno	Brown/ Rainbow Trout	1 Apr. to 30 Sep.	Day tickets: Flemings, Grocer, 42 Main Street, Balerno. Tel: 0131-449 3833. Season permits: Dalmeny Estate Office, South Queensferry, W. Lothian.	Average weight of fish caught: 1–2 lbs. Fly fishing only. Bank fishing only. Season tickets issued by ballot – applications must be in by 1 March.
Loch Venachar	Callander	Brown Trout	15 Mar. to 6 Oct.	J. Bayne, Main Street, Callander. Tel: (01877) 330218.	Boats for hire.
Loch Voil	Balquhidder	Brown Trout Salmon Sea Trout Char	15 Mar. to 6 Oct.	Stronvar Country House Hotel, Balquhidder FK19 8PB. Tel: (01877) 384688. C.M. Oldham & I.T. Emslie, Muirlaggan, Balquhidder, Lochearnhead FK19 8PB. Tel: (01877) 384219.	Hotel's guests only. Advanced bookings necessary. Popular flies: Blae & Black, Kate McLaren, Grouse & Claret, Black Spider, Greenwell's Glory, Butcher, Professor (size 12). Other baits: spinners, rapala, toby, kynoch killer for salmon. 5 boats are available.
West Water	West Linton	Wild Brown Trout	May to Aug.	East of Scotland Water, Fishing Desk, 55 Buckstone Terr., Edinburgh EH10 6XH. Tel: 0131-445 4141.	Average weight of fish caught: 14 oz. Fly fishing only. 1 boat available.

TAYSIDE

RIVERS AND LOCHS

Constituent Area Tourist Boards
City of Dundee Tourist Board
Director, City of Dundee Tourist Board,
Tourism Information Department,
4 City Square,
Dundee DD1 3BA.
Tel: (01382) 623141, Ext. 4384.

Perthshire Tourist Board
Director of Tourism,
Tourist Information Centre,
45 High Street,
Perth PH1 5TJ.
Tel: (01738) 627958.

Angus Tourist Board
Tourist Manager,
Tourist Information Centre,
Market Place,
Arbroath,
Angus DD11 1HR.
Tel: (01241) 876680.

River Purification Board
Tay River Purification Board
1 South Street,
Perth PH2 8NJ.
Tel: (01738) 627989.

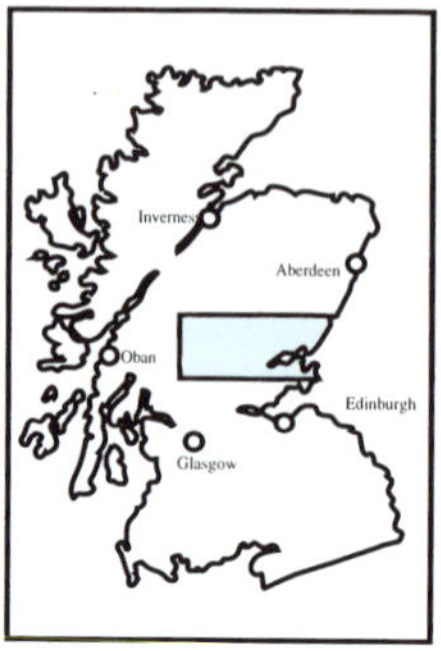

RIVERS

Water	Location	Species	Season	Permit available from	Other information
Braan	Amulree	Brown Trout	15 Mar. to 6 Oct.	Amulree Tearoom, Post Office, Amulree. Tel: (01350) 725200.	Fly fishing only.
	Cochill Burn	Brown Trout	15 Mar. to 6 Oct.	Kettles of Dunkeld, Atholl Street, Dunkeld. Tel: (01350) 727556.	Fly fishing only.
Dean	Strathmore	Brown Trout	15 Mar. to 6 Oct.	Strathmore Angling Improvement Assoc., Mrs. M.C. Milne, 1 West Park Gdns, Dundee. Tel: (01382) 667711.	Fly fishing only.
Devon	Hillfoots, Tillicoultry to Crook of Devon	Salmon Sea Trout Brown Trout	15 Mar. to 31 Oct. 15 Mar. to 6 Oct.	Country Pursuits, 46 Henderson Street, Bridge of Allan. Tel: (01786) 834495.	Fly fishing only from: 15 March to 12 April.
Dochart (Map IV C2)	Killin	Brown Trout	15 Mar. to 6 Oct.	J.H. Rough, J.R. News, Main Street, Killin. Tel: (01567) 820362. Clachaig Hotel, Killin. Tel: (01567) 820270.	All legal lures permitted. Fly only on lower beat.
Earn (Map IV D2)	Crieff	Salmon Sea Trout Brown Trout	1 Feb. to 15 Oct. 15 Mar. to 6 Oct.	Crieff Angling Club, Adam Boyd Newsagents, 39 King Street, Crieff. Tel: (01764) 653871.	No shrimp, prawn, diving minnow or floats. No bait before 1 May.
	By Crieff	Salmon Sea Trout Brown Trout	1 Feb. to 31 Oct. 15 Mar. to 6 Oct.	Country Pursuits, 46 Henderson Street, Bridge of Allan. Tel: (01786) 834495.	(Lower Strowan Beat) Permit available for season (day per week throughout session).
Ericht	Glenericht	Salmon Brown Trout	1 Apr. to 15 Oct. 15 Mar. to 6 Oct.	Bridge of Cally Hotel, Blairgowrie, Perthshire. Tel: (01250) 886231.	Fly fishing only.
	Craighall (upper)	Salmon Brown Trout	15 Jan. to 15 Oct. !5 Mar. to 6 Oct.	A.L. Rattray, Craighall, Blairgowrie PH10 7JB. Tel: (01250) 874749 or (01250)875080.	Subject to availability.

Water	Location	Species	Season	Permit available from	Other information
Fillan	by Crianlarich	Salmon Brown Trout	15 Jan to 15 Oct. 16 Mar. to 16 Oct.	Portnellan House, by Crianlarich FK20 8QS. Tel: (01838) 300284.	
Garry (Map IV C1)	Blair Atholl	Brown Trout	15 Mar. to 6 Oct.	Highland Shop, Blair Atholl. Tel: (01796) 481303.	Any legal method permitted.
Isla	Strathmore	Brown Trout	15 Mar. to 6 Oct.	Strathmore Angling Improvement Association, Mrs. M.C. Milne, 1 West Park Gardens, Dundee. Tel: (01382) 667711.	Fly fishing only on upper beats.
Lochay (Map IV C2)	Killin	Brown Trout Pike Perch	15 Mar. to 6 Oct.	J.H. Rough, J.R. News, Main Street, Killin. Tel: (01567) 820362.	Fly only on upper beat.
Lunan	Arbroath	Sea/ Brown Trout	15 Mar. to 6 Oct.	Arbroath Cycle and Tackle Centre, 274 High Street, Arbroath. Tel: (01241) 873467.	Fly, bait or spinning.
Lyon (Map IV B2)	Aberfeldy	Salmon	15 Jan. to 15 Oct.	Fortingall Hotel, Fortingall, by Aberfeldy. Tel: (01887) 830367.	No Sunday fishing. Max. rods on each of 2 beats. Maps, tackle, etc. available.(6 miles single bank.)
	Tirinie Fishings	Salmon Brown Trout	15 Jan. to 15 Oct. 15 Mar. to 6 Oct.	Coshieville Hotel, by Aberfeldy PH15 2NE.	Max. 4 rods. No bait fishing. No Sunday fishing. Boat & ghillie available for hire.
South Esk (Map III F5)	Kirriemuir	Salmon Sea Trout	16 Feb. to 31 Oct.	H. Burness, Kirriemuir Angling Club, 13 Clova Road, Kirriemuir. Tel: (01575) 573456.	No permits on Saturdays. No Sunday fishing. Fly only in parts in low water. Booking advisable. Map available.
Tay (Map IV C2)	Aberfeldy	Salmon Sea Trout	15 Jan. to 15 Oct.	Country Pursuits, 46 Henderson Street, Bridge of Allan. Tel: (01786) 834495.	(Killiechassie Beat) 4 rods maximum. Ghillie available.No prawns/ shrimps after 1Sep.
		Salmon Sea Trout	5 Jan. to 15 Oct.	Country Pursuits, 46 Henderson Street, Bridge of Allan. Tel: (01786) 834495.	(Derculich Beat) Maximum 3 rods. Ghillie available. No bait.
		Salmon Sea Trout	15 Jan. to 15 Oct.	Country Pursuits, 46 Henderson Street, Bridge of Allan. Tel: (01786) 834495.	(Lower Farleyer) 4 rods maximum. Ghillie available.
		Salmon Sea Trout	15 Jan. to 15 Oct.	Country Pursuits, 46 Henderson Street, Bridge of Allan. Tel: (01786) 834495.	(Moness Beat) Maximum 3 rods. Boat & ghillie available.
		Salmon Sea Trout	15 Jan. to 15 Oct.	Country Pursuits, 46 Henderson Street, Bridge of Allan. Tel: (01786) 834495.	(Lower Bolrocks Beat) 4 rods max. Boat & ghillie available.
		Trout Salmon	15 Mar to 6 Oct. 15 Jan to 15 Oct.	Tom Sharp, Laigh of Cluny, Steading, Edvadynate, Aberfeldy PH15 2JU.. Tel/Fax: (01887) 840469.	(Weem Water Beat). 6 rods max 1 1/4 single bank fishing. Private beat day or weekly permits. Booking advisable.

Water	Location	Species	Season	Permit available from	Other information
Tay cont.	Grandtully	Salmon Brown Trout Grayling	15 Jan. to 15 Oct. 15 Mar. to 6 Oct.	Country Pursuits, 46 Henderson Street, Bridge of Allan. Tel: (01786) 834495.	Fly or spinning. Boat and ghillie available. Booking advisable. Rod hire and tackle. 5-rod beat.
		Salmon Sea Trout	15 Jan. to 15 Oct.	Country Pursuits, 46 Henderson Street, Bridge of Allan. Tel: (01786) 834495.	(Findyate Beat) Maximum 3 rods. Boat and ghillie available. No prawns/shrimps after 1 Sep. Good Spring beat.
		Salmon Sea Trout	15 Jan. to 15 Oct.	Country Pursuits, 46 Henderson Street, Bridge of Allan. Tel: (01786) 834495.	(Clochfoldich Beat) Maximum 3 rods. Boat & ghillie available. No prawns/shrimps after 1 Sep. Good Spring Beat.
	Dalguise	Salmon	15 Jan. to 15 Oct.	Country Pursuits, 46 Henderson Street, Bridge of Allan. Tel: (01786) 834495. Finlayson Hughes, 29 Barossa Place, Perth. Tel: (01738) 630926.	$1^1/_4$ miles both banks. Boats & ghillies available.
	Dunkeld	Salmon Brown Trout	15 Jan. to 15 Oct. 15 Mar. to 6 Oct.	Stakis Hotels Ltd., Dunkeld House Hotel, Dunkeld. Tel: (01350) 727771.	Two boats with two rods. Experienced ghillies. 8 bank rods. Tuition. No salmon fishing on Sundays. Booking advisable.
		Brown Trout Grayling	15 Mar. to 6 Oct.	Kettles of Dunkeld, Atholl Street, Dunkeld. Tel: (01350) 727556.	Fly fishing only. Tackle hire.
		Salmon Sea Trout	15 Jan. to 15 Oct.	Country Pursuits, 46 Henderson Street, Bridge of Allan. Tel: (01786) 834495.	(Upper Newtyle Beat) Maximum 5 rods. Boat & ghillie available.
		Salmon Sea Trout	15 Jan. to 15 Oct.	Country Pursuits, 46 Henderson Street, Bridge of Allan. Tel: (01786) 834495.	(Lower Newtyle Beat) Maximum 5 rods. Boat & ghillie available.
	Stanley	Salmon Sea Trout Brown Trout	15 Jan. to 13 Oct. 12 Mar. to 6 Oct.	Tayside Hotel, Stanley, nr. Perth. Tel: (01738) 828249. Tackle & Guns, 920 Pollokshaws Road, Glasgow. Tel: 0141-632 2005. (Jan.–May Spring salmon)	Day permits available May–Jul. Ghillies by arrangement. Advisable to book in advance.
	Perth	Salmon Sea Trout Flounder Roach	15 Jan. to 15 Oct.	Director of Leisure & Recreation, Perth & Kinross District Council, 3 High Street, Perth. Tel: (01738) 639911, Ext. 3603. (Monday to Friday) Tourist Information Centre, 45 High Street, Perth PH1 5TJ. Tel: (01738) 638353. Weekends & public holidays.	Advisable to book in advance. Only 20 permits per day. Only 2 permits in advance by any one person. No weekly permits.
Tilt	Blair Atholl	Salmon	End May to 15 Oct.	The Highland Shop, Blair Atholl. Tel: (01796) 481303.	(Private beat, 3 miles) Booking advised. Fly or spinning only.

Water	Location	Species	Season	Permit available from	Other information
Tummel (Map IV C2)	Pitlochry	Salmon	15 Jan. to 15 Oct.	Pitlochry Angling Club, c/o Tourist Information Centre, Pitlochry. Tel: Mr. Gardiner (01796) 472157 (evenings/weekends).	Permits available Monday to Saturday. Booking in advance is advisable.
Tummel cont.	Pitlochry to Ballinluig	Brown Trout Grayling	15 Mar. to 6 Oct.	Tourist Information Centre, Pitlochry. Mitchells of Pitlochry, 23 Atholl Road, Pitlochry. Tel: (01796) 472613. Season tickets and enquiries to: Pitlochry Angling Club, Secretary, Mr. Harriman, Sunnyknowe, Nursing Home Brae, Pitlochry Tel: (01796) 472484 (evenings and weekends).	Pitlochry angling water. Five miles of river, both banks. Maps and rules on permits. Grayling permits available in the winter.
	Moulinearn to Ballinluig	Salmon Sea Trout	15 Jan. to 15 Oct.	Pitlochry Angling Club, c/o Tourist Information Centre, Pitlochry. Tel: Mr. Gardiner (01796) 472157 (evenings and weekends).	Only available July & August.
Tummel (Upper)	Kinloch Rannoch	Brown Trout	15 Mar. to 6 Oct.	Lochgarry Cottage. Tel: (01882) 632354. Innerhadden Keeper. Tel: (01882) 632339. Local shops and hotels.	Average weight of fish caught: 12 oz. Other baits: spinning and live.

LOCHS & RESERVOIRS

Water	Location	Species	Season	Permit available from	Other information
Loch Bainnie	Spittal of Glenshee	Brown Trout	18 Mar. to 11 Aug.	Invercauld Estates Office, Braemar AB35 5XQ. Tel: (01339) 741224.	Boat available from: Mr. G. Kerr, Gamekeeper, Wester Binzean, Glenshee. Tel: Glenshee 206. No spinning or use of live bait.
Ben Vrackie Loch	By Pitlochry	Brown Trout	15 Mar. to 30 Sep.	Mr. Seaton, Gamekeeper's House, Baledmund Estate, Pitlochry.	Average weight of fish caught: 8 oz. Any legal method permitted.
Blair Walker Pond	Blair Atholl	(Stocked) Brown/ Rainbow Trout	15 Mar. to 6 Oct.	The Highland Shop, Blair Atholl. Tel: (01796) 481303.	Fly only.
Butterstone Loch	Dunkeld	Rainbow/ Brown Trout	20 Mar. to 22 Oct.	The Bailiff, Lochend Cottage, Butterstone, by Dunkeld. Tel: (01350) 724238.	Fly fishing only.
Castlehill Reservoir	Glendevon	Brown Trout	1 Apr. to 30 Sep.	Fife Regional Council, Craig Mitchell House, Flemington Road, Glenrothes. Tel: (01592) 754411. Glendevon Treatment Works. Tel: (01259) 781453.	Fly fishing only. Boat or bank fishing.
Loch Dochart	By Crianlarich	Salmon Brown Trout	15 Jan. to 15 Oct.	Portnellan House, by Crianlarich FK20 8QS. Tel: (01838) 300284.	Fly only. Boats available.
Dunalastair Reservoir	Kinloch Rannoch	Brown Trout Pike	15 Mar. to 6 Oct. 15 Mar. to 30 Nov.	Lochgarry Cottage. Tel: (01882) 632354. Dunalastair Hotel. Tel: (01882) 632323.	Six boats. No bank fishing. Fly fishing only for trout – average weight 1 lb 9 oz. 9am to dusk.

Water	Location	Species	Season	Permit available from	Other information
Loch Earn	St. Fillans/ Lochearnhead	Brown Trout Charr Rainbow Trout	15 Mar. to 6 Oct.	P.O., Drummond Arms Hotel, Four Seasons Hotel (all St. Fillans). Clachan Cottage Hotel, 45 Bar & Rest., P.O., Village shop (all Lochearnhead).	12-14 ozs - Regular stocking with brown trouts up to 3lbs. 6 boats available without board engines. Drummond Estates boat hire. Tel: (01567) 830400.
Loch Eigheach	Moor of Rannoch	Brown/ Rainbow Trout Brown Trout	Mar. to Oct. 15 Mar. to 6 Oct.	St. Fillans Post Office, St. Fillans. Rannoch & District Angling Club, John Brown, The Square, Kinloch Rannoch. Tel: (01882) 632268.	Average weight of fish caught: 12 oz–2 lbs. Loch is regularly stocked. Bank fishing only.
Errochty Dam	Nr. Blair Atholl	Brown Trout Pike	15 Mar. to 6 Oct. All year	The Highland Shop, Blair Atholl. Tel: (01796) 481303.	Any legal method.
Loch Faskally	Pitlochry	Salmon Brown Trout Pike Perch	May to 15 Oct. 15 Mar. to 6 Oct.	Mr. D. McLaren, Pitlochry Boating Station, Loch Faskally, Pitlochry. Tel: (01796) 472919/472759.	Any legal lure for salmon and trout. Boats available. Cafe facilities. Fishing tackle bait when available.
Loch Freuchie	Amulree	Brown Trout Pike	15 Mar. to 6 Oct.	Amylree Tearoom, Post Office, Amulree. Tel: (01350) 725200.	Fly fishing only. Coarse fishing.
Glendevon (Upper & Lower Reservoir)	Glendevon	Brown Trout	1 Apr. to 30 Sep.	Fife Regional Council, Craig Mitchell House, Flemington Road, Glenrothes. Tel: (01592) 754411. Glendevon Treatment Works. Tel: (01259) 781453.	Fly fishing only. No Sunday fishing. Bank fishing on Lower Glendevon.
Glenfarg	Glenfarg	Brown Trout	1 Apr. to 30 Sep.	Fife Regional Council, Craig Mitchell House, Flemington Road, Glenrothes. Tel: (01592) 754411. Glenfarg Treatment Works. Tel: (01577) 830561.	Fly fishing only. No Sunday fishing. Boat available.
Heathery-ford	Just off Junc. 6 on M90 at Kinross	Brown/ Rainbow Trout	Mid-Mar. to Dec.	Kinross Trout Fishery, office on site. Tel: (01577) 864212.	All bank fishing, top quality trout. Trout master water. Fly fishing only.
Holl	Lomond Hills	Brown Trout	1 Apr. to 30 Sep.	Fife Regional Council, Craig Mitchell House, Flemington Road, Glenrothes. Tel: (01592) 754411.	Fly fishing only. No Sunday fishing. Boat available.
Loch Lubhair	Nr. Crianlarich	Salmon Brown Trout	15 Jan. to 13 Oct.	Portnellan House, by Crianlarich FK20 8QS. Tel: (01838) 300284.	Popular flies: Black Pennel, Black & Peacock, Mullard, Claret. Any legal method.
Loch Kinardochy	Tummel Bridge	Brown Trout	15 Mar. to 6 Oct.	Mitchells of Pitlochry, 23 Atholl Road, Pitlochry PH16 5BX. Tel: (01796) 472613.	Fly fishing from boat only. Advance booking recommended.
Lochan-na-Laraig	Killin	Trout	15 Mar. to 6 Oct.	J.H. Rough, J.R. News, Main Street, Killin. Tel: (01567) 820362.	All legal lures.
Loch Lee	Glen Esk	Brown Trout Arctic Char	1 May to 12 Aug.	Head Keeper, Invermark, Glenesk, by Brechin DD9 7YZ Tel: (01356) 670208.	Average weight of fish caught: 8 oz to 12 oz. 3 boats – 3 rods per boat. No Sunday fishing.
Loch Leven	Kinross	Rainbow/ Brown Trout	2 Apr. to 6 Oct.	Loch Leven Fisheries, The Pier, Kinross. Tel: (01577) 863407.	Fly and boat fishing.

Water	Location	Species	Season	Permit available from	Other information
Lintrathern Reservoir	Kirriemuir	Brown Trout	1 Apr. to 6 Oct.	Lintrathen Angling Club, Jack Yule, 61 Hillrise, Kirriemuir, Angus DD8 4JS. Tel: Loch (01575) 560327. Tel: Home (01575) 573816. Club bookings: Dr. Parratt, 91 Strathearn Road, Broughty Ferry, Dundee. Tel: (01382) 677305. (Not after start of season.)	20 boats & 2 disabled boats. Sunday fishing. Max. catch 15 fish per boat. Telephone for details of sessions and backwater dam. Bank fishing.
Mill of Criggie Trout Fishery	St. Cyrus, Montrose	Rainbow/ Brown Trout	All year	Eric & Rennie McVicar, Mill of Criggie, St. Cyrus, Montrose DD10 0DR. Tel/Fax: (01674) 850457.	Fly fishing only (bait for under 12's). Tuition (trout & salmon), courses, tackle hire. Bothy. Package holidays with varied accommodation.
Monikie	Monikie	Brown Trout	Start Apr. to 6 Oct.	Tel: (01382) 370300.	Average weight of fish caught: 1 lb 4 oz. Popular flies: Bibio, Kate McLaren, Ace of Spades. Boats: (10) Island Pond, (4) North Pond, (4) Crombie. Fly only. Boat only.
Loch nan Ean	Dalmunzie	Brown Trout	18 Mar. to 11 Aug.	Invercauld Estates Office, Braemar AB35 5XQ. Tel: (01339) 741224.	No spinning or use of live bait permitted.
Loch Rannoch	Kinloch Rannoch	Brown Trout Arctic Char Pike Perch	15 Mar. to 6 Oct.	Local shops and hotels. Loch Rannoch Conservation Association, R. Legate (Sec.), Glenrannoch House. Tel: (01882) 632307.	Fly and spinners only. No live bait. Average weight of fish caught: 8 oz to 1 lb. Boats from Dunalastair Hotel. Ghillie service. Rod hire. Small tackle shop.
		Brown Trout Pike Perch	15 Mar. to 6 Oct.	E.M. Beattie (Sec.), 2 Schiehallion Place, Kinloch Rannoch. Tel: (01882) 632261.	Average weight of fish caught: 8 oz to 1 lb. No live bait allowed.
Rescobie Loch	Forfar	Brown/ Rainbow Trout	15 Mar. to 31 Oct.	Bailiff, Rescobie Loch, South Lodge, Reswallie, by Forfar DD8 2SA. Tel: (01307) 818384.	Fly fishing only.
Sandy-knowes Fishery	Bridge of Earn	Rainbow Trout	1 Mar. to 25 Dec.	E. Christie, The Fishery Office, Sandyknowe Fishery, Bridge of Earn. Tel: (01738) 813033.	Bank fly fishing only. Session times: 10am–2pm, 2pm–6pm, 6pm–10pm. Bag limit 4 trout per session.
Loch Tay	Killin	Brown Trout Salmon	15 Mar. to 5 Oct. 15 Jan. to 15 Oct.	J.H. Rough, J.R. News, Main Street, Killin. Tel: (01567) 820362. Clachaig Hotel, Killin. Tel: (01567) 820270.	All legal lures permitted.
	Milton Morenish	Salmon Trout	15 Jan. to 15 Oct. 15 Mar. to 6 Oct.	Loch Tay Highland Lodges, Milton Morenish, by Killin. Tel: (01567) 820323.	3 boats available with outboards. Sixteen boats available. Ghillie and rod hire. Special offers for midweek fishing.
Loch Tummel	West of Pitlochry	Trout Pike Perch	Apr. to Oct.	Queen's View Visitor Centre, Strathtummel, by Pitlochry PH16 5NR.	
Loch Turret	Crieff	Salmon Sea Trout	1 Apr. to 30 Sep.11 Feb. to 30 Sep.	East of Scotland Water, Forth Valley Division, Balmore Treatment Works, Balmore, Torrance, Glasgow G64 4AJ. Tel: (01360) 620511. Adam Boyd Newsagents, 39 King Street, Crieff. Tel: (01764)	Four boats with outboards. Fly only.No prawn. Fly fishing Sep. No lead attached to fly.

NORTHEAST and SPEY

RIVERS AND LOCHS

Constituent Area Tourist Boards
Aviemore and Spey Valley Tourist Board
Area Tourist Officer,
Tourist Information Centre,
Grampian Road, Aviemore,
Inverness-shire PH22 1PP.
Tel: (01479) 810363.

Banff and Buchan Tourist Board
Tourism Manager,
Tourist Information Centre,
Collie Lodge,
Banff AB4 1AU.
Tel: (01261) 812419.

Kincardine and Deeside Tourist Board
Tourist Officer,
Tourist Information Centre,
Bridge Street, Banchory,
Kincardineshire AB31 2SX.
Tel: (01330) 822000.

City of Aberdeen Tourist Board
Director, City of Aberdeen Tourist Board,
St. Nicholas House,
Broad Street,
Aberdeen AB9 1DE.
Tel: (01224) 632727.

Gordon District Tourist Board,
Director,
Gordon District Tourist Board,
St. Nicholas House,
Broad Street,
Aberdeen AB9 1DE.
Tel: (01224) 632727.

Moray Tourist Board
Chief Tourist Officer,
Tourist Information Centre,
17 High Street,
Elgin,
Morayshire IV30 1EG.
Tel: (01343) 542666.

River Purification Board
North East River Purification Board
Greyhope House,
Greyhope Road,
Torry,
Aberdeen AB1 3RD.
Tel: (01224) 248338.

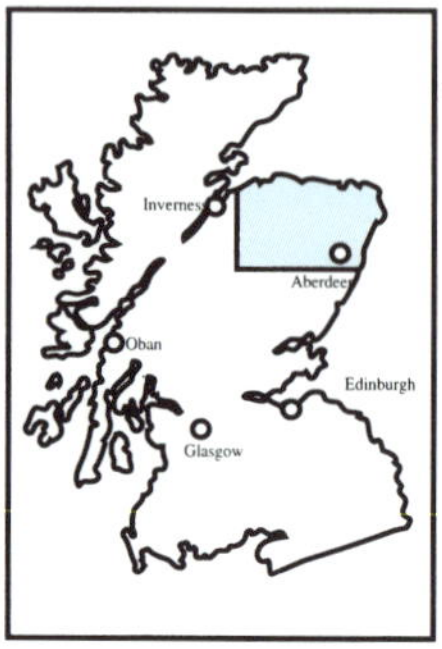

RIVERS

Water	Location	Species	Season	Permit available from	Other information
Avon (Map III E2)	Ballindalloch	Salmon Sea Trout	11 Feb. to 30 Sept.	Delnashaugh Inn, Ballindalloch, Banffshire AB37 9AS. Tel: (01807) 500255.	No prawn. Fly fishing Sep. No lead attached to fly.
	Tomintoul	Salmon Sea Trout	Feb. to end Sep.	Gordon Hotel, Tomintoul, Banffshire AB37 9ET. Tel: (01807) 580206.	No prawn. Fly fishing Sep. No lead attached to fly.
Bogie	Huntly	Salmon Sea Trout	11 Feb. to 31 Oct. 1 Apr. to 6 Oct.	Clerk of Fishings, Huntly Fishings Committee, Murdoch, McMath & Mitchell, 27/29 Duke Street, Huntly. Tel: (01466) 792291.	Permit covers Bogie, Deveron and Isla.
Carron	Stonehaven	Salmon Sea Trout Brown Trout	1 May to 31 Aug.	David's Sports Shop, 31 Market Square, Stonehaven. Tel: (01569) 762239.	Visitors' permits for Sea pool to railway viaduct. Further info.: Mr. A.G. Kellas, 44 Farburn Drive, Stonehaven AB3 2 BZ. Tel: (01569) 764227.

Water	Location	Species	Season	Permit available from	Other information
Clunie	Braemar	Brown Trout	15 Mar. to 20 Sep.	Ballater Angling Association, Tourist Information Centre, Braemar.	Fly fishing only.
Cowie	Stonehaven	Sea Trout Salmon Brown Trout	1 May to 31 Aug.	David's Sports Shop, 31 Market Square, Stonehaven. Tel: (01569) 762239.	Visitors' permits for Sea pool to railway viaduct. For further information: Mr. A.G. Kellas, 44 Farburn Drive, Stonehaven AB3 2BZ. Tel: (01569) 764227.
Dee (Map III F3)	Aboyne	Salmon Sea Trout	1 Mar. to 30 Sep.	Glen Tanar Estate, Brooks House Glen Tanar, Aboyne AB34 5EU. Tel: (013398) 86451. Fax: (013398) 86047	No Sunday fishing. Day permits available.
Deveron (Map III F2)	Huntly	Salmon Sea Trout Brown Trout	11 Feb. to 31 Oct. 1 Apr. to 6 Oct.	Clerk of Fishings, Huntly Fishings Committee, Murdoch, McMath & Mitchell, 27/29 Duke Street, Huntly. Tel: (01466) 792291.	Permits cover Deveron.
		Salmon Sea Trout Brown Trout	11 Feb. to 31 Oct.	Castle Hotel, Huntly AB54 4SH. Tel: (01466) 792696.	2 rods on hotel's own beat. Other private beats also available. Fly and spinning only.
		Salmon Sea Trout Brown Trout	11 Feb. to 31 Oct.	Forbes Country Matters, 47 Gordon Street, Huntly AB54 5EQ.	Huntly, Rothiemay, Bridge of Marnoch and other private beats. Daily and weekly lets. No shrimp or prawn.
	Turriff	Salmon Sea Trout Brown Trout	11 Feb. to 31 Oct.	Turriff Angling Assoc., I. Masson, The Cross, 6 Castle Street, Turriff. Tel: (01888) 562428.	No day tickets. Six weekly available to visitors. Restrictions on spinning.
Don (Map III F3)	Manar Beat	Salmon Sea Trout Brown Trout	11 Feb. to 31 Oct. 1 Apr. to 30 Sep.	J.J. Watson, 44 Market Place, Inverurie. Tel: (01467) 620321.	No worm, shrimp or prawn. Limit of 4 rods per day.
	Strathdon	Salmon Brown Trout	11 Feb. to 31 Oct.	Colquhonnie Hotel, Strathdon. Tel: (01975) 651210.	Fly and spinning only.
	Kintore	Salmon Sea Trout Brown Trout	11 Feb. to 31 Oct.	Kintore Arms Inn, Kintore. Tel: (01467) 632216. J.A. Copland, Newsagent, 2 Northern Road, Kintore. Tel: (01467) 632210.	No worm until 1 Apr. No natural minnow. No shrimp or prawn. Reductions for school children and OAPs.
	Inverurie	Salmon Sea Trout Brown Trout	11 Feb. to 31 Oct. 1 Apr. to 30 Sep.	J.J. Watson, 44 Market Place, Inverurie. Tel: (01467) 620321.	No worm until 1 Apr. No shrimp or prawn. Reductions for school children and OAPs. Booking advised.
	Inverurie (Keithhall & Ardmurdo Beats)	Salmon Sea Trout Brown Trout	11 Feb. to 31 Oct. 1 Apr. to 30 Sep.	J.J. Watson, 44 Market Place, Inverurie. Tel: (01467) 620321.	No worm until 1 Apr. No shrimp or prawn. Reductions for school children and OAPs. Booking advised. Saturday - members only.

Water	Location	Species	Season	Permit available from	Other information
Dulnain (Map III D3)	Grantown-on-Spey	Salmon Sea Trout Brown Trout	11 Feb. to 30 Sep. 15 Mar. to 30 Sep.	Strathspey Angling Assoc., Mortimer's, 3 High Street, Grantown-on-Spey. Tel: (01479) 872684.	Visitors resident in Grantown, Cromdale, Duthill, Carrbridge, Dulnain Bridge and Nethy Bridge areas. 12 miles of river.
Findhorn (Broom of Moy Beat) (Map III D2)	Forres	Salmon Sea Trout	11 Feb. to 30 Sep.	J. Mitchell, Springbank, Findhorn, Forres. Tel: (01309) 690406.	Popular flies: all shrimp. Stoats Tail, Dunkeld, Munro Killer. Spinning or worming allowed. Let by the week. Some day rods in early part of season.
Gairn	Nr. Ballater	Brown Trout	15 Mar. to 20 Sep.	Ballatet Angling Association. Countrywear, Bridge Street, Ballater.	Fly fishing only.
Glen of Rothes	By Elgin	Rainbow Brook Brown Trout	All year (Except browns)	Glen of Rothes Trout Fishery, Glen of Rothes, Rothes, Moray AB38 7AG. Tel: (01340) 831888.	Average weight is 2lb. Lures conventional, wet flies, dry flies, advice available on site. Additional loch for bait fishing. Bank fishing only.
Isla	Huntly	Salmon Sea Trout Brown Trout	11 Feb. to 31 Oct. 1 Apr. to 6 Oct.	Clerk of Fishings, Huntly Fishings Committee, Murdoch, McMath & Mitchell, 27/29 Duke Street, Huntly. Tel: (01466) 792291.	Permit covers Isla, Deveron and Bogie.
Muckle Burn	By Forres	Salmon Sea Trout	11 Feb. to 30 Sep.	I. Grant, Tackle Shop, 97D High Street, Forres. Tel: (01309) 672936.	Reductions for juniors.
Spey (Map III D3)	Aberlour	Salmon Sea Trout Brown Trout	11 Feb. to 30 Sep.	J.A.J. Munro, 93–95 High Street, Aberlour. Tel: Aberlour 871428.	3 tickets per hotel (Aberlour, Lour & Dowans or 6 day tickets, first come first served). One fish above bridge (9am–5pm), one fish below bridge (9am–midnight), other fish sold for club funds. No day tickets on Saturdays or local holidays.
	Grantown-on-Spey	Salmon Sea Trout Brown Trout	11 Feb. to 30 Sep. 15 Mar. to 30 Sep.	Strathspey Angling Assoc., Mortimer's, 3 High Street, Grantown-on-Spey. Tel: (01479) 872684.	7 miles both banks. No prawn. No Sunday fishing. Visitors must reside in Grantown, Cromdale, Duthill, Carrbridge, Dulnain Bridge or Nethy Bridge.
		Salmon Sea Trout	11 Feb. to 30 Sept.	Strathspey Estate Office, Heathfield, Grantown -on-Spey. Tel: (01479) 872520	No live bait. Fly only from May 1.
	Nethy Bridge Boat of Garten	Salmon Sea Trout Brown Trout	11 Feb. to 30 Sep.	Abernethy Angling Improvement Assoc., Boat of Garten. Allen's, Deshar Road, Boat of Garten. Tel: (01479) 831372.	6.25 miles both banks. No Sunday fishing. Visitors should reside in Boat of Garten, Nethy Bridge, Carrbridge or Dulnain Bridge. No shrimp or prawn allowed.
	Boat of Garten	Salmon Sea Trout Brown Trout	11 Feb. to 30 Sep. 15 Mar. to 30 Sep.	Allen's, Deshar Road, Boat of Garten. Tel: (01479) 831372.	

Water	Location	Species	Season	Permit available from	Other information
		Salmon Sea Trout	11 Feb. to 30 Sep.	Strathspey Estate Office, Heathfield, Grantown-on-Spey. Tel: (01479) 872520.	No live bait. Fly only from May 1.
	Aviemore	Salmon Sea Trout Brown Trout	11 Feb to 30 Sept.	Rothiemurchus Estate, Inverdruie, Aviemore PH22 1QH. Tel: (01479) 810703. M.J. Campbell, Kinrana, Aviemore. Tel: (01479) 311292. The Rowan Tree Restaurant & Guesthouse. Tel: (01479) 810207.	Beats on River Spey.
		Salmon Sea Trout Brown Trout	11 Feb. to 30 Sep.	Abernethy Angling Improvement Assoc., Speyside Sports, 64 Grampian Road, Aviemore. Tel: (01479) 810656.	Day tickets & weekly tickets available. No Sunday fishing.
	Kincraig	Brown Trout Salmon Sea Trout	11 Feb. to 30 Sep.	Alvie Estate Office, Kincraig, by Kingussie. Tel: (01540) 651255/651249. Dalraddy Caravan Park, by Aviemore. Tel: (01479) 810330.	Fly fishing or spinning.
Ugie (Map III G1)	Peterhead	Salmon Sea Trout Brown Trout	11 Feb. to 31 Oct.	Dicks Sports, 54 Broad Street, Fraserburgh. Tel: (01346) 514120. Robertson Sports, 1–3 Kirk Street, Peterhead AB4 6RT. Tel: (01779) 472584.	Bag limit 8 fish per day. Fly, spinning or worm entire season. No shrimps, prawns or illegal baits.
Ury	Inverurie	Salmon Sea Trout Brown Trout	11 Feb. to 31 Oct. 1 Apr. to 30 Sep.	J.J. Watson, 44 Market Place, Inverurie AB5 3XN. Tel: (01467) 620321.	No worm till 1 Apr. No natural minnow. No shrimp or prawn. Reductions for school children and OAPs. Sunday fishing – trout only.
Ythan (Map III G2)	(Estuary) Newburgh	Salmon Sea Trout	11 Feb. to 31 Oct.	The Ythan Fishery, Mrs. Forbes, 3 Lea Cottages, Newburgh, Ellon, Aberdeenshire AB41 0BN. Tel: (01358) 789297.	Limited fishing available. Details from Mrs. Forbes.
	Fyvie	Salmon Sea Trout	11 Feb. to 31 Oct.	Fyvie Angling Assoc., Sec. J.D. Pirie, Prenton South Road, Old Meldrum AB51 0AB. Tel: (01651) 872229.	No shrimps or prawns. No worming May to August.

LOCHS & RESERVOIRS

Water	Location	Species	Season	Permit available from	Other information
Aboyne Loch	Aboyne	Pike Perch		The Warden, Aboyne Loch, Holiday Park. Tel: (01339) 886244.	Fishing parties restricted on Sat. and Sun.
Loch Alvie	Aviemore	Brown Trout Pike	15 Mar. to 6 Oct. All year	Alvie Estate Office, Kincraig,Kingussie. Tel: (01540) 651255/651249. Dalraddy Caravan Park, by Aviemore. Tel: (01479) 810330.	1 boat. Fly fishing or spinning only.
Avielochan	Aviemore	Rainbow/ Brown Trout Wild Brown Trout Rainbow Trout	1 Apr. to 30 Sep.	Mrs. MacDonald, Avielochan, Aviemore. Tel: (01479) 810847. Allen's, Deshar Road, Boat of Garten. Tel: (01479) 831372. Speyside Sports, Aviemore. Tel: (01479) 810656.	Boat available. Fly fishing only. Sunday fishing 9am–5pm, 5pm–10pm. Fly fishing only. Stocked rainbow trout up to 7lbs.

Water	Location	Species	Season	Permit available from	Other information
Loch of Blairs	Forres	Brown/ Rainbow Trout	30 Mar. to 30 Sep.	I. Grant, Tackle Shop, 97D High Street, Forres. Tel: (01309) 672936.	Average weight of fish caught: 1 lb 8 oz. Popular flies: lures, conventional wet flies, dry flies. Two sessions. Boat fishing.
Brucklay Fishery	Maud	Rainbow Trout	1 Apr. to 30 Sep.	Brucklay Estate Office, Shevado, Maud AB42 8QN. Tel: (01771) 613263.	6 acre loch with bank and boat fishing. Average weight of fish caught: 2 lbs 8 oz. Fly fishing only.
Crimon-mogate Loch	Fraserburgh	Brown/ Rainbow Trout	All year	Crimonmogate, Lonmay, Fraserburgh. Tel: (01374) 224492.	Average weight of fish caught: 2 lbs 8 oz. Fly and lure fishing.
Loch Dallas	Boat of Garten	Brown/ Rainbow Trout	1 Apr. to 30 Sep.	Mortimer's, 3 High Street, Grantown-on-Spey. Tel: (01479) 872684. Allan's Store, Boat of Garten. Tel: (01479) 831372.	Fly fishing only (10am–6pm). Boat fishing. No Sunday fishing. 1 boat (2 rods).
Loch Ericht	Dalwhinnie	Brown Trout	15 Mar. to 6 Oct.	Badenoch Angling Assoc., Loch Ericht Hotel, Dalwhinnie. Tel: (01528) 522257.	Bank fishing only.
Glenlatter-ach Reservoir	By Elgin	Stocked Brown Trout	1 May. to 30 Sep.	.The Warden, Millbuies Lochs, Longmorn, Elgin. Tel: (01343) 860234.	Fly fishing only. 3 boats available. Bank fishing.
Lochin-dorb	Between Forres & Grantown	Brown Trout	1 May to 30 Sep.	Frank & Wendy Anderson, Underkeeper's Cottage, Lochindorb, Grantown-on-Spey, Tel: (01309) 651270.	Free fishing from bank. Boats available during season.
Loch Insh	Kincraig	Salmon Sea Trout Brown Trout Char Pike	11 Feb. to 30 Sep. 15 Mar. to 6 Oct. All year	Alvie Estate Office, Kincraig, Kingussie. Tel: (01540) 651255/651249. Dalraddy Caravan Park, by Aviemore. Tel: (01479) 810330.	One boat. Boat fishing only. Fly fishing or spinning.
		Salmon Sea Trout Brown Trout Arctic Char Pike	May to Sep.	Loch Insh Watersports, Boat House, Kincraig. Tel: (01540) 651272.	Boats are available.
Loch Laggan	Laggan	Brown Trout	15 Mar. to 6 Oct.	Loch Ericht Hotel, Dalwhinnie. Tel: (01528) 522257.	Bank fishing.
Loch of Logie	Fraserburgh	Brown/ Rainbow Trout	All year	Crimonmogate, Lonmay, Fraserburgh. Tel: (01374) 224492.	Average weight of trout caught: 2 lbs 8 oz. Fly and lure fishing.
Loch McLeod	Nr. Grantown-on-Spey	Brown/ Rainbow Trout	1 Apr. to 30 Sep.	Strathspey Estate Office, Heathfield, Grantown-on-Spey. Tel: (01479) 872529.	Bank fishing only. No fishing on Sundays. 2 rods per day. Fly fishing only (10am–6pm).
Millbuies Loch	By Elgin	Brown/ Rainbow Trout	Late Mar. to mid-Oct.	The Warden, Millbuies Loch, Longmorn, Elgin. Tel: (01343) 860234.	Boat fishing. Fly fishing only. Four boats available.

Water	Location	Species	Season	Permit available from	Other information
Loch Mor	Dulnain Bridge	Brown/ Rainbow Trout	Apr. to Sep.	Mortimer's, 3 High Street, Grantown-on-Spey. Tel: (01479) 872684.	Fly fishing only.
Loch Na Bo	Lhanbryde	Brown Trout	1 Apr. to 30 Sep.	D. Kinloch, Gardener's Cottage, Loch-na-Bo, Lhanbryde, Elgin. Tel: (01343) 842214.	Fly fishing only.
Pitfour Lake	Nr. Peterhead	Rainbow/ Brown Trou tTench, Carp Perch	All year (except for Browns)	Saplinbrae House Hotel, Old Deer, nr. Peterhead. Tel: (01771) 623515.	7 boats, bank fishing, fly only for trout. No spinning. No dogs.
Rothiemurchus Estate (Fish farm lochs)	Aviemore	Rainbow Trout Brown Trout Pike	Check with manager, Aviemore.	Rothiemurchus Fish Farm, by Aviemore PH22 1 QH. Tel: (01479) 810703.	Stocked rainbow trout loch. Open all year except when frozen. Additional private lochs available.
Loch Saugh	Fettercairn/ Drumtochty Glen	Brown Trout	15 Mar. to 6 Oct.	Brechin Angling Club, W.G. Balfour, 9 Cookston Crescent, Brechin DD9 6BP. Tel: (01356) 622753. Ramsay Arms Hotel, Fettercairn. Tel: (01561) 340334. Drumtochty Arms Hotel, Auchenblae AB30 1XR. Tel: (01561) 320210. David Rollston-Smith, Fishing Tackle, Guns & Sport, 180 High Street, Montrose. Tel: (01674) 672692. G. Carroll Angling Supplies, Brechin.	Fly fishing only from bank.
Glen Tanar Loch	Glen Tanar	Rainbow Trout	Mar. to Dec.	Glen Tanar Estate, Brooks House, Glen Tanar, Aboyne AB34 5EU. Tel: (013398) 86451. Fax: (013398) 86047.	3 boats. Boat fishing by day or evening.
Loch Vaa	Aviemore	Brown/ Rainbow Trout	1 Apr. to 30 Sep.	Mortimer's, 3 High Street, Grantown-on-Spey. Tel: (01479) 872684.	Boat fishing only. 2 boats - 2 rods per boat. Fly fishing only. No Sunday fishing. Fishing 10am–6pm only.
Loch Vrotichan	Cairnwell	Brown Trout	18 Mar. to 11 Aug.	Invercauld Estates Office, Braemar AB35 5XQ. Tel: (01339) 741224. Tourist Information Centre, Braemar. Tel: (013397) 41600. Tourist Information Centre, Ballater. Tel: (0139397) 55306.	Fly fishing only.

GREAT GLEN and SKYE

Constituent Area Tourist Boards
Fort William and Lochaber Tourism Ltd.
Area Tourist Officer,
Tourist Information Centre,
Cameron Centre, Cameron Square,
Fort William,
Inverness-shire PH33 6AJ.
Tel: (01397) 703781.

Isle of Skye and South West Ross Tourist Board
Area Tourist Officer,
Tourist Information Centre,
Meall House,
Portree,
Isle of Skye IV51 3BG.
Tel: (01478) 612137.

Inverness, Loch Ness and Nairn Tourist Board
Area Tourist Officer,
Tourist Information Centre,
Castle Wynd,
Inverness IV2 3BG.
Tel: (01463) 234353.

River Purification Board
Highland River Purification Board
Graesser House,
Fodderty Way,
Dingwall.
Tel: (01349) 62021.

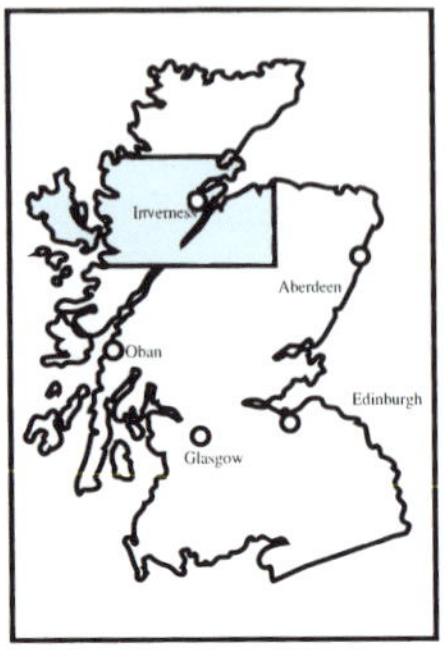

RIVERS

Water	Location	Species	Season	Permit available from	Other information
Brogaig	Glencoe	Sea Trout Brown Trout	1 Mar. to 31 Oct.	Jansport, Wentworth Street, Portree, Skye. Tel: (01478) 612559.	
Coe		Salmon Sea Trout	15 Apr. to 15 Oct.	National Trust for Scotland, Visitor Centre, Glencoe. Tel: (01855) 811307.	No Sunday fishing.
Croe (Map 11C5)		Salmon Brown Trout	1 Mar. to 30 Sep.	National Trust for Scotland, Morvich Farm, Inerinate, by Kyle. Tel: 901559) 511231.	Fly fishing only.
Farrar (Map 11E4)	Struy	Salmon Brown Trout	Jun. to 15 Oct. 15 Mar. to 30 Sep.	Culligran Estate, Glen Strathfarrar, Struy, nr. Beauly IV4 7JX. Tel/Fax: (01463) 761285.	Fly fishing only.
Garry (upper) (Map 11D6)	Garry Gualach to Poulary Bridge	Salmon Sea Trout Brown Trout	15 Mar. to 14 Oct. 15 Mar. to 6 Oct.	Mr. Isaacson, Garry Gualach Country Holidays, Invergarry.	Fly only 1 May to end of season.
Glass (map 11E4)	Struy	Salmon Sea Trout	Jun. to 15 Oct. 15 Mar. to 30 Sep.	Culligran Estate, Glen Strathfarrar, Struy, nr. Beauly IV4 7JX. Tel/Fax: (01463) 761285.	Fly fishing only.
Lealt	North Skye	Salmon Sea Trout Brown Trout	1 Mar. to 31 Oct.	Jansport, Wentworth Street, Portree, Skye. Tel: (01478) 612559.	

Water	Location	Species	Season	Permit available from	Other information
Moidart (Map 11B7)	West of Fort William	Salmon Sea Trout	11 Feb. to 31 Oct.	Mrs. N. Stewart, Kinlochmoidart House, Kinlochmoidart, nr. Fort William.	Fly only. Short (approx. 5 miles) spate river.
Moriston	Glenmoriston Estuary beat	Salmon	15 Jan. to 15 Oct.	Vincent Tait, Head Gamekeeper. Tel: (01320) 351219.	Fly and spinning only.
	Dundreggan Beat	Salmon Brown Trout	1 May to end Sep. Mar. to Sep.	Vincent Tait, Head Gamekeeper. Tel: (01320) 351219.	Fly and spinning only.
Nairn (Map 111 F4)	Nairn/ Culloden Moor	Salmon Sea Trout	11 Feb. to 7 Oct.	Nairn Angling Association, P. Fraser, High Street, Nairn. Tel: (01667) 453038. Clava Lodge Holiday Homes, Culloden Moor, Inverness IV1 2EJ. Tel: (01463) 790228.	
Ness (Map 11 F4)	Inverness Town Water	Salmon Sea Trout	15 Jan. to 15 Oct.	Graham's Tackle, 37 Castle Street, Inverness. Tel: (01463) 233178.	3 miles of river immediately above the tide.
Nevis (Map II D7)	Fort William	Salmon Sea Trout		Rod & Gun Shop, 18 High Street, Fort William. Tel: (01397) 702656.	Spinning permitted in afternoon only.
Polloch	Strontian	Salmon Sea Trout	1 May. to 31 Oct.	Post Office, Strontian.	Average weight of fish caught: Salmon 6 lbs, Sea Trout 1 lb, Brown Trout 1 lb. Popular flies: dark flies. Worm and spinning allowed. No prawn fishing.
Snizort	Skye	Salmon Sea Trout Brown Trout	1 Jul. to 15 Oct.	Skeabost House Hotel, Skeabost, Isle of Skye. Tel: (01470) 532202.	Discounts for residents.
Spean (Map II E7)	Nr. Fort William	Salmon Sea Trout Brown Trout	15 Jan. to 15 Oct.	Rod & Gun Shop, 18 High Street, Fort William. Tel: (01397) 702656.	Major tributary of the Lochy.
Staffin	North Skye	Salmon Sea Trout	1 Mar. to 31 Oct.	Jansport, Wentworth Street, Portree, Skye. Tel: (01478) 612559.	
Strontian	Strontian	Salmon Sea Trout Brown Trout	1 May. to 31 Oct.	Post Office, Strontian.	Average weight of fish caught: Salmon 6 lbs to 10 lbs, Sea Trout 1 lb. Popular flies: Blue Charm, Hair Fly. Worm (if river in spate) and spinning. No prawns.

LOCHS & RESERVOIRS

Water	Location	Species	Season	Permit available from	Other information
Loch Abhana	By Cannich	Brown Trout	Apr. to 6 Oct.	Glen Affric Hotel, Cannich. Tel: (01456) 415214.	Fly fishing only. Boat or bank.
Ardtornish Estate Waters	Morvern	Salmon Sea Trout Brown Trout	Apr. to Oct.	Ardtornish Estate Office, Morvern, by Oban, Argyll. Tel: (01967) 42128	Six boats for hire.
Loch Arkaig	Fort William	Sea Trout Brown Trout Salmon (occasional) Pike	Mar. to Oct.	Locheil Estate Fishings, 33 High Street, Fort William.Tel: (01397) 702433.Rod & Gun Shop, 18 High Street,Fort William. Tel: (01397) 702656.Mrs Yates, No. 2 Clunes, Achnacarry, . Tel: (01397) 712719.	

Water	Location	Species	Season	Permit available from	Other information
Loch Beanna-chran	Strathfarrar	Brown Trout	15 Mar. to 6 Oct.	Glen Affric Hotel, Cannich. Tel: (01456) 415214.	Fly fishing only. 1 boat. No bank fishing.
Loch Benevean (Bheinn a' Mheadhoin)	Glen Affric	Brown Trout	15 Mar. to 6 Oct.	Glen Affric Hotel, Cannich. Tel: (01456) 415214.	Fly fishing only. 6 boats available. No bank fishing.
Loch Dochfour	Inverness	Brown Trout	15 Mar. to 6 Oct.	Dochfour Estate Office, Dochgarroch, by Inverness. Tel: (01463) 861218. Dochgarrod Shop & P.O.	No Sunday fishing. Bank fishing only. Fly only.
Loch Doilet	Strontian	Salmon Sea Trout Brown Trout	1 May to 31 Oct.	George Fisher, Polloch Lodge, Strontian. Tel: (01967) 402412. General Store, Strontian. Post Office, Strontian.	Average weight of fish caught: Salmon 6 lbs, Sea Trout 1 lb. Popular flies: black flies. Worm and spinning available. No prawns. Boats available from: Jim Bannerman, Tel: (01967) 402408 or (01967) 402412.
Glen Affric Hill Lochs	Tomich Strathglass	Brown Trout	15 Mar. to 6 Oct.	Caledonian Hotel, Beauly. Tel: (01463) 782278.	Fly only. Boats available. Some salmon fishing.
Glen-moriston Hill Lochs (21)	Glenmoriston	Brown Trout	May to Oct.	Vincent Tait (Gamekeeper), Levishie, Glenmoriston. Tel: (01320) 351219 (Eve.).	1 boat available.
Guisachan Hill Lochs	Tomich	Brown/ Rainbow Trout	Apr. to Sep.	Tomich Hotel, Tomich, by Beauly. Tel: (01456) 415399.	Fly fishing only. Brown trout, Rainbow Trout on 8 lochs.
Loch Inchlaggan & Loch Garry	Invergarry	Brown Trout Arctic Char	May to Sep.	Mr. P. Thomas, Ardochy Lodge, Glengarry, Invergarry PH35 4HR. Tel: (01809) 511232.	Boats available. Loch Inchlaggan fly only.
Loch Insh	Kincraig	Salmon Trout Arctic Char Pike	May to Sep.	Loch Insh Watersports, Boat House, Kincraig. Tel: (01540) 651272.	Boats are available.
Loch Lundrava	Nr. Fort William	Brown Trout	15 Apr. to 30 Sep.	Mrs. A. MacCallum, Lundavra Farm, Fort William. Tel: (01397) 702582.	Average weight of fish caught: 8 oz.Fly fishing only. 2 boats available. Bank fishing.
Loch Lungard	Glen Cannich	Brown Trout	15 Mar. to 6 Oct.	Glen Affric Hotel, Cannich. Tel: (01456) 415214.	Fly fishing only. No bank fishing. Boats available from Loch Mullardoch.
Loch Mealt	North Skye	Brown Trout Arctic Char	15 Mar. to 30 Sep.	Jansport, Wentworth Street, Portree, Skye. Tel: (01478) 612559.	
Loch Monar	Glen Strathfarrar	Brown Trout	15 Mar. to 6 Oct.	Glen Affric Hotel, Cannich. Tel: (01456) 415214.	Fly fishing only. Boat for hire. No bank fishing.
Loch Morar (and hill lochs)	Morar	Salmon Sea Trout Brown Trout	15 Mar. to 6 Oct.	The Morar District Salmon Fishery Board, Superintendent, Viv de Fresnes. Tel: (01687) 462388.	6 boats for hire, and ghillie if required.

Water	Location	Species	Season	Permit available from	Other information
Loch Mullardoch	Cannich	Brown Trout	15 Mar. to 6 Oct.	Glen Affric Hotel, Cannich. Tel: (01456) 415214.	Fly fishing only. 4 boats. No bank fishing.
Loch Ness	From Urquhart Bay, Loch Ness	Brown Trout Sea Trout Ferox Salmon	1 Apr. to 31 Oct.	Office - Borlum Farm, Drumnadrochit IV3 6XN. Tel/Fax: (01456) 450358.	Average weight of fish caught: 2lb. Ghillie provided. Boats available.
Loch Ruthven	Farr	Brown Trout	15 Mar. to 6 Oct.	J. Graham & Co., 37/39 Castle Street, Inverness. Tel: (01463) 233178.	Fly fishing only.
South Skye Fishings (various lochs)	South Skye	Sea Trout Brown Trout Arctic char	Apr. to Oct.	Hotel Eilean Iarmain at weekends. Tel: (01471) 833332.	Fishing on approx. 20 lochs both wild and stocked, also two small spate rivers.
Storr Lochs (and hill lochs)	North Skye	Brown Trout	1 Apr. to 30 Sep.	Jansport, Wentworth Street, Portree, Skye. Tel: (01478) 612559.	Further information: Sec., Portree Angling Assoc., Hillcroft, Treaslane, by Portree.
White-bridge Lochs (Knockie, Bran & Killin)	Whitebridge	Brown Trout	Mar. to Oct.	Whitebridge Hotel, Stratherrick, Gorthleck, Inverness-shire. Tel: (01456) 486226.	Boats available. Fly fishing only.

NORTH OF SCOTLAND

RIVERS AND LOCHS

Constituent Area Tourist Boards
Caithness Tourist Board
Area Tourist Office,
Tourist Information Centre,
Whitechapel Road,
Wick,
Caithness KW1 4EA.
Tel: (01955) 602596.

Sutherland Tourist Board
Area Tourist Officer,
Tourist Information Centre,
The Square,
Dornoch,
Sutherland IV25 3SD.
Tel: (01862) 810400.

Ross and Cromarty Tourist Board
Area Tourist Officer,
Information Centre,
North Kessock,
Black Isle, Ross-shire IV5 1XB.
Tel: (01463) 730505.
River Purification Board
Highland River Purification Board
Graesser House,
Fodderty Way,
Dingwall IV15 9QY.
Tel: (01349) 62021.

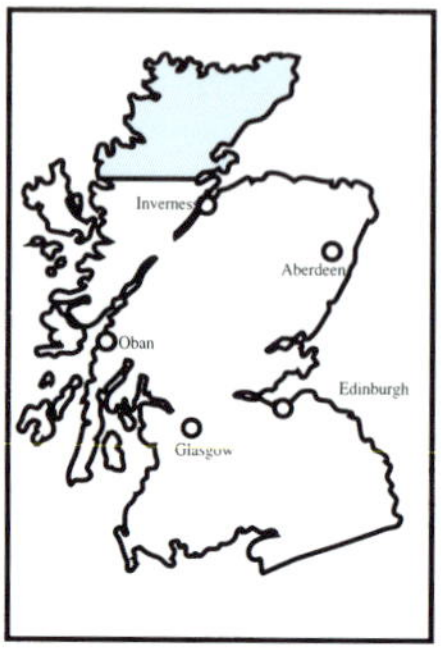

RIVERS

Water	Location	Species	Season	Permit available from	Other information
Alness (Map I D5)	Alness	Salmon Sea Trout	15 May to 16 Oct.	Novar Estates, Estate Office, Evanton, Ross-shire. Tel: (01349) 830208.	Fly fishing only. 6 beats on rotation. 4 rods per beat.
Beauly (Map II E4)	Muir of Ord	Salmon Sea Trout Brown Trout	May to Sep.	Ord House Hotel, Muir of Ord. Tel: (01463) 870492.	River and loch fishing available.
Blackwater	Strathpeffer	Salmon Sea Trout	Apr. to end Sep.		Further info. from: Craigdarroch Lodge Hotel, Contin, by Strathpeffer. Tel: (01997) 421265.
Borgie (Map I D2)	Tongue	Salmon	12 Jan. to 30 Sep.	Borgie Lodge Hotel, Skerray, Tongue, Sutherland. Tel/Fax: (01641) 521332.	Fly fishing only. Average weight 8lbs. 3 rotating beats of 2 rods. Day ticket water for 3 rods and tackle hire.
Brora (Lower) (Map I E4)	Brora	Salmon Sea Trout	1 Feb. to 15 Oct.	Mr. & Mrs. Hammond, Sciberscross Lodge, Strath Brora, Rogart. Tel: (01408) 641246.	Popular flies: Orange, black, red Waddingtons, Willie Gunn.
Carron (Map II C4)	Various beats upstream from Ardgay	Salmon Sea Trout	11 Jan. to 30 Sep.	Finlayson Hughes, 29 Barossa Place, Perth PH1 5EP. Tel: (01738) 630926.	Fly only. Finlayson Hughes handle fishing on five substantial and productive beats.
Cassley (Map I C4)	Glencassley Water	Salmon Sea Trout	11 Jan. to 30 Sep.	Bell Ingram, Bonar Bridge, Sutherland IV24 3EA. Tel: (01863) 766683.	Fly only. Approx. 9 miles of the upper river (left bank only).
	Glenrossal Beat	Salmon Sea Trout	11 Jan. to 30 Sep.	Glenrossal Estate, Rosehall, Sutherland IV27 4BG. Tel: (01549) 84203.	Fly only. 2.5 miles of left bank of the lower river.

Water	Location	Species	Season	Permit available from	Other information
Conon (Map II E3)	Rosehall	Salmon Sea Trout	11 Jan. to 30 Sep.	Achness Hotel, Rosehall, Sutherland IV27 4BD. Tel: (01549) 84239.	Fly only. Over a mile of very productive double bank fishing.
	Upper Cassley Beats 1 & 2	Salmon Sea Trout	11 Jan. to 30 Sep.	Bell Ingram, Bonar Bridge, Sutherland IV24 3EA. Tel: (01863) 766683.	Fly only. 2 extensive beats (right bank only) of the upper river.
	Contin	Salmon Sea Trout	Mar. to Apr.	Coul House Hotel, Contin, by Strathpeffer. Tel: (01997) 421487.	Lower/middle/upper Brahan, lower Fairburn beats various times. Ghillies, boats. Fly and spinning.
	Maryburgh	Brown/ Rainbow Trout Pike	15 Mar. to 6 Oct.	Seaforth Highland Estate, Brahan, Dingwall. Tel: (01349) 865505.	Stocked pond. Loch fishing and river in the lower, middle and upper Conon. Fishing available in the stocked pond and loch all year round.
	Muir of Ord	Salmon Sea Trout Brown Trout	May to Sep.	Ord House Hotel, Muir of Ord. Tel: (01463) 870492.	River and loch fishing available.
	Strathpeffer	Salmon Brown Trout	1 Apr. to 30 Sep.		Further information from: Craigdarroch Lodge Hotel, Contin, by Strathpeffer. Tel: (01997) 421265.
	Dingwall	Salmon Sea Trout	25 Jan. to 30 Sep.	The Sports & Model Shop, High Street, Dingwall. Tel: (01349) 862346.	Popular flies: Greenwell's Glory, Peter Ross, Black Pennel. Fly fishing only. Thigh waders only.
Lower Conon	Contin	Salmon Sea Trout	26 Jan. to 30 Sep.	Dingwall & District A.C., c/o Sports & Model Shop, High Street, Dingwall. Tel: (01349) 862346.	Fly only. Thigh waders only.
Doinard (Map I C2)	Durness	Salmon Sea Trout		Cape Wrath Hotel, Durness, Sutherland. Tel: (01971) 511274.	Please phone in advance. especially in high season.
Glass	Evanton	Brown Trout	15 Mar. to 6 Oct.	Novar Estates, Estate Office, Evanton, Ross-shire. Tel: (01349) 830208.	Fly fishing only.
Halladale (Map I E2)	Forsinard	Salmon	11 Jan. to 30 Sep.	Miss A. Imlach, The Strath Halladale Partnership, Bunahoun, Forsinard, Sutherland KW13 6YU. Tel/Fax: (01641) 571271.	Fly fishing only (spate river).
	Tongue	Salmon	11 Jan. to 30 Sep.	Borgie Lodge Hotel, Skerray, Tongue, Sutherland. Tel/Fax: (01641) 521332.	Fly fishing only. 4 rotating beats, 3 rods per beat. Tackle hire.
Helmsdale (Map I E3)	Helmsdale	Salmon Sea Trout	11 Jan. to 30 Sep.	Strathullie Crafts & Fishing Tackle, Dunrobin Street, Helmsdale KW8 6AH. Tel: (01431) 821343.	Association beat. Fly fishing only.
Kirkaig (Map I B4)	Lochinver	Salmon	1 May to 15 Oct.	Inver Lodge Hotel, Lochinver IV27 4LU. Tel: (01571) 844496.	
Oykel (Map I C4)	Sutherland	Salmon Sea Trout	End June to 30 Sep.	Inver Lodge Hotel, Lochinver IV27 4LU. Tel: (01571) 844496.	2 top beats only (3 miles).

Water	Location	Species	Season	Permit available from	Other information
Thurso (Map I F2)	Thurso/ Halkirk	Salmon Trout	11 Jan. to 5 Oct.	Thurso Fisheries Ltd., Estate Office, Thurso East, Thurso. Tel: (01847) 893134.	Fly fishing only. Twelve 2 rod beats in rotation.
Torridon (Map II C3)	Achnasheen	Salmon Sea Trout	11 Feb. to 31 Oct.	Torridon Hotel, Torridon, Wester Ross IV22 2EY. Tel: (01445) 87242.	Small spate river.
Ullapool	Ullapool	Salmon Sea Trout Brown Trout	May to 30 Sep.	Ullasports, West Argyle Street, Ullapool. Tel: (01854) 612621.	
Wester	By Wick	Salmon Sea Trout Brown Trout	1 Mar. to 31 Oct.	Mrs. G. Dunnet, Auckhorn Lyth, by Wick KW1 4UD. Tel: (01955) 631208. Hugo Ross Tackle Shop, 56 High Street, Wick. Tel/Fax: (01955) 604200.	
Wick (Map I G2)	Wick	Salmon Sea Trout Brown Trout	11 Feb. to 21 Oct.	Hugo Ross Tackle Shop, 56 High Street, Wick. Tel/Fax: (01955) 604200.	Fly/worm fishing. Spate river with good holding pools.

LOCHS

Water	Location	Species	Season	Permit available from	Other information
Loch A'chroisg	Achnasheen	Pike Perch Brown Trout	No close season	Ledgowan Lodge Hotel, Achnasheen. Tel: (01445) 720252.	Free to customers.
Loch a'Ghriama	Overscaig	Brown Trout	30 Apr. to 30 Sep.	Overscaig Lochside Hotel, Loch Shin, by Lairg IV27 4NY. Tel: (01549) 431203.	Boats available. No Sunday fishing.
Loch an Ruthair	By Kinbrace	Brown Trout	Apr. to 30 Sep.	Head Keeper, Achentoul Estate, Kinbrace. Tel: (01431) 831227.	Average weight of fish caught: 8 to 12 oz. Popular flies: Soldier Palmer, Black Pennel. Bait fishing and spinning allowed. 2 boats available.
Loch Achall	By Ullapool	Salmon Sea Trout Brown Trout	1 May to 30 Sep. 15 Mar, to 6 Oct.	Ullasports, West Argyle Street, Ullapool. Tel: (01854) 612621.	Popular flies: Soldier Palmer, Butcher, Grouse & Claret. 3 boats available. Bank fishing.
Lochs Airigh Leathaid	By Westerdale, Halkirk	Brown Trout	Apr. to Sep.	Ulbster Arms Hotel, Halkirk. Tel: (01847) 831206.	Fly only. Average weight: 1 lb 2 oz.
Loch Ascaig	Helmsdale	Salmon Sea Trout Brown Trout	1 Jun. to 30 Sep. 15 Mar. to 6 Oct.	M. Wigan, Borrobol, Kinbrace KW11 6UB. Tel: (01431) 831264.	Popular flies: Loch Ordie, Soldier Palmer. Fly fishing only. 3 boats available.
Loch Badagyle	Nr. Achiltibuie	Sea Trout Brown Trout Arctic Char	1 Apr. to 30 Sep.	Polly Estates Ltd., Inverpolly, Ullapool IV26 2YB. Tel: (01854) 622452.	Fly fishing only. Boats with or without motors are available.
Loch Badanloch (& other hill lochs)	Kinbrace	Brown Trout	15 Mar. to 6 Oct.	Brian Lyall, Badanloch, Kinbrace, Sutherland. Tel: (01431) 831232.	Average weight of fish caught: 8 oz. 9 boats. Fly only. Sunday fishing. Private beat at top of River Helmsdale for 2 rods per day.

Water	Location	Species	Season	Permit available from	Other information
Loch Beannach	Lairg	Brown Trout	30 Apr. to 30 Sep.	Boat permits: R. Ross (Fishing Tackle), Main Street, Lairg IV27 4DB. Tel: (01549) 402239.	Average weight of fish caught: 1 lb. Popular flies: Kate McLaren, Loch Ordie. Strictly fly fishing only. Boats available from R. Ross.
Loch Bad na H-Achlaise (Green Loch)	Nr. Achiltibuie	Brown/Sea Trout	1 Apr. to 30 Sep.	Polly Estates Ltd., Inverpolly, Ullapool IV26 2YB. Tel: (01854) 622452.	Fly fishing only. No Sunday fishing.
Loch Bad na h'Erba	Sciberscross	Wild Brown Trout	1 Apr. to 30th Sept.	Mr. & Mrs. Hammond, Sciberscross Lodge, Strath Brora, Rogart IV28 3YQ. Tel: (01408) 641246.	Average weight of fish caught: 12 oz.. Popular flies: Black Pennel, Ke-He, Loch Ordie, Dunkeld. Boats are available.
Black Loch	Nr. Achiltibuie	Brown Trout	1 Apr. to 30 Sep.	Polly Estates Ltd., Inverpolly, Ullapool IV26 2YB. Tel: (01854) 622452.	Fly fishing only. No Sunday fishing. Boat available.
Borgie & Skerray Hill Lochs (Mapl D2)	Tongue	Brown Trout	15 Mar. to 6 Oct.	Borgie Lodge Hotel, Stkerray, Tongue, Sutherland. Tel/Fax: (01641) 521332.	8 - 10 ozs, fish up to 4lbs. Fly only. Bank and boat fishing.
Loch Borralan	Ledmore	Brown/ Rainbow Trout Arctic Char	15 Mar. to 6 Oct.	Te Alt Bar, The Altnacealalgach, Ledmore, by Lairg. Tel: (01854) 666220.	Any legal method permitted. Boat and bank fishing.
		Brown Trout Arctic Char	1 Apr. to 30 Sep.	Ledmore Estate, Blarmhor, Elphin, by Lairg. Tel: (01854) 666207.	Baits: Any legal mathod permitted. Boats available with outboards. Bank fishing available.
Loch Borralie	Durness	Brown Trout	Apr. to end Sep.	Cape Wrath Hotel, Durness, Sutherland. Tel: (01971) 511274.	Limestone loch. Fly fishing only. Boats available. Please phone in advance, especially in high season.
Loch Broom (Map II D2)	By Ullapool	Salmon Sea Trout	Apr. to Oct.	Ullasport, West Argyle Street, Ullapool. Tel: (01854) 612621.	
Loch Brora	Brora	Salmon Sea Trout Brown Trout	Apr. to Oct.	Rob. Wilson Rods & Guns, Rosslyn Street, Brora. Tel: (01408) 621373.	Boats available. Fly only. Ghillies available.
		Salmon Sea Trout Brown Trout Char	1 May to 15 Oct.	Mr. & Mrs. Hammond, Sciberscross Lodge, Strath Brora, Rogart IV28 3YQ. Tel: (01408) 641246.	Popular flies: General Practitioner, Stoats Tail, Dunkeld. Boat available with outboard, if required.
Loch Cam	Ledmore	Brown Trout Arctic Char	1 Apr. to 30 Sept.	Ledmore Estate, Blarmhor, Elphin, By Lairg. Tel: (01854) 666207.	Any legal method permitted. Boats available with outboards. Bank fishing available.
Loch Caise	Forsinard	Brown Trout	1 May to 30 Sep.	Forsinard Hotel, Forsinard. Tel: (01641) 571221.	

Water	Location	Species	Season	Permit available from	Other information
Loch Caladail	Durness	Brown Trout	Apr. to end Sep.	Cape Wrath Hotel, Durness, Sutherland. Tel: (01971) 511274.	Limestone loch. Fly fishing only. Boats available. Please phone in advance, especially in high season.
Loch Calder	Thurso	Brown Trout	15 Mar. to 6 Oct.	Harper's Fishing Tackle, 57 High Street, Thurso. Tel: (01847) 893179.	Average weight of fish caught: 12 oz to 1 lb (fish up to 7 lbs). Popular flies: Bibio, Black Pennel, Kate McLaren,. Spinning and bait fishing permitted, but fly fishing preferred. Boats available.
Caol Loch	Forsinard	Brown Trout	1 May to 30 Sep.	Forsinard Hotel, Forsinard. Tel: (01641) 571221.	Boat and bank fishing. Use standard pattern loch flies.
Cape Wrath & hill lochs (30-plus)	Durness	Brown Trout	Apr. to end Sep.	Cape Wrath Hotel, Durness, Sutherland. Tel: (01971) 511274	Please phone in advance, especially in high season.
Cherigal Loch	By Westerdale Halkirk	Brown Trout	Apr. to Sep.	Ulbster Arms Hotel, Halkirk. Tel: (01847) 831206.	Fly only. Average weight: 12 oz.
Col Loch Beg		Wild Brown Trout	1 Apr. to 15 Oct.	Garvault Hotel, by Kinbrace. Tel: (01431) 831224.	Average weight of fish caught: 8 oz. Popular flies: Loch Ordie, Black Spider, Black Pennel. Fly fishing only.
Col Loch Mhor		Wild Brown Trout	1 Apr. to 15 Oct.	Garvault Hotel, by Kinbrace. Tel: (01431) 831224.	Average weight of fish caught: 8 oz. Popular flies: Loch Ordie, Black Spider, Black Pennel. Fly fishing only.
Loch Craggie	Tongue	Wild Brown Trout (occ. Salmon)	15 Mar. to 6 Oct.	Ben Loyal Hotel, Tongue. Tel: (01847) 611216. Post Office, Tongue. Tel: (01847) 611201.	Fly fishing available. Boat available. Average weight of fish caught: 8 oz. to 1 lb. Popular flies: Pennel, Goats Toe, Zulu.
		Brown Trout	Mar. to Sep.	Altnaharra Hotel, by Lairg IV27 4UE.	
		Salmon Sea Trouit Brown Trout	15 Mar. to 6 Oct.	Borgie Lodge Hotel, Skerray, Tongue, Sutherland. Tel/Fax: (01641) 521332.	8 oz. Fly, spinning, trolling. Dapping good for salmon. 1 boat with outboard and outriggers.
Loch Croispol	Durness	Brown Trout	Apr. to end Sep.	Cape Wrath Hotel, Durness, Sutherland. Tel: (01971) 511274.	Limestone loch. Fly fishing only. Boats available. Please phone in advance, especially in high season.
Loch Culag (and numerous other lochs)	Lochinver	Brown Trout	Mid-May to 6 Oct.	Inver Lodge Hotel, Lochinver, Sutherland. Tel: (01571) 844496.	7 lochs with boats. 2 lochs for residents of hotel only. (Check for details).
The Dam Lochs	Nr. Ullapool	Brown Trout	15 Mar. to 6 Oct.	Ullasport, West Argyle Street, Ullapool. Tel: (01854) 612621.	Fly fishing only.
Loch Doir na H-Airb (Stac Loch)	Nr. Achiltibuie	Brown/Sea Trout	1 Apr. to 30 Sep.	Polly Estates Ltd., Inverpolly, Ullapool IV26 2YB. Tel: (01854) 622452.	Fly fishing only. No Sunday fishing.

Water	Location	Species	Season	Permit available from	Other information
Dornoch & District A.C. (7 lochs)	Dornoch	Salmon Sea Trout Brown Trout	15 Mar. to 6 Oct.	Dornoch & District A.A., William A. McDonald, Castle Street, Dornoch. Tel: (01862) 810301.	No Sunday fishing. Fly fishing only. 7 boats available.
Dornoch Lochans	Dornoch	Rainbow Trout	All year	M. & B. MacGillivray, Davochfin, Dornoch IV25 3RW. Tel: (01862) 810600.	Open all year: 10am to dusk. Sundays: 2–6pm. 2 lochans fly only. 2 for bait (provided). Instruction and tackle available. Popular flies: Ace of Spades, Black Pennel, Nymphs, etc.
Lochan Dubh na H-Amaite	Sciberscross	Wild Brown Trout	1 Apr. to 30th Sept.	Mr. & Mrs. Hammond, Sciberscross Lodge, Strath Brora, Rogart IV28 3YQ. Tel: (01408) 641246.	Average weight of fish caught: 1 lb. Popular flies: Black Pennel, Ke-He, Loch Ordie, Dunkeld. Boat available.
Dubh-nan-Geodh	Westerdale Halkirk	Brown Trout	Apr. to Sep.	Ulbster Arms Hotel, Halkirk. Tel: (01847) 831206.	Fly only. Average weight of fish caught: 1 lb 10 oz.
Dunnet Head Loch	Dunnet Head (B855)	Brown Trout	May to Oct.	Dunnet Head Tearoom, Brough Village, Dunnet Head. Tel: (01847) 851774.	Loch well stocked. Fly from bank only. No Sunday fishing. Sea fishing from rocks.
Eileanach Loch	By Westerdale, Halkirk	Brown Trout	Apr. to Sep.	Ulbster Arms Hotel, Halkirk. Tel: (01847) 831206.	Fly only. Average weight: 9 oz.
Eun Loch	By Westerdale, Halkirk	Brown Trout	Apr. to Sep.	Ulbster Arms Hotel, Halkirk. Tel: (01847) 831206.	Fly only. Average weight: 1 lb 8 oz.
Forsinard Loch (& many others)	Forsinard	Brown Trout	1 May to 30 Sep.	Forsinard Hotel, Forsinard, Sutherland. Tel: (01641) 571221.	Fly fishing only. Bank and boat fishing (5 boats). Sea trout up to 3.5 lbs.
	Kyle of Tongue	Salmon Sea Trout Sea Bass	11 Feb. to 31 Oct.	Ben Loyal Hotel, Tongue. Tel: (01847) 611216. Post Office, Tongue. Tel: (01847) 611201.	No Sunday fishing. Bank fishing only.
Gainimh Loch	By Westerdale, Halkirk	Brown Trout	Apr. to Sep.	Ulbster Arms Hotel, Halkirk. Tel: (01847) 831206.	Fly only. Average weight: 7 oz.
Loch Ganneigh		Wild Brown Trout	1 Apr. to 15 Oct.	Garvault Hotel, by Kinbrace. Tel: (01431) 831224.	Average weight of fish caught: 8 oz. Popular flies: Loch Ordie, Black Spider, Black Pennel. Fly fishing only.
Loch Glascar-noch	Aultguish	Brown Trout Pike	Mar. to Sep. All year	Tel: (01997) 455254 to obtain permission.	
Loch Glass	Head of River Glass	Brown Trout	15 Mar. to 6 Oct.	Novar Estates, Estate Office, Evanton, Ross-shire. Tel: (01349) 830208.	Bank fishing only. Any legal method.
Garbh Loch	Forsinard	Brown Trout	1 May to 30 Sep.	Forsinard Hotel, Forsinard. Tel: (01641) 571221.	Bank and boat fishing. Popular flies: Black Pennel, Ke-He, Invicta.

Water	Location	Species	Season	Permit available from	Other information
Golspie A.C. Waters (Lochs: Brora, Lundie, Horn, Buidhe)		Salmon Sea Trout Brown Trout	1 Apr. to 15 Oct.	Golspie A.C., Lindsay & Co., Main Street, Golspie. Tel: (01408) 633212.	Fly fishing only. Bank and boat fishing. No Sunday fishing.
Loch Heilan	Castletown	Brown Trout	May to Sep.	H.T. Pottinger, Greenland Mains, Castletown, Thurso. Tel: (01847) 821210.	Bank and boat fishing.
Loch Hempriggs	South of Wick	Brown Trout	14 Mar. to 14 Oct.	Thrumster Filling Station. Tel: (01955) 651252. Hugo Ross Fishing Tackle Shop, 56 High Street, Wick. Tel/Fax: (01955) 604200.	Average weight of fish caught: 12 oz to 1 lb.
Hill Lochs (32)	Around Assynt	Brown Trout	15 Mar. to 6 Oct.	Tourist Information Centre, Lochinver. Tel: (01571) 844330.	Mainly fly fishing. There are 6 lochs where spinning or bait can be used. Bank fishing only.
Loch Hope (Map I D2)	Nr. Tongue	Salmon Sea Trout	Mid-Apr. to Sep. Jun. to Sep.	Altnaharra Hotel, by Lairg IV27 4UE. Tel: (01549) 411222.	Average weight of fish caught: Salmon 8 lbs, Sea Trout 3 lbs. Popular flies: Salmon - Invicta, Pennel. Sea Trout - Peter Ross. Fly only. 6 boats are available.
Lochs Kernsary Tournaig Goose	Gairloch	Brown Trout	15 Mar. to 6 Oct.	National Trust for Scotland, Inverewe Visitor Centre, Poolewe, Ross-shire. Tel: (01445) 781229.	
Kyle of Tongue & local lochs	Tongue & Farr	Salmon Sea Trout Brown Trout		Tongue Stores & Post Office, Main Street, Tongue. Tel: (01847) 611201.	Sunday fishing for brown trout only. Boats available from: Ben Loyal Hotel, Tongue.
	Tongue	Salmon Sea Trout Sea Bass	11 Feb. to 31 Oct.	Borgie Lodge Hotel, Skerray, Tongue, Sutherland. Tel/Fax: (01641) 521332.	Tackle hire. Bank and boat fishing.
Leckmelm Hill Lochs	Ullapool	Brown Trout	May to Sep.	Leckmelm Holiday Cottages, Leckmelm, Ullapool. Tel: (01854) 612471.	Bank fishing only. No Sunday fishing.
Loch Loyal	Tongue	Salmon Sea Trout Wild Brown Trout	15 Mar. to 6 Oct.	Ben Loyal Hotel, Tongue. Tel: (01847) 611216. Post Office, Tongue. Tel: (01847) 611201.	Fly fishing only. Bank or boat fishing (2 boats available).
		Brown Trout	Mar. to Sep.	Altnaharra Hotel, by Lairg IV27 4UE. Tel: (01549) 411222.	Average weight of fish caught: 8 oz to 1 lb. Popular flies: Pennel, Goats Toe, Zulu. 1 boat available.
		Salmon Sea Trout Brown Trout Perox	15 Mar. to 6 Oct.	Borgie Lodge Hotel, Skerray, Tongue, Sutherland. Tel/Fax: (01641) 521332.	8 oz. Fly, spinning, worming and trolling. Outriggers available one with outboard.
Loch Lurgainn	Nr. Achiltibuie	Brown/Sea Trout	1 Apr. to 30 Sep.	Polly Estates Ltd., Inverpolly, Ullapool IV26 2YB. Tel: (01854) 622452.	Fly fishing only. No Sunday fishing. Boats with or without motors available.

Water	Location	Species	Season	Permit available from	Other information
Loch Maree	Wester Ross	Salmon Sea Trout Brown Trout	May to Oct.	Loch Maree Hotel, Achnasheen IV22 2HL. Tel: (01445) 760288.	Several boats available.
				Kinlochewe Holiday Chalets, c/o Castlegate House, Castlegate. Tel: (01445) 760256.	2 boats available. Fly only end June onwards.
Loch Meadie (Map I E1)	By Westerdale, Halkirk	Brown Trout	Apr. to Sep.	Ulbster Arms Hotel, Halkirk. Tel: (01847) 831206.	Fly only. Average weight: 10 oz.
	Tongue	Brown Trout	Mar. to Sep.	Altnaharra Hotel, by Lairg IV27 4UE. Tel: (01549) 411222.	Average weight of fish caught: 8 oz to 1 lb. 1 boat available.
		Brown Trout	15 Mar. to 6 Oct.	Borgie Lodge Hotel, Skerray, Tongue, Sutherland. Tel/Fax: (01641) 521332.	8 oz. Fly only. Bank or boat fishing. Average basket 20 fish.
Loch Merkland	Overscaig	Brown Trout	30 Apr. to 30 Sep.	Overscaig Lochside Hotel, Loch Shin,by Lairg IV27 4NY. Tel: (01549) 431203.	Boat available. Fly only. No Sunday fishing.
Loch Migdale	By Bonar Bridge	Brown Trout	May to 31 Oct.	Dunroamin Hotel, Bonar Bridge, Sutherland. Tel: (01863) 766236.	1 boat available.
More Loch	By Westerdale, Halkirk	Brown Trout	Apr. to Sep.	Ulbster Arms Hotel, Halkirk. Tel: (01847) 831206.	Fly only. Average weight: 9 oz.
Loch Morie	Head of River Alness	Brown Trout	15 Mar. to 6 Oct.	Novar Estates, Estate Office, Evanton, Ross-shire. Tel: (01349) 830208.	Bank fishing only. Any legal method.
Loch na Dail (Polly Loch)	Nr. Achiltibuie	Brown/Sea Trout	1 Apr. to 30 Sep.	Polly Estates Ltd., Inverpolly, Ullapool IV26 2YB. Tel: (01854) 622452.	Fly fishing only. No Sunday fishing. Boat available.
Loch nan Clar		Wild Brown Trout	1 Apr. to 15 Oct.	Garvault Hotel, by Kinbrace. Tel: (01431) 831224.	Average weight of fish caught: 8 oz. Fly fishing only.
Loch Naver		Salmon Brown Trout	Mar. to end Sep.	Altnaharra Hotel, by Lairg IV27 4UE. Tel: (01549) 411222.	Average weight of fish caught: Salmon 8 lbs, Brown Trout 8oz. 3 boats available.
Loch Palm		Wild Brown Trout	1 Apr. to 15 Oct.	Garvault Hotel, by Kinbrace. Tel: (01431) 831224.	Average weight of fish caught: 8 oz. Fly fishing only.
Loch Rangag	Latheron	Brown Trout	1 Apr. to 30 Sep.	John Anderson, Lochend Cottage, Latheron, Caithness. Tel: (01593) 741230.	Average weight of fish caught: 12 oz. Fly fishing only. Boats are available.
Rhiconich (50 lochs)	Nr. Kinlochbervie	Salmon Sea Trout Brown Trout	15 Feb. to 15 Oct.	Rhiconich Hotel, Kinlochbervie. Tel: (01971) 521224.	Fly fishing only. 7 boats available.
Loch Rhifail		Wild Brown Trout	1 Apr. to 15 Oct.	Garvault Hotel, by Kinbrace. Tel: (01431) 831224.	Average weight of fish caught: 8 oz. Fly fishing only.
Loch Rhimsdale		Wild Brown Trout	1 Apr. to 15 Oct.	Garvault Hotel, by Kinbrace. Tel: (01431) 831224.	Average weight of fish caught: 8 oz. Fly fishing only.

Water	Location	Species	Season	Permit available from	Other information
Loch Rhuard	Latheron	Brown Trout	1 Apr. to 30 Sep.	John Anderson, Lochend Cottage, Latheron, Caithness. Tel: (01593) 741230.	Average weight of fish caught: 12 oz. Fly fishing only. Boats are available.
Loch Rossail		Wild Brown Trout	1 Apr. to 15 Oct.	Garvault Hotel, by Kinbrace. Tel: (01431) 831224.	Average weight of fish caught: 8 oz. Fly fishing only.
Loch St. Johns	Caithness	Wild Brown Trout	7 Apr. to 30 Sep.	Hugo Ross Fishing Tackle, 56 High Street, Wick. Tel/Fax: (01955) 604200.	Boats are available from Hugo Ross.
Sarclet Loch	Thrumster	Brown Trout	15 Mar. to 14 Oct.	Thrumster Filling Station. Tel: (01955) 651252.	Average weight of fish caught: 8 oz to 1 lb plus. Popular flies: Cocky Bundu, Soldier Palmer, Loch Ordie, Black Pennel.
Scourie Lochs	N.W. Sutherland	Salmon Sea Trout Brown Trout	1 May to 15 Oct.	Scourie Hotel, Scourie IV27 4SX. Tel: (01971) 502396.	Fly fishing only. Boats available.
Loch Sgeirach		Wild Brown Trout	1 Apr. to 15 Oct.	Garvault Hotel, by Kinbrace. Tel: (01431) 831224.	Average weight of fish caught: 8 oz. Fly fishing only.
Loch Shin (Map I D4)	Overscaig	Brown Trout Ferox Trout	30 Apr. to 30 Sep.	Overscaig Lochside Hotel, Loch Shin, by Lairg IV27 4NY. Tel: (01549) 431203.	Boats and outboards available.
	Lairg	Brown Trout Char	15 Apr. to 30 Sep.	Sutherland Sporting company, Main Street, Lairg IV27 4AR. Tel: (01549) 402229.	Average weight of fish caught: 7 oz. Popular flies: Kate McLaren. Spinning and worming permitted, fly preferred. Boats and engines available from boathouse from 1 June.
Loch Sionascaig (& 9 other lochs)	Ullapool	Brown Trout	1 Apr. to 30 Sep.	Polly Estate Office, Inverpolly, Ullapool IV26 2YB. Tel: (01854) 622452.	Boats and outboards available. No Sunday fishing. Fly fishing only, trawling for ferox permitted. Noted for large ferox.
Loch Skerray (Map I D2)	Tongue	Brown Trout	15 Mar. to 6 Oct.	Borgie Lodge Hotel, Skerray, Tongue, Sutherland. Tel/Fax: (01641) 521332.	1 lb. Fly only. Boats av ailable. Trout up to 4 lbs but hard to catch.
Skyline Loch	Forsinard	Brown Trout	1 May to 30 Sep.	Forsinard Hotel, Forsinard, Sutherland. Tel: (01641) 571221.	Popular flies: Black Zulu, Silver Butcher.
Loch Slain (Map 1 D2)	Tongue	Salmon Sea Trout Brown Trout Char	15 Mar. to 6 Oct.	Borgie Lodge Hotel, Skerray, Tongue, Sutherland. Tel/Fax: (01641) 521332.	12 oz to 1 lb. Fly fishing only. 1 boat. No bank fishing.
Loch Sletill	Forsinard	Brown Trout	1 May to 30 Sep.	Forsinard Hotel, Forsinard, Sutherland. Tel: (01461) 571221.	Fly fishing only. Bank and boat fishing.
Loch Stack	N.W. Sutherland	Salmon Sea Trout Brown Trout	1 May to 15 Oct.	Scourie Hotel, Scourie IV27 4SX. Tel: (01971) 502396.	Fly fishing only. Boats are available. Ghillie mandatory on loch.
Loch Staink	Tongue	Brown Trout	Mar. to Sep.	Altnaharra Hotel, by Lairg IV27 4UE. Tel: (01549) 411222.	Average weight of fish caught: 8 oz to 1 lb. 1 boat available.

Water	Location	Species	Season	Permit available from	Other information
Loch Stemster	Latheron	Brown Trout	1 Apr. to 30 Sep.	John Anderson, Lochend Cottage, Latheron, Caithness. Tel: (01593) 741230.	Average weight of fish caught: 12 oz. Fly fishing only. Boats are available.
Loch Strath-Kinaird	By Ullapool	Salmon Sea Trout	Apr. to Oct.	Ullasport, West Argyle Street, Ullapool. Tel: (01854) 612621.	
Tarvie Lochs	By Contin	Brown/ Rainbow Trout		Sports & Model Shop, High Street, Dingwall. Tel: (01349) 862346.	Main loch: Fly fishing only. Boat available. Troutmaster water. Small loch only: coarse methods.
Loch Tarvie	By Strathpeffer	Brown Trout Rainbow Trout	15 Mar. to 6 Oct. All year	The Tarvie Lochs Trout Fishery, Tarvie, by Strathpeffer IV14 9EJ. Tel: (01997) 421250.	Average weight of fish caught: Rainbow 2 lbs 4 oz, Brown 1 lb 12 oz - Troutmaster water. Fly fishing only. Boat fishing only. Open all year, except Xmas. Tuition and tackle hire available.
Loch Uidh Tarraigean (Upper Polly Lochs)	By Achiltibuie	Brown Trout	1 Apr. to 30 Sep.	Polly Estates Ltd., Inverpolly, Ullapool IV26 2YB. Tel: (01854) 622452.	Fly fishing only. No Sunday fishing.
Ulbster Estate Lochs (9 hill lochs)	Halkirk	Brown Trout	15 Mar. to Sep.	Ulbster Arms Hotel, Halkirk, Caithness. Tel: (01847) 831206.	No Sunday fishing. Fly fishing only. 1 boat on each of 5 lochs.
Loch Urigill	Ledmore	Brown Trout Arctic Char	1 Apr. to 30 Sept.	Ledmore Estate, Blarmhor, Elphin, By Lairg. Tel: (01854) 666207.	Baits: Any legal mathod permitted. Boats available with outboards. Bank fishing available.
Loch Watenan	Ulbster	Brown Trout	1 Mar. to 30 Sep.	Mr. J. Swanson, Aspen Bank, Banks Road, Watten. Tel: (01955) 621208.	Fly fishing only. 1 boat available.
Loch Watten	Watten Village	Brown Trout	1 May to 30 Sep.	Hugo Ross Fishing Tackle, 56 High Street, Wick. Tel/Fax: (01955) 604200.	Boats for hire from tackle shop. Fish min. size 10". No Sunday fishing. Fly only.
		Brown Trout	1 May to 1 Oct.	J.A. Barnetson, Lynegar Farm, Watten. Tel: (01955) 621205/621308.	Average weight of fish caught: 12 oz. 3 boats available.
	(A882) Between Wick & Thurso	Stocked Brown Trout	1 May to 30 Sep.	John F. Swanson, Aspen Bank, Banks Lodge, Watten. Tel: (01955) 621326/621208.	Average weight of fish caught: 12 oz to 1 lb. Fly fishing only. 4 boats available.
Loch Wester	By Wick	Salmon Sea Trout Brown Trout	1 Mar. to 31 Oct.	Mrs. G. Dunnet, Auckhorn Lyth, by Wick KW1 4UD. Tel: (01955) 631208. Hugo Ross Fishing Tackle, 56 High Street, Wick. Tel/Fax: (01955) 604200.	Fly fishing only. Boats available 1 Jul. to 31 Oct.
Yarrows Loch	Thrumster	Brown Trout	15 Mar. to 14 Oct.	Thrumster Filling Station. Tel: (01955) 651252.	Average weight of fish caught: 12 oz to 1 lb Boats are available – ask Thrumster Filling Station.

WESTERN ISLES RIVERS AND LOCHS

Area Tourist Boards
Western Isles Tourist Board
Area Tourist Officer,
Western Isles Tourist Board,
26 Cromwell Street,
Stornoway,
Isle of Lewis PA87 2XY.
Tel: (01851) 703088.

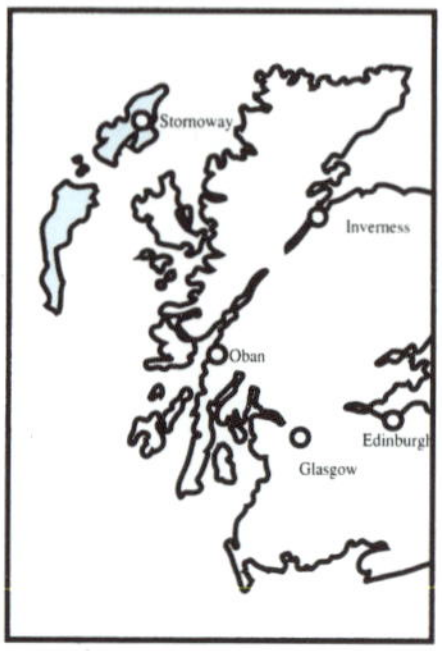

River Purification Authority
Western Isles Island Area
No formal board constituted.

RIVERS

Water	Location	Species	Season	Permit available from	Other information
LEWIS River Blackwater	13 miles West of Stornoway	Salmon Sea Trout Brown Trout	1 Jul. to 14 Oct. 15 Mar. to 30 Sep.	The Manager, Garynahine Estate Office, Isle of Lewis. Tel: (01851) 621314.	Fly fishing only from bank.

LOCHS

Water	Location	Species	Season	Permit available from	Other information
LEWIS Beag-Na-Craoibhe	Stornoway	Brown Trout	15 Mar. to 6 Oct.	Sportsworld, 1–3 Francis Street, Stornoway. Tel: (01851) 705464.	Bank fishing only. 1 boat available.
Loch Bruiche Breivat	Nr. Stornoway	Brown Trout Arctic Char	15 Mar. to 30 Sep.	Estate Office, Scaliscro, Timsgarry, Isle of Lewis. Tel: (01851) 672325.	Popular flies: Brown Muddler, Invicta, Soldier Palmer. Boats are available.
Breugach	Stornoway	Brown Trout	15 Mar. to 6 Oct.	Sportsworld, 1–3 Francis Street, Stornoway. Tel: (01851) 705464.	Bank fishing. Two boats available.
Loch Coirigeroid	Nr. Stornoway	Brown Trout Arctic Char	15 Mar. to 30 Sep.	Estate Office, Scaliscro, Timsgarry, Isle of Lewis. Tel: (01851) 672325.	Popular flies: Brown Muddler, Invicta, Soldier Palmer. Boats are available.
Loch Fhir Mhaoil	Nr. Stornoway	Salmon Sea Trout Brown Trout	Jun. to 15 Oct.	Estate Office, Scaliscro, Timsgarry, Isle of Lewis. Tel: (01851) 672325.	Spinning and worm fishing permitted. Boats are available.
Keose (and other lochs in Keose Glebe fishings)	10 miles South of Stornoway	Brown Trout	15 Mar. to 30 Sep.	M. Morrison, 'Handa', 18 Keose Glebe, Lochs, Isle of Lewis HSQ 9JX. Tel: (01851) 830334. Sportsworld, 1–3 Francis Street, Stornoway. Tel: (01851) 705464. Tourist Office, 26 Cromwell Street, Stornoway. Tel: (01851) 703088.	Boat and equiptment available.
Loch Langavat	Nr. Stornoway	Salmon Sea Trout Brown Trout Arctic Char	15 Mar. to 15 Oct.	Estate Office, Scaliscro, Timsgarry, Isle of Lewis. Tel: (01851) 672325.	Spinning and worming permitted. Boats are available.

Water	Location	Species	Season	Permit available from	Other information
Loch MacLeod	Nr. Stornoway	Salmon Sea Trout Brown Trout	1 Jul. to 14 Oct. 15 Mar. to 30 Sep.	The Manager, Garynahine Estate Office, Isle of Lewis. Tel: (01851) 621314.	
Loch na Craoibhe	Achmore	Brown Trout	15 Mar. to 6 Oct.	Sportsworld, 1–3 Francis Street, Stornoway. Tel: (01851) 705464.	Bank fishing. 1 boat available.
Loch nam Falcag	Achmore	Brown Trout	15 Mar. to 6 Oct.	Sportsworld, 1–3 Francis Street, Stornoway. Tel: (01851) 705464.	Bank fishing. 1 boat available.
Loch nan Culaidhean	Nr. Stornoway	Salmon Sea Trout Brown Trout	1 Jul. to 14 Oct. 15 Mar. to 30 Sep.	The Manager, Garynahine Estate Office, Isle of Lewis. Tel: (01851) 621314.	
Lochs Sgibacleit, Shromois, Airigh Thormaid	Nr. Stornoway	Salmon Sea Trout Brown Trout	May to 30 Oct.	Estate Office, Scaliscro, Timsgarry, Isle of Lewis. Tel: (01851) 672325.	Spinning and worm fishing permitted. Boats are available.
Loch Tarbart	Nr. Stornoway	Salmon Sea Trout Brown Trout	1 Jul. to 14 Oct. 15 Mar. to 30 Sep.	The Manager, Garynahine Estate Office, Isle of Lewis. Tel: (01851) 621314.	
Loch Tungavat	Nr. Stornoway	Brown Trout	15 Mar. to 15 Oct.	Estate Office, Scaliscro, Timsgarry, Isle of Lewis. Tel: (01851) 672325.	Average weight of fish caught: 6 to 8 oz. Popular flies: Soldier Palmer, Butcher, Invicta. Boats are available.
Vatandip	Stornoway	Brown Trout	15 Mar. to 6 Oct.	Sportsworld, 1–3 Francis Street, Stornoway. Tel: (01851) 705464.	Bank fishing. 1 boat available.
BENBECULA **Loch Eilean Iain**	Benbecula	Brown Trout	Mar. to Sep.	South Uist Estates Ltd., Estate Office, South Uist.	Average weight of fish caught: 1 to 3 lbs. Popular flies: Soldier Palmer, Black Pennel, Ke-He. Worm. Fly. 1 boat available.
Loch Hermidale	Benbecula	Brown Trout		South Uist Estates Ltd., Estate Office, South Uist. Colin Campbell Sports, Benbecula. Tel: (01870) 602236. Bornish Stores, Bornish, South Uist. Tel: (01878) 710366.	Average weight of fish caught: 12 oz to 1 lb. Popular flies: Black Spider, Blue Zulu, Peter Ross, Invicta. 1 boat is available.
South Langavat (Heorovay-Olavat) and numerous other lochs	Benbecula	Brown Trout	15 Mar. to 30 Sep.	Bornish Stores. Tel: (01878) 710366. Colin Campbell Sports Ltd., Balivanich. Tel: (01870) 602236.	Fly only. Boats available.
Loch Olavat (East, West, North)	Benbecula	Brown/Sea Trout		South Uist Estates Ltd., Estate Office, South Uist.	Popular flies: Black Pennel, Invicta, Peter Ross, Grouse & Claret. 2 boats are available.

Water	Location	Species	Season	Permit available from	Other information
SOUTH UIST Loch Druim an Lasgair	South Uist	Brown Trout	15 Mar. to 6 Oct.	South Uist Estates Ltd., Estate Office, South Uist.	Average weight of fish caught: 12 oz to 1 lb. Popular flies: Soldier Palmer, Butchers, Black Spider.
East Loch Bee	South Uist	Brown Trout	Mar. to Sep.	South Uist Estates Ltd., Estate Office, South Uist. Colin Campbell Sports, Benbecula. Tel: (01870) 602236. Bornish Stores, Bornish, South Uist. Tel: (01878) 710366.	Average weight of fish caught: 12 oz to 1 lb 8 oz. Popular flies: Black Pennel, Ke-He, Bloody Butcher. 2 boats are available.
All hill and Machair lochs	South Uist	Salmon Sea Trout Brown Trout	Jul. to mid Oct. Jul. to Oct. Apr. to Sept.	Resident Manager, Lochboisdale Hotel, Lochboisdale, South Uist. Tel: (01878) 700332. South Uist Estates Ltd., Estate Office, South Uist.	14 boats available on lochs. Fly fishing only.
Loch Snaid	South Uist	Brown Trout		South Uist Estates Ltd., Estate Office, South Uist.	Average weight of fish caught: 12 oz to 1 lb. Popular flies: Grouse & Claret, Black Pennel, Black Spider, Butchers.
NORTH UIST Lochs & Sea Pools in North Uist		Salmon Sea Trout Brown Trout	25 Feb. to 15 Oct. 15 Mar. to 31 Oct. 15 Mar. to 30 Sep.	The Manager, Lochmaddy Hotel, North Uist. Tel: (01876) 500331.	Average weight of fish caught: Salmon 5 lbs 5 oz, Sea Trout 2 lbs 5 oz, Brown Trout 8 oz. Fly fishing only. No Sunday fishing. Boats are available on most lochs.
ISLE OF HARRIS Laxdale System	Isle of Harris	Salmon Sea Trout Brown Trout	15 Mar. to 15 Oct.	Tony Scherr, Borve Lodge Estates, Isle of Harris. Tel: (01859) 550202.	Fly fishing only. Permits cannot be reserved in advance.

NORTHERN ISLES LOCHS

Area Tourist Boards
Orkney Tourist Board
Information Centre,
6 Broad Street,
Kirkwall,
Orkney KW15 1NX.
Tel: (01856) 872856.

Shetland Islands Tourism
Area Tourist Officer,
Δ12
Shetland Islands Tourism,
Information Centre,
Market Cross, Lerwick,
Shetland ZE1 0LU.
Tel: (01595) 3434.

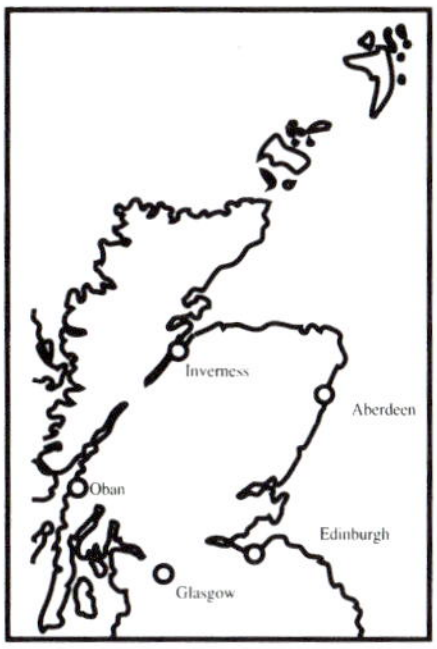

LOCHS

Water	Location	Species	Season	Permit available from	Other information
ORKNEY Board-house	Mainland	Brown Trout	15 Mar. to 6 Oct.	None required.	Boats available locally. All legal methods permitted. Anglers are recommended to join Orkney Trout Fishing Association, Kirkwall, who make facilities available to visitors.
Harray	Mainland	Brown Trout	15 Mar. to 6 Oct.	None required.	See Orkney for further information.
Hundland	Mainland	Brown Trout	15 Mar. to 6 Oct.	None required.	See Orkney for further information.
Kirbister	Mainland	Brown Trout	15 Mar. to 6 Oct.	None required.	See Orkney for further information.
Stenness	Mainland	Sea Trout Brown Trout	25 Feb. to 31 Oct. 15 Mar. to 6 Oct.	None required.	See Orkney for further information.
Swannay	Mainland	Brown Trout	15 Mar. to 6 Oct.	None required.	See Orkney for further information.
SHETLAND (1000 lochs & voes)	Shetland Islands	Sea Trout Brown Trout	25 Feb. to 31 Oct. 15 Mar. to 6 Oct.	Rod and Line Tackle Shop, Harbour St., Lerwick. Tel: (01595) 695055.	Average weight of fish caught: Brown Trout 12oz. Popular flies: all dark flies, Black Pennel, Grouse & Claret, Ke-He, Invicta, Blue Zulu (Sizes 10 & 12). Other baits: spinning where permitted with mepps spoons and toby lures. Boats available on 5 popular lochs:

Water	Location	Species	Season	Permit available from	Other information
Various	Yell Island	Brown Trout	15 Mar. to 6 Oct.	No permit required.	Average weight of fish caught: 8 oz to 8 lbs plus. Popular flies: Bibio, Silver Invicta. Spinning permitted.
Loch Benston	East Mainland	Brown Trout	15 Mar. to 6 Oct.	Rod and Line Tackle Shop, Harbour St., Lerwick. Tel: (01595) 695055.	Average weight of fish caught: 1 1/2 lb. Fly fishing only. A boat is available. Tackle for hire/sale in town. A good loch early in the season.
Loch Girlsta	East Mainland	Brown Trout Ferox Char	15 Mar. to 6 Oct.	Rod and Line Tackle Shop, Harbour St., Lerwick. Tel: (01595) 695055.	Average weight of fish caught: 1 to 2 lbs. Fly and spinning. The loch is at its best late in the season around July and August.
Huxter Loch	Isle of Whalsay	Brown Trout	15 Mar. to 6 Oct.	Brian J. Poleson, Sheardaal, Huxter, Symbister, Whalsay.	Average weight of fish caught: 12 oz. Fly fishing only. 1 boat available.
Ibister Loch	Isle of Whalsay	Brown Trout	15 Mar. to 6 Oct.	Brian J. Poleson, Sheardaal, Huxter, Symbister, Whalsay.	Average weight of fish caught: 10 to 12 oz. Fly fishing only. 1 boat available.
Loch Spiggie	South Mainland	Sea/ Brown/ Brook Trout	1 Apr. to 30 Sep.	Rod and Line Tackle Shop, Harbour St., Lerwick. Tel: (01595) 695055.	Strictly fly fishing only. A boat is available. Certain areas of the loch have restricted access.

Game Angling

CLUB	SECRETARY
Aberfeldy Angling Club	V. Hackel, P.O. Box 2000, Aberfeldy.
Airdrie Angling Club	Jimmy Potter, Sharp Avenue, Coatbridge, Lanarkshire.
Berwick & District Angling Association	D. Cowan, 129 Etal Road Tweedmouth, Berwick. Tel: (01289) 306985.
Blairgowrie, Rattray & District Angling Association	W. Matthew, 9 Mitchell Square, Blairgowrie, Perthshire. Tel: (01250) 873679.
Castle Douglas & District Angling Association	Stanley Kaye, 2 Cairnsmore Road, Castle Douglas, Kirkcudbrightshire. Tel: (01556) 502695.
Dalbeattie Angling Association	J. Moran, 12 Church Crescent, Dalbeatttie DG5 4BA. Tel: (01556) 502292.
Devon Angling Association	R. Breingan, 33 Redwell Place, Alloa, Clackmannanshire FK10 2BT. Tel: (01259) 215185.
Dumfries & Galloway Angling Association	L. Chalmers, 50 Brooms Road, Dumfries. Tel: (01387) 267647.
Dunkeld & Birnam Angling Association	Mr . A. Steele, 21 Willowbank, Little Dunkeld, Perthshire. Tel: (01350) 727428.
Dunoon & District Angling Club	A. H. Young, "Ashgrove", 28 Royal Crescent, Dunoon PA23 7AH, Tel: (01369) 705732.
Eckford Angling Association	The Buccleugh Estates Ltd., Estate Office, Bowhill, Selkirk. Tel: (01750) 20753.
Eye Water Angling Club	W. S. Gillie, 2 Tod's Court, Eyemouth, Berwickshire. Tel: (01890) 750038.
Fyvie Angling Association	J.D. Pirie, Prenton, South Road, Oldmeldrum, Aberdeenshire AB51 0AB. Tel: (01651) 872229.
Galashiels Angling Club	Mr. S. Grzybowski, 3 St. Andrew Street, Galashiels. Tel: (01896) 755712.
Goil Angling Club	Mr. Ian Given, 'Bonnyrigg', 25 Churchill Drive, Bishopton, Renfrewshire, Tel: (01505) 863531.
Gordon Fishing Club	J. Fairgrieve, Burnbrae Eden Road, Gordon. Tel: (01573) 410357.
Greenlaw Angling Club	Mr. T. Waldie, 26 East High Street, Greenlaw, Berwickshire, TD10 6UF. Tel: (01361) 810542.
Hawick Angling Club	D. Smith, (Secretary) "Wellogate Bank", Wellogate Brae, Hawick, TD9 9NE. Tel: (01450) 373142.
Inverness Angling Club	Mr. K. MacDonald, Swanston Avenue, Inverness. Tel: (01463) 240095.
Jedforest Angling Association	J. Tait, 9 Boundaries, Jedburgh TD8 6EX. Tel: (01835) 863871.
Kelso Angling Association	Euan Robson, 33 Tweedsyde Park, Kelso TD5 7RF. Tel: (01573) 225279.

Killin, Breadalbane Angling Club	J. H. Rough,. J.R.News, Main Street, Killin, Perthshire FK21 8UJ. Tel: (01567) 820362.
Kilmaurs Angling Club	T. C. McCabe, 8 East Park Crescent, Kilmaurs, Ayrshire. Tel: (01563) 538652.
Kyles of Bute Angling Club	A. H. Richardson, Allt Beag, Tignabruaich, Argyll PA21 2BE. Tel: (01700) 811486.
Ladykirk & Norham Angling Association	Mr. R. G. Wharton, 8 St. Cuthbert's Square, Norham, Berwick-upon-Tweed, TD15 2LE. Tel: (01289) 382467.
Lairg Angling Club	J. M. Ross, St. Murie, Church Hill Road, Lairg, Sutherland IV27 4BL. Tel: (01549) 402010.
Lauderdale Angling Associated Waters	D. M. Milligan, The Torrs, Portling, Dalbeattie, Kirkcudbrightshire DG5 4PZ.
Loch Keose & Associated Waters	M. Morrison, Handa, 18 Keose Glebe, Lochs, Isle of Lewis, HS2 9JX. Tel: (01851) 830334.
Loch Lomond Angling Improvement Association	Colin McCrory, P.O. Box 3559, Uddingston, G71 7SJ. Tel: (01506) 633033.
Loch Rannoch Conservation Association	Richard Legate, Glenrannoch House, Kinloch Rannoch. Tel: (01882) 632307.
Morebattle Angling Club	K. Rothwell, Eildon View, Mainsfield Avenu(Morebattle, Kelso TD5 8QP. Tel: (01573) 440247.
New Galloway Angling Association	A. Carnie, Carsons Knowe, New Galloway, Tel: (01644) 420760.
Peebleshire Salmon Fishing Association	Blackwood & Smith W. S., 39 High Street, Peebles. Tel: (01721) 720131.
Peebleshire Trout Fishing Association	D.G. Fyfe, 39 High Street, Peebles. Tel: (01721) 720131.
Perth & District Anglers' Association	Mr D. Brand, "Langholme"' Braehead, Almondbank, by Perth PH1 3LN. Tel/Fax: (01738) 583288.
Pitlochry Angling Club	R. Harriman, Sunnyknowe, Nursing Home Brae, Pitlochry, Perthshire. Tel: (01796) 472484.
Rannoch & District Angling Club	J. Brown, The Square, Kinloch Rannoch, Perthshire. Tel: (01882) 632268.
River Almond Angling Association	H. Meikle, 23 Glen Terrace, Deans, Livingston, West Lothian. Tel: (01506) 411813.
St. Andrews Angling Club	Peter F. Malcolm, 54 St. Nicholas St., St. Andrews, Fife. Tel: (01334) 476347.
St. Marys Loch Angling Association	Mr. N. MacIntyre, "Whincroft", 8 Rosetta Road, Peebles EH45 8JU. Tel: (01721) 722278.
Stormont Angling Club	Mrs. Shirley Wood, Scone Estates Office, Scone Palace, Perth PH2 6BD. Tel: (01738) 552308.
Turriff Angling Association	I. Masson, 6 Castle Street, Turiff AB53 7BJ. Tel: (01888) 562428.

Scotland's Spring Spawners - a coarse fishing perspective

by Ron Woods, Scottish Carp Group

Coarse fishing starts right on the border. In the west the River *Sark*, and its sister stream the *Kirtle*, have a good head of dace and a few chub, though much better specimens of the latter are found nearby in the lower reaches of the *Annan*. In the east, the *Tweed* separates Scotland and England. Sadly, its great roach and dace shoals are no more, but the Tweed and its tributaries, particularly the *Jed* and the *Teviot*, still yield excellent grayling.

Stillwater coarse fishing is scarce in Borders Region - although a few lochs like *Cauldshiels* and *Bowdens* have modest stocks of pike and perch - but it abounds in Dumfries and Galloway. *Castle Loch* at Lochmaben, Scotland's top bream water, also produces good roach and pike. West of Dumfries lie *Loch Rutten*, and *Loch Arthur* also holding bream, roach and pike. Nearby is *Loch Ken*, well known both for quality roach on long-range feeder tactics and its prolific stocks of pike. Many smaller coarse fisheries in Dumfries and Galloway are owned and stocked by hotels and guest houses, often with carp and tench in addition to the more common species. Good fishing is available at *Cowans Farm Guesthouse, Kirkgunzeon, Torwood House* and the *Three Lochs Caravan Park*, Glenluce, and the *Palakona Guest House*, Newton Stewart. These waters can also be fished on day tickets.

Moving north, the grayling angler will find sport in the Rivers *Ayr* and *Gryffe*, and particularly in the middle reaches of the *Clyde* and its tributaries. From Motherwell down to Glasgow Green the Clyde is a good mixed coarse fishery with dace, roach, perch and pike plus a few bream and chub. Pike, roach and perch are well distributed in the central belt and good specimens of all three can be taken in waters as far apart as *Kilbirnie Loch* and *Castle Semple Loch* in Ayrshire and the lower reaches of the river *Forth* near Stirling. The *Forth and Clyde Canal*, stretching from near Dumbarton in the west to Grangemouth in the east, offers not only these species but also good summer tench fishing and the occasional bream.

Carp and tench are less common in Scotland than in the south, but several waters across the central belt, mostly in public parks, have been stocked in the last few years. At Kilwinning, *Eglinton Country Park Loch* holds bream, perch, pike and a small head of carp; although it is best known for its roach. As well as roach and bream, Glasgow's *Hogganfield Loch* has a large but elusive head of carp which reach at least mid-twenties. *Strathclyde Park Loch* near Motherwell has a few carp in addition to its main stock of roach and bream. The *Monklands Canal* at Drumpellier Country Park near Coatbridge is well stocked with all species, including small carp and some tench. *Lanark Loch* has some nice tench as well as a good head of carp up to low twenties. The carp of *Duddingston Loch* in Edinburgh's Holyrood Park, home of the Scottish record, are large and challenging although the pleasure angler can enjoy year round roach and perch sport there.

Northwest of Glasgow lies Scotland's premier pike water, *Loch Lomond*. Tommy Morgan's 47lb 11oz specimen is still the recognised Scottish record, and at Glasgow's Kelvingrove Museum you can see the skull of a fish nearly twice as heavy. Numerous twenties and a few thirties come out every year, probably more to livebaits than to lures or deadbaits. A boat will give you the edge, but please treat this and indeed other lochs with *great* respect. Lomond is deep, exposed, and liable to rapid changes in surface conditions with even small increases or shifts in the wind. Never go out without proper safety equipment, and wear lifejackets at all times. Lomond's pike are not its only asset: good roach and perch are present, particularly near the river mouths, plus dace and a few bream. The *Endrick Water*, which flows into Lomond below Balmaha, can also produce good nets of dace and roach with a few bonus chub.

Further north are several waters from *Loch Ard* in the Trossachs to *Loch Clunie* and *Loch Marley* in Perthshire which can yield good pike and perch. A little further still lies *Loch Awe*, arguably as good a pike fishery as Lomond - certainly from April to September - though perhaps producing more middleweights in the 10-15 lb bracket and a few less twenties. Bank fishing in the shallow bays with ledgered deadbaits is productive, and while livebaits and a boat are often useful they are less advantageous here than on Lomond. Perch are also present, and can reach specimen proportions. To the east are the rivers of the *Tay* system, especially the *Earn* and the *Tummel*, which offer superb winter grayling sport with individual fish up to three pounds. There are pike and roach also in the Tay itself. Finally into the Highlands, where the only coarse fish in any numbers are pike, found in the lochs of the Great Glen and as far north as *Loch Achilty* and *Loch Garve* in Ross & Cromarty. In these and a few more remote Highland waters there are undoubtedly some very big pike which have never seen a bait...yet.

Although coarse fishing is now the fastest-growing branch of angling in Scotland, most of our waters are still far less heavily fished than their English counterparts. Fish of all species are generally fit and well fed; and rarely show the scars of previous captures. They are not usually tackle-shy, but many Scottish waters are much larger and less densley stocked than commercial fisheries down south. Location is therefore the key, together with sensible feeding practices taking account of the generally lower water knowledge is always useful, and tackle dealers who take a particular interest in coarse fishing include *Mike's Tackle Shop* in Edinburgh, *Anglers' Rendezvous* and *Scottish Angling Centre* in Glasgow, *PD Tackle* in Cumbernauld Village, *JB Angling* in Kirkintilloch, and *Ronnie MacLeod* in Motherwell.

Unfortunately, some game fishing interests see themselves in conflict with coarse species. At best this means the cost of coarse fishing is often negligible, but it can be difficult to convince owners that you are not seeking to poach their trout or salmon and the restrictions some of them place on tackle or baits can hamper effective coarse fishing methods. At worst, proprietors have massacred prime stocks such as the Tweed and Tay roach populations. Things are changing, however, and a growing number of dedicated coarse waters or mixed fisheries are available. There are also several coarse fishing clubs.

For details of general coarse fishing clubs call the Scottish Federation for Coarse Angling, Steve Clerkin, Tel: (01592) 642242. Specialist anglers can contact the Scottish Carp Group, Ron Woods, Tel: (01968) 674792 or the Regional Association of the Pike Anglers' Club of GB - Alistair McPhee, Tel: (01259) 210877.

Big baits - big ideas?

by Jim McLanaghan

The discovery of the mark came about in a rather peculiar way. Our venue was the extreme South West of Scotland, our quarry tope and pollack. A couple of years earlier my brother and I had come across a reef with some very deep and extensive kelp cover and this was literally within casting distance of the shore, although we were in my 16ft dinghy.

The pollack fishing had been superb with fish to 10lbs on spinning gear, providing heart stopping excitement as they crash-dived to the kelp bed only a few metres below. During a lull in the action I decided to put down a conger bait, fully accepting that a snag-up was almost inevitable. Diving into my tackle box I grabbed the first trace that came to hand - a tope trace, 7ft-8ft long - and down that went. I retrieved my line ten minutes later - minus the trace which was lying somewhere below, hooked to a large tree of kelp.

The next trace was a proper conger trace 2 ft long and it duly descended into the depths with a mackerel head as bait - but I stopped it just above the kelp and no more. I put the rod down, set the ratchet plus light clutch and picked up my pollack rod when the scream of a reel had me jumping almost out of my skin. My old ABU12 was losing line at an incredible speed. Only two things move at such speed in Scottish waters (apart from Trident subs) tope and shark, so without any preamble I lifted the rod, set the clutch and STRUCK - HARD! Whatever I had hooked into had obviously never read of line tension, clutch settings or any such rubbish since it carried on as if nothing had happened, rocketing for the horizon. Realising I had hooked something with skin like sandpaper, I became acutely aware of the length, or lack of lengh of my trace and started to cringe.

I had tamed a lot of good tope with my ABU12 in the years past but whatever I'd hooked now was not for taming and after a few minutes the line went slack as the fish's tail slapped agaist my main line and chaffed through it. Back came my line for the second time in less than 10 minutes - minus the trace. The pollack fishing was now ended. We had bigger fish to fry, or at least catch.

Tope - ready for returning after taking a whole mackerel.

Hoping that the big fish was still in the vicinity, the floats had our total undivided attention for the next 20 minutes or so and then it was back to see if the pollack had returned - they had. Casting my 1 oz lure across the tide, there was a tentative pluck, then nothing. Then, a lunging diving take and my Mitchell 300 reel squealed in protest at the line being stripped from it. As the fish stopped, a louder more strident urgent tone imposed itself upon us. Looking round for the source of the noise I saw my brother's reel and rod literally bouncing with tension as line melted from the spool and up through the rings. As the rod swept up and back we both felt a great deal more confident, his trace was OK. His reel was fractionally larger and his line 30% stronger than mine.

The fish slowed once it was hooked but took several long runs and dived as the run shortened till after 20 minutes the fish

Not ALL baits get big fish.

lay exhausted beside the boat. I gawped - the tope was huge and as I lifted it into the boat I checked to see if my trace was there also - it wasn't. The fish was weighed, photographed, then returned alive and at 65 lbs it registered 90% of the Scottish Record, and all because of an abortive attempt at congering! This fish and its location intrigued us since most of our previous tope had come from deeper water with strong tide runs and none closer than 600 yds from shore. Was there something that we were missing? Tope and pollack in the same piece of pond - this seemed to be too good to be true or was it a fluke? Over the rest of the season we fished the mark on several occasions and we added some rubby dubby (groundbait) of minced mackerel which in the very light tide dispersed nice and slowly. Using the technique of small floats we had tope on EVERY trip!! Indeed, we had multiple catches each time, not all huge fish, but none under 35 lbs.

I tried a similar ploy some years ago during a boat competition. The skipper put the anchor down and promptly went to sleep. I put on a huge mackerel bait - and did the same. I ended up with the largest fish of the festival. My son and his friend were fishing off Dunbar, down towards St. Abbs Head, and the cod had been slow, so in desperation Dave, my son's friend, put on a whole herring. Being in the middle of winter he hoped for a good cod or even a ling but was totally unprepared when his rod was almost wrenched from his hand and the take was so vicious that the spool on his reel never even turned. On the retrieve his trace was shredded and his herring gone - the culprit almost certainly a porbeagle shark but on the wrong gear.

Three tales of big baits with completely different targets and outcomes but with a single common thread, they all attracted big fish. It is reasonably fair to say that all anglers hope to hook "the big one" some day but how often - if ever - do they really fish for them. This attitude as Roy Castle used to say, calls for dedication, single mindedness and even fanaticism but it catches fish. In Scottish waters a big bait can result in a BIG FISH just about anywhere around our coastline - even from the shore 150 lbs skate are possible.

Finally, always be prepared to change tactics and/or tackle should you encounter something big, even if he has taken your bait he'll probably want more - try again as we did - it could pay off. Oh yes, people often ask me what I consider a BIG BAIT, well, the minimum is half a mackerel and then on up to a 5 lb cod.

Tight lines

BORDERS

The Scottish Borders provide some of the best sea angling in the UK. Based on Eyemouth, which has the largest fishing fleet in the South of Scotland, and the smaller fishing villages of Burnmouth and St Abbs, the clear unpolluted waters are well stocked with a wide variety of seafish. So clear is the water that one of the first Marine Reservations has been established off Eyemouth. The rugged coastline with its unique fauna make a spectacular background to your day's fishing. It should be noted that sea angling is not permitted off St. Abbs Head National Reserve (Petticowick-Long Carr). Eyemouth is only nine miles north of Berwick-upon-Tweed,
just off the A.1. Its colourful boats, fish auction and sandy beach make it a popular resort during the summer. Well known for its excellent rock fishing, the town is also a useful point of access to the north and south. Boat fishing has developed over the years due to the efforts of Eyemouth Sea Angling Club who now run a number of shore and boat competitions throughout the season.
The club operates the coast from Burnmouth harbour in the south to the harbour at St Abbs in the north.
Types of fish: Shore - cod, mackerel, coalfish, flounder, plaice, sole, haddock,whiting, catfish, ling and wrasse. Boat - the same species can be caught as on shore but larger specimens.
Boats: A large number of fishing boats are usually available from Eyemouth, St Abbs and Burnmouth for parties of anglers at weekends.

DUMFRIES AND GALLOWAY

Solway Firth to Isle of Whithorn

The area is renowned for its strong tides which can create difficulties for boat angling in the wrong conditions. Local advice should be sought before sailing and as a further safety measure the Coastguard should be advised of any intended trips If a boat trip is cancelled or an angler prefers shore fishing, the coastline abounds with excellent shore marks which produce a great diversity of species. Summer months are undoubtedly the most productive but the winter cod fishing can also be very good with many large fish being taken.

Kippford

Better known as a yachting centre Kippford still offers good angling opportunities Shore marks around Kippford yield bags of flatfish and dogfish in the summer with the occasional bass. The area excels in the winter with catches of big cod. The Scottish shore caught record cod came from here. Boat fishing during the summer tends to give more variety with mackerel, thornback and dogfish, both spur and spotted featuring in the catches.
Bait: Lug and ragworm can be dug locally and cockles and mussels picked from the shore.
Season: May to September for comfort and variety. November to February for big cod but wrap up well!

Kirkcudbright

About 5 miles from the open sea on the Dee estuary, Kirkcudbright is at the centre of an excellent shore fishing area. Rocky points in Kirkcudbright bay along the Dundrennan shore to the east and Borgue to the west, give good varied fishing especially during the summer. Dogfish feature heavily in local club matches with the occasional conger, bull huss and thornback. Settled conditions and clear water give good bags of pollack and garfish, and mullet are attracted to ground bait. The estuary produces bags of plaice, dabs flounders, eels and coalfish giving good sport at the harbour. The bay also fishes well for cod and whiting in the winter. Boat fishing can be good with launching sites at

at the
harbour, Ross Bay and Brighouse but these are restricted by the tides. One charter boat operates from Kirkcudbright. Boat catches are as varied as the shore, but there is always the chance of a tope.
Bait: Lug and ragworm are available locally along with cockles and mussels. Mackerel and herring can be bought in the town.
Tackle: A limited amount available from: Watson Mckinnel in Kirkcudbright. A better selection from: "Patties",
109 Queensberry Street,
Dumfries,
"Reel em In",
Friars Vennel, Dumfries.
Charter Boat: "Howzat" Howard Williams.
Tel: (01557) 330367.
Further Information:
Information Centre,
Kirkcudbright.
Tel: (01557) 330494.

Garlieston & The Isle of Whithorn

Situated on the east side of the Machars Peninsula, the area is sheltered from the prevailing westerly winds giving good shore and boat fishing. Rock marks give good bags of dogfish, pollack and wrasse with conger and mullet also being taken. Burrow Head gives good fishing when the weather is fine. The summer months are the best for both shore and boat fishing. Boats can be launched from both harbours on a suitable tide and charter boats operate from the Isle of Whithorn. The biggest attraction for boat anglers is tope which can sometimes be caught in numbers. Some big fish are caught every year and most are released. Spurdog and thornback sometimes take bate meant for tope.
Tackle: Some available locally from: A. McGhie, Radio Shop, George Street, Whithorn. J.M. William, Grocer & Harbour Master, The Harbour,
Isle of Whithorn.
Tel: (01988) 500246.
Bait: Lug, rag and shellfish available locally.
Boats: Craig Mills,
Main Street,
Isle of Whithorn DG8 8LN.
Tel: (01988) 500393 - (Manu Kea). Rab McCreadie - (Crusader).
Local Clubs:
Kirkcudbright & District SAC, Stuart Ross, "Fanore", 53 St. Cuthbert Street, Kirkcudbright.
Tel: (01557) 330845.
Peever Sea Anglers,
Jack McKinnel,
20 Merse Strand,
Kirkcudbright.
Tel: (01557) 331505.

Luce Bay

There are some good shore marks, namely Sandhead Sands for Flatfish, Dogfish and Bass in season. Terrally Bay for these species plus Codling, Whiting, Spurdogfish. Around East and West Tarbet bays at the Mull of Galloway good rock fishing may be had for Lesser Spotted Dogfish, Bull Huss, Spurdogfish, Conger Eels, Wrasse, Whiting, Pollack, Coalfish, Flatfish and Mackerel in season, normally from late April to December.
Boats: W. Carter, Castle Daly Angling Centre, Auchenmalg, Glenluce.
Tel: (01581) 500250.
(Self drive boats for hire & hotel accommodation).
Bait: Lug can be dug in most sandy bays around Luce Bay, especially at Sandhead. Some shellfish available, mussels and cockles with razorfish on spring tides.
Launching Sites: Difficult to launch without four wheel drive vehicle.
Sites: Yacht Club at Drummore high water only. Cailiness Road picnic site. Back of harbour Drummore. East Tarbet Bay usually necessary to rope the trailer over shingle. £3 charge at local farm.
Safety: Dinghy anglers should be aware of the strong tides in the area, especially around the Mull of Galloway area.

Port William

Port William is situated on the east side of Luce Bay and has a good, though tidal harbour. It is the starting point for many anglers wishing to fish the lower part of Luce Bay. The once famous shore mark of Monreith Bay, still a good bass beach, lies just to the south of Port William.
Types of fish: Tope, spurdog, rays, cod, pollack, flatfish from boats. Bass wrasse, codling and pollack from the shore.
Tackle: Available in village.
Bait: Lugworm, shellfish and molluscs along beach. Mackerel in bay.
Season: May-October.

Drummore

Drummore, the main port for anglers wishing to fish

the western side of Luce Bay lies 5 miles north of the Mull of Galloway. Hotels and guest houses cater for anglers. There are many good shore marks on sandy beaches north of Drummore, while the Mull of Galloway provides excellent shore fishing over rocky ground. The Mull, the most southerly point of Scotland, is an area of very strong tides and is not recommended as a fishing area to anglers with small boats incapable of at least 10 knots, especially during ebb tides.
Types of fish: Pollack, wrase from rocky shores, flatfish, bass, mullet and rays from sandy beaches. Pollack, coalfish, cod, whiting, wrasse, lesser spotted dogfish, bull huss, spurdog, tope, rays, conger from boats.
Boats: "On yer Marks" Ian or Sue Burrett, Cardrain Cottage, Drummore.
Tel: (01776) 840346.
Charter Boats:
Stuart Aylott -
Tel: (01776) 840226.
Bait: All types available on shore at low tide. Mackerel from Mull of Galloway shore marks.

Port Logan

Port Logan is the small community which is situated abut 7.5 miles north of the Mull of Galloway on the west side of the Galloway Peninsula. An area with many good shore marks both to the north and south of the village. It is one of the few relatively easy launching sites on this coastline south of Portpatrick. A good alternative for the angler with his own boat when easterly winds prevent fishing in Luce Bay. Like the Mull of Galloway an area of strong ties,
especially off Crammoc Head, to the south of Port Logan Bay.
Types of fish: As for the southern part of Luce Bay with occasional haddock. Herring in June and July. Ideal to launch dinghies at Port Logan from concrete slipway onto hard sand where two wheel drive vehicles can run onto beach. Slack water occurs one and a half hours before high and low water.
Boats: Ian Burrett, Cardrain Cottage, Drummore.
Tel: (01776) 840346.

Portpatrick

The small fishing port and holiday resort of Portpatrick lies on the west coast of Wigtownshire, 8 miles from Stranraer. There is good shore fishing from the many rocky points north and south of the resort, the best known being the Yellow Isle, half a mile north of the harbour. Sandeel Bay, a little further north, and Killintringan Lighthouse are also worth fishing. Small slipway only used at high tide.
Types of fish: Pollack, coalfish, plaice, flounder, codling, mackerel, dogfish, conger, wrasse and tope occasionally.
Boats: Brian Tyreman, Pinminnoch Cottage, Portpatrick DG9 9AB.
Tel: (01776) 810468 "Cornubia".
Bait: None sold locally. Lugworm and some ragworm can be dug east of the railway pier, Stranraer.
Season: May-December.
Further Information from: Mr. R. Smith, 24 Millbank Road, Stranraer.
Tel: (01776) 703691.

Stranraer & Loch Ryan

Stranraer, at the head of Loch Ryan, offers the angler, as a rail and bus terminal, a good stepping off point for many sea angling marks and areas in this part of Scotland, with Sandhead on Luce Bay (8 miles) to the south, Portpatrick (8 miles) to the west and Lady Bay (8 miles) on the west side of Loch Ryan with Cainryan (6 miles) and Finnart Bay (10 miles) on the opposite side of the loch. Best Shore marks being Cairnryan Village, South of Townsend Thoresen ferry terminal. Old House Point and Concrete Barges north of Cairnryan Village, Finnart Bay on East Mouth of Loch, Wig Bay, Jamiesons Point and Lady Bay on west side of Loch Ryan. Boats may be launched at Wig Bay Slipway, Lady Bay and at Stranraer Market Street.
Access Safety: Most landowners will grant permission to cross lands to fish if this is requested and will advise best routes to avoid crossing crops. Most rock marks are safe but caution is needed in wet conditions as they may become slippy. In Loch Ryan anglers fishing from rocks or beaches should be aware of the wash from ferries and seacat as these can

be dangerous if caught in the drive up the beaches or rocks. **Please note:** No fishing is allowed on the jetty at Cairnryan at any times and the owners are going to take legal action against anglers who break through the boundary fence to obtain access. The jetty is unsafe and no insurance is in force.

Types of fish: taken from shore pollack, codling, coalfish, plaice, dabs, wrasse, whiting, conger eel, lesser spotted dogfish, flounder, with spurdog, thornback ray and bull huss at times. Occasional tope. Taken from boat: Pollack, codling, coalfish, plaice, dabs, wrasse, whiting, conger eel, lesser spotted dogfish, flounder with spurdog thornback ray and bull huss at times. Turbot, monkfish and spotted and cuckoo ray in the deeper water.

Boat: Mike Watson, Main Street, Stranraer. Tel: (01776) 853225.

Tackle: The Sports Shop, George Street, Stranraer. Tel: (01776) 702705, (frozen bait stocked).

Bait: Lugworm can be dug in most sandy bays, with the cockle shore at Stranraer the most popular. Loch Ryan Sea Angling Association has a lease on the cockle shore at Stranraer to restrict bait digging and the conditions are that anglers are only allowed to dig sufficient bait for one day's fishing. Ragworm can be dug in places. Cultured ragworm on sale at sports shop in Stranraer along with a good assortment of frozen baits. Mussels can be obtained on most beaches. Mackerel are caught from shore and boat in season.

Season: Sea fishing is carried out all year but from May to October the best for daylight with a lot of night fishing giving better results.

Local Clubs: Loch Ryan Sea Angling Association, Paul Paterson, 46 Antrim Avenue, Stranraer. Tel: (01776) 703529. Sealink S.A.C., Niven Dickson, Seabank Road, Stranraer. Tel: (01776) 704895.

Further information from above or: Mr. R. Smith, 24 Millbank Road, Stranraer. Tel: (01776) 703691.

STRATHCLYDE SOUTH

Loch Ryan to Ardrossan

The angling potential of much of the coast between Loch Ryan and Girvan remains unknown, the many rocky shores, small headlands and sandy beaches probably only attracting the anglers in an exploratory mood, or those seeking solitude in pursuit of their hobby.

Girvan

Girvan has a sheltered port and is a family holiday resort. From the end of the pier good fishing can be had for fair-sized plaice, flounders and spotted dog. Night fishing is good for rock cod. Just one mile to the south of the town lies the noted Horse Rock, only about 50 yards from the main Stranraer road. Access to the rock may be gained from about half tide. Except during very high tides and during storms it is a good shore mark providing access to water of about 20 feet on the sea-side even at low tide.

Types of fish: Plaice, codling, rays, flounder, pollack and ling, whiting, gurnard (mostly from boat) and tope, however very few people fish for them. (Mullet in the harbour during the summer months).

Boats: M. McCrindle, 7 Harbour Street, Girvan KA26 9AJ. Tel: (01465) 713219. Tony Wass, 22 Templand Road, Dalry KA24 5EU. Tel: (01294) 833724.

Baits: Lugworm and ragworm can be dug at beach nearby or fresh mackerel from boat.

Tackle: Available from Girvan Chandlers, 4 Knockcushon Street, Girvan KA26 9AG.

Season: March to October.

Further information from: Brian Burn (S.F.S.A.). Tel: (01292) 264735.

Ayr

Ayr is a popular holiday town on the estuaries of the Rivers Ayr and Doon, 32 miles south-west of Glasgow. Good shore fishing can be had on the Newton Shore, north of the harbour for flounders and the odd doggie during the summer months with a few coallies, codling and whiting throughout the winter, especially when there is a good storm. Some flounders and eels are taken from the harbour and at times excellent

mullet can be caught from the tidal stretches of the river Ayr. Boat fishing in the bay can be very productive for mackerel and herring from May to October. Usually from July to November the boat fishing improves with the arrival of codling, pollack, ling, coallies, plaice, dabs, sea scorpions and spotted dogs.
Tackle: Available from Gamesport, 60 Sandgate, Ayr.
Bait: Lug and rag can be dug at the Newton Shore with Doonfoot beaches producing lug and peeler crab during summer months.
Boats: Ayr Sea Angling Centre
Tel: (01292) 285297. There is also a good public slipway for dinghies to launch. Difficulty can be had on exceptionally low tides at low water.
Further information: Brian Burn (S.F.S.A).
Tel: (01292) 264735.

Prestwick & Troon
Just north of Ayr, Prestwick and Troon offers some reasonable shore fishing at certain times of the year. Prestwick beaches fish for codling, flounders and coallies from usually November to January especially on evening tides. Flounders, the odd coallie and spotted dog can be caught throughout the summer months. The Ballast Bank at Troon can produce conger, pollock, doggies, wrasse and the odd codling throughout the summer months with the better chance of a few codling and coallies during the winter. Troon pier is a favourite mark for herring and mackerel during the summer and there is always the chance of a conger or two from this area.
Bait: Lug and rag can be dug on Prestwick shore and mussels beds also at Troon and Barassie beaches.
Boats: Jimmy Wilson, 27 Wallace Avenue, Troon.
Tel: (01292) 313161.
Dinghies can be launched from Troon Marina, however there is a launching charge.
Further information: John Fitchett
Tel: (01292) 314057.

Irvine
Irvine is Scotland's only "New Town" by the sea. The harbour which is situated at the mouth of the River Irvine and River Garnock is no longer used by commercial shipping. There is plenty to do for the non angling members of the family in the nearby Magnum Leisure Centre, Maritime Museum and shopping centre. The long sandy beaches to the north and south of the harbour are good for flounders, dabs and eels especially evening flood tides. Irvine Bay is a good boat fishing area with several reefs of varying sizes within easy reach of the harbour. The sandy stretches can often produce good bags of flatfish. Further afield from Irvine is Troon wreck and Lady Isle where good pollack can be caught.
Type of fish: Cod, ling, pollack, flatties, L.S.D. and of course mackerel and herring.
Tackle: Irvine Angling World.
Tel: (01294) 313336.
Young and Son, Saltcoats.
Tel: (01294) 605344.
Bait: Lugworm and ragworm can be dug in the harbour. Frozen baits can be bought from local Tackle shops.
Boats: Norrie Mason, New Town Marine, c/o 19 Grange Road, Stevenston, Ayrshire KA21 3EA.
Tel: (01294) 605524.
Season: All year round.

Saltcoats & Ardrossan
Saltcoats with the neighbouring towns of Stevenston and Ardrossan, is situated on the Ayrshire coast 30 miles south-west of Glasgow. Shore fishing is possible in the South Bay and around the harbours. Approximately 3 miles north is Ardneil Bay which can produce a few codling over the rough ground.
Types of fish: Pollack, wrasse, doggies, eels, cod, saithe, flatties and herring.
Further information: Please obey any private fishing signs within the area and remember dinghy anglers. No fishing within 50 meters of Ore terminal at Hunterston.
Boats: Robert Reid-
Tel: (01294) 601844.
Bait: Ragworm available from Saltcoats Harbour, Fairlie Pier. Lugworm from Ardrossan north shore and Farlie sand flats.
Tackle: Light tackle is all you require for most species in the area. Fixed spool or

multiplier, light rod - 8-10lb line, spinning or bait .
Season: May to October
Local Club Ardrossan & District Sea Angling Club.
Further Information from: Bud McClymont, 41 Come Crescent, Saltcoats KA21 6JL
Tel: (01294) 461830.

Largs

Largs is within easy reach of several good fishing banks, including the Piat Shoal, the Skelmorlie Patch and the east shore of Cumbrae.
Types of fish: Dogfish, flounders, gurnard, dragonets, pollack, mackerel, plaice, coalfish and dabs.
Boats: Are readily available from local hirers.
Tackle: Hastie of Largs Ltd, Department Store, 109 Main Street, Largs. Tel: (01475) 673104
Bait: Lug, rag, cockles and mussels are available from Fairlie Flats. Sea trout are caught regularly on the shore.

Gourock

The coastline from Largs to Greenock was probably the most popular area in Scotland for shore angling, with many anglers from the Midlands of England and beyond making regular trips north. Now the fishing is generally poor. At Wemyss Bay, angling is not permitted from the pier, but odd good catches can still be had to the south, and the Red Rocks, about a mile to the north, are noted for odd codling and other species. At Inverkip there is a sandy beach around the entrance to the marina where flounders, odd dabs and eels can be taken. Cloch Point, where the Firth turns east, is well known for its fishing potential, although the current can be fierce, and because of the rough bottom,
relatively heavy lines are necessary. The coastline from Cloch along Gourock Promenade to the swimming pool car park provides fair fishing and is easily accessible. Further inland at Greenock Esplanade, flounders, dabs, eels and coallies are among the species available, although the water here is shallower, and this area is more productive at night. This stretch of coastline provides the dinghy angler with easy access to many of the Clyde marks, including the Gantocks, where outsize cod and coalfish were taken many years ago, mainly on pirks. The bay beside the power station holds flatfish and the ground off Greenock Esplanade is popular for coallies, some pollack and dabs. Dinghy owners should note that no anchoring is permitted in the main navigation channels, and several other regulations must also be adhered to.
Types of fish: Coalfish (known locally as saithe), odd codling, conger eel, dab, dogfish, flounder, occasional ling, plaice,
pollack (Iythe), pouting, whiting and wrasse. Grey mullet, herring and mackerel can also be caught during the summer months.
Tackle: Inversports, 27a Kempock Street, Gourock, Brian Peterson & Co., 12 Kelly Street, Greenock. Findlay & Co., 58 Lynedoch Street, Greenock.
Bait: Lug, rag, mussels, cockles and crabs can all be obtained from the shoreline.
Boats: J Crowther, Inverclyde Boat Owners Association, 164 Burns Road, Greenock. Tel:(01475) 634341 can advise.

Isle of Arran

The island of Arran, lying in the outer Firth of Clyde, may be reached from the mainland by ferries running from Ardrossan to Brodick, the largest community on the island. Good shore fishing is found around the whole of the island, much of which remains unexplored.

Lamlash

Lamlash is the main centre for sea angling on the island, probably because of its situation on the shores of Lamlash Bay, the large horse-shoe shaped bay which is almost landlocked by the Holy Isle. This gives excellent protection to the bay from easterly winds. Lamlash is also the starting point for boat trips to the excellent fishing grounds of Whiting Bay and those around Pladda to the south.
Types of fish: Codling, whiting, coalfish, pollack, conger, rays, flatfish, mackerel, dogfish,
plaice, dabs, gurnard, wrasse and odd haddock.
Bait: Obtainable from many beaches.
Season: March-November.

Corrie
Corrie is situated on the north east coast of the island.
Types of fish: Codling, haddock, conger, rays, dogfish, ling, pollack, gurnard, garfish, mackerel and wrasse.

Whiting Bay
This bay, which takes its name from the whiting, is very open to the sea. There are excellent fishing banks from Largiebeg Point to King's Cross Point.
Boats: Dinghies can be hired from the Jetty, Whiting Bay or by arrangement with Jim Ritchie,
Tel (01770) 700382.
Bait: Cockles, mussels, lugworm, ragworm, limpets and crabs are abundant on the banks from half tide.

Lochranza
Lochranza is situated at the northern end of the island. The loch is surrounded by hills opening out on to Kilbrannan Sound.
Types of fish: Cod, conger, wrasse and pollack from the shore. Codling, conger, some haddock, plaice and dabs from boat.
Tackle: Available from boat hirers.
Bait: Mussels, cockles, lugworm and ragworm obtainable.

Brodick
Good fishing in Brodick Bay from Markland Point to Clauchlands Point.
Types of fish: Codling, plaice and other flatfish, conger, wrasse and pollack can be had from the shore while cod, conger, rays, dogfish, ling, pollack, gurnard, garfish and other round fish can be fished from boats.
Bait: Mussels are obtainable from the rocks around Brodick Pier or may be purchased from boat hirers.

Isle of Cumbrae, Millport
There is good fishing at a bank between the South East Point of Millport Bay (Farland Point) and Keppel Pier, Fintry Bay and Piat Shoal provide good sport. West of Portachur Point in about 15/ 20 fathoms and in Dunagoil Bay. S.W. Bute are good. Fairlie Channel directly seaward of Kelburn Castle is about 12/15 fathoms. East shore northwards about 10 fathoms line.
Types of fish: Saithe, conger, coalfish, dogfish, mackerel and flatfish.
Tackle: Available locally from boat hirers.
Bait: Mussels, worms, etc., on shore Boat hirers and local shops provide bait.

STRATHCLYDE NORTH

Helensburgh
Helensburgh is a small seaside town on the Firth of Clyde at the southern end of the Gareloch, easily reached by train or car.
Types of fish: Shore and boat flounder, coalfish, conger, dogfish, whiting, dab, pollack and mackerel.
Tackle: Lochside Bait + Tackle, 112A East Princes Street, Helensburgh .
Tel: (01436) 677796.
Bait: Ragworm, lugworm, may be dug locally. Mussels and crabs can be gathered from the shore. Fresh & frozen bait can be purchased from Lochside Bait & Tackle, 112A East Princes Street, Helensburgh.
Tel:(01436) 677796.
Season: All year.
Further information from: Mr M.J. Partland, Drumfork S.A.C., 142 East Clyde Street, Helensburgh G84 7AX.
Tel: (01436) 671937.

Garelochhead
Garelochhhead is the village at the head of the Gareloch, with the whole shoreline within easy reach. Upper and lower loch Long and Loch Goil are only a few miles away.
Types of fish: Coalfish, pollack, dab, flounder, plaice, whiting, pouting, mackerel, and lesser spotted dogfish.
Tackle: Lochside Bait & Tackle, 112A East Princes Street, Helensburgh.
Tel: (01436) 677796.
Bait: Garelochhead - cockles and mussels. Roseneath - lugworm, ragworm and cockles. Rhuragworm. Kilcreggan - ragworm. Coulport - cockles. Fresh & frozen bait can be bought from: Lochside Bait & Tackle, 112A East Princes Street, Helensburgh.
Tel: (01436) 677796.
Season: All year.
Further information from: Mr M.J. Partland, Drumfork S.A.C.,142 East Clyde Street.Helensburgh G84 7AX.
Tel: (01436) 671937.

Arrochar, Loch Long
The village lies at the northern end of the loch, and has waters sheltered by the high surrounding hills.
Types of fish: Shore conger, pollack, coalfish. Boat - whiting, dabs, conger, pollack, coalfish, mackerel, dogfish and odd rays.
Tackle: Lochside Bait & Tackle, 112A East Princes Street, Helensburgh. Tel: (01436) 677796.
Bait: Fresh herring and mackerel, mussels and cockles usually available from the pier. Artificial baits, lures etc., available from shops in village. Fresh and frozen bait can be bought from Lochside Bait & Tackle, 112A East Princes Street, Helensburgh. Tel: (01436) 677796.
Season: All year.
Further information from: Mr M.J.Partland, Drumfork S.A.C., 142 East Clyde Street, Helensburgh G84 7AX . Tel: (01436) 671937.

Clynder
Clynder is the fishing centre on the sheltered west side of the Gareloch and one mile north of the popular Rhu Narrows.
Types of Fish: Conger, rays, plaice, flounders, dogfish, whiting, pouting and mackerel.
Tackle: Lochside Bait + Tackle, 112A East Princes Street, Helensburgh Tel (01436) 677796.
Boats: C Moar (01436) 831336.
Bait: Cockles, mussels, lug, ragworm, can be dug. Fresh & frozen bait can be bought from Lochside Bait & Tackle, 112A East Princes Street, Helensburgh. Tel: (01436) 677796.
Season: All year.
Further information from: Mr M.J. Partland, Drumfork, S.A.C., 142 East Clyde Street, Helensburgh G84 7AX. Tel: (01436) 671837.

Isle of Bute, Rothesay
The holiday resort of Rothesay, situated on the island of Bute, only a 30 minute crossing by roll on / roll-off ferry from Wemyss Bay, is sheltered from the prevailing south - westerly winds. Several boat hirers cater for sea anglers. There are also many excellent shore marks. The deep water marks at Garroch Head can be productive for both shore and boat anglers.
Types of fish: Shore - cod, coalfish , pollack, plaice, mackerel, wrasse. Boat - cod, pollack, plaice. mackerel, conger, coalfish, wrasse, whiting and ling.
Tackle: Available from Bute Arts and Tackle, 94-96 Montague Street, Rothesay, Isle of Bute, Tel: (01700) 503598.
Bait: Lugworm, ragworm, cockles and mussels can be obtained from beaches around the island, and no angler should set forth without feathers or tinsel lures and a few good heavy spinners. Herring is also useful bait.
Season: July-October.

Kilchattan Bay
Sheltered bay waters at the south end of the Isle of Bute renowned for its good all year round fishing.
Types of fish: Cod, pollack, plaice, mackerel, conger, dogfish, wrasse, whiting.
Bait: Worm, fresh cockle available locally.
Season: July to October.

Mainland Ardentinny
Ardentinny is a small unspoiled village picturesquely situated on the west shore of Loch Long, 12 miles from Dunoon by car.
Types of fish: Cod, mackerel from the shore. Cod, conger, haddock, ray, plaice, flounder, whiting, coalfish and mackerel from boats.
Bait: Cockles, mussels, lug and ragworm easily dug in bay .
Season: All year, winter for large cod.

Dunoon
Types of fish: Most of the shoreline around Dunoon provides catches of cod, coalfish, pollack, flounder, mackerel, plaice. Using ragworm & lugworm, cockle, mussel, razorfish and peeler crab. Boat fishing takes mostly cod, pollack, coalfish dogfish, dabs, plaice, flounder. Also conger over wrecks or rough ground at night.
Boats: Gourock skippers fish Dunoon waters. Approx 3 miles from Dunoon is Holy Loch.
Bait: Can be bought at shops most of the year or obtained in East Bay shore.
Further information from: John Murray, Tel: (01475) 738241.

Tighnabruaich & Kames
Tighnabruaich, on the Kyles of Bute, is famed for its beauty and Highland scenery. Access to some good fishing banks on the west side of the Bute and around the Kyles.
Types of fish: Mackerel and coalfish from the shore, flatfish, whiting, dogfish, pollack, gurnard and several species of wrasse. Conger fishing can be arranged.
Bait: Supplies of fresh bait (lug, cockle, mussel, clams etc.,) are locally available.
Boats: Motor dinghies available for hire. Local fisherman can take parties of anglers by arrangement.
Contact: Andy Lancaster, Kames Hotel.
Tel; (01700) 811489.
Season: Spring to Autumn.

Loch Fyne
This is the longest sea-loch in Scotland, penetrating into the Highlands from the waters of the lower Firth of Clyde. The depth of the water within the loch varies enormously with depth of around 100 fathoms being found not only at the seaward end but also at the head of the loch of Inveraray. Much of the shore angling potential remains unknown although access to both shores is made relatively easy by roads running down each side. Boat launching facilities are less easy to find because of the rugged shoreline. Best side is Inveraray to Furnace. Quarry is now out of bounds.
Types of fish: Mackerel, codling, pollack, flatfish, conger (at night).

Inveraray
Inveraray stands on its west shore near the head of Loch Fyne.
Types of Fish: Mackerel, pollack, codfish, ling, dogfish, conger eel and plaice.
Bait: Mussels and worms available from shore at low tide.
Season: June-September.

Tarbert (Loch Fyne)
The sheltered harbour and the adjacent coast of the loch near the lower end of the loch on the west shore are good fishing grounds for the sea angler.
Types of fish: Mackerel, coalfish and sea trout from the shore. Mackerel, cod, coalfish and whiting from boats.
Boats: Evening out with the boats of the herring fleet can be arranged.
Tackle: Local shops.
Bait: There is an abundance of shellfish and worms on the mud flats.
Season: June, July and August.

Oban
Good catches can be occasionally be taken in Kerrera Sound near the Cutter Rock and the Ferry Rocks. Fishing is much better off the south and west coasts of Kerrera Island and Shepherds Hat, Maiden Island and Oban Bay give good mackerel fishing in July and August. These places are very exposed and should only be attempted in good settled weather. Many large skate, up to 200lbs average, are regularly taken from the Firth of Lorn.
Best shore marks: Salmore Point, North Connel at road bridge, Bonawe Quarry, rail bridge at Loch Cerran, Easdale Rocks.
Types of fish: Boat & Shore Tope, conger, whiting, codling, cod, pollack, coalfish, skate, thornback, ray, spurdog, dogfish, mackerel, ling, wrasse and gurnard.
Tackle requirements: From light spinning to beachcasters. Boat rods mainly 20lbs class, but for skate 50lbs class. All sea and game anglers necessities stocked at "The Anglers Corner."
Boats: Ronnie Campbell, 14 Kenmore Cottages, Bonawe, Argyll.
Tel: (01631) 750213 (launching for Loch Etive best at Oban).
Bait: Mussels and lugworm etc. can be dug from the Kerrera beaches. Frozen and preserved baits can be bought from The Angler's Corner, 2 John Street, Oban. Tel: (01631) 566374 or from Binnie Bros. Fishmongers, 8 Stevenson Street, Oban. Tel: (01631) 566374.
Season: May-November.
Boats: Launching is available at Oban and 2 miles south at the Puffin Dive Centre.
Further information from: Ross Binnie.
Tel: (01631) 566734.

Isle of Islay
This is the southernmost of the islands. Several of the larger communities like Port Ellen and Port Askaig

have good harbours.
Types of fish: Boat - cod, haddock, whiting, mackerel, dogfish, flounder, conger, rays.
Tackle: Available from J. Campbell, Sub-Post Office, Bridgend.
Bait: Lugworm plentiful on most beaches. Clam skirts from fish factory waste. Bait can be purchased from fishing boats at the piers.
Season: June-October.
Further information from: Bowmore Tourist Office.
Tel: (01496) 810254.

Isle of Mull (Salen)
Salen is situated on the east coast of Mull facing the sound of Mull in a central position, 11 miles from Craignure and 10 miles from Tobermory. The village is sited between Aros River and a headland forming Salen Bay. The Sound of Mull is one of the main skate marks in the Argyll area. Many 100lbs., plus skate have now been taken. One of the contributing factors is the sheltered nature of the Sound, which can allow practically uninterrupted angling. This area has also yielded a number of fine tope, the largest of which was a specimen of 50lbs. It is worth noting that cod and haddock seldom frequent the sound and should not be expected. This is an area recommended for dinghy owners.
Type of fish: Coalfish, pollack, wrasse, flounder, mullet sea trout and mackerel from the shore. Ray, skate, ling, pollack, coalfish, spurdog, tope, conger, gurnard and odd codling from boats.
Tackle: Available from the Tackle and Books, Main Street, Tobermory, 10 miles away.
Bait: Easily obtainable from shoreline. Mackerel bait from Tackle and Books, Main Street, Tobermory.
Season: March-November.
Further information from: Mr. Duncan Swinbanks, Tackle and Books, 10 Main Street, Tobermory.

Isle of Mull (Tobermory)
The principal town on Mull, it is situated on a very sheltered bay at the north eastern tip of the island. Apart from hitting the headlines in the national press with its treasure, Tobermory has been extensively covered in the angling press. It is Scotland's most popular centre for skate fishing. Every year and average of 50 ton-up specimens are caught, tagged and returned alive. It is this thoughtful conservation that has maintained the quality of fishing in the area. Large tope of between 35lbs. and 45lbs., can be numerous. Ten Scottish records, red gurnard, grey gurnard, blonde ray, spotted ray, spurdogfish, angler fish, turbot, common skate and two wrasse have come from these Mull waters. Every year catches of migratory fish can be made. Coalfish, whiting, haddock and cod are encountered.
Types of fish: Tope, skate, rays, pollack, coalfish, ling, conger, gurnard, spurdog, cod, haddock, flatfish (plaice, dabs and turbot) and whiting from boats. Coalfish, pollack, cod, wrasse, flounder, grey mullet, sea trout, conger, thornback and mackerel from the shore.
Boats: Andrew Jackson, Laggerbay, Acharacle, Argyll PH36 4JW.
Tel: (01972) 500208, has a purpose built 38 ft. sea angling boat for fishing parties with boat rods and reel available. There are 14-16 ft. dinghies for hire for fishing in and around the bay.
Tackle: A tackle shop, with a complete range of stock is on the Main Street.
Bait: Herring and mackerel available from Tackle and Books, Tobermory. Mussels and lugworms are easily obtainable from the shoreline.
Season: May-November.

Further information from: Mr. Duncan Swinbanks, Tackle and Books, 10 Main Street, Tobermory.

Isle of Coll
Coll is one of the smaller islands seaward of Mull. Fishing vessels concentrate on the Atlantic side, but good sport can be had on the Mull side and even at the mouth of Arinagour Bay where the village and hotel lie and the mail steamer calls. Fishing from rocks at several spots round the island can give good results.
Types of fish: Mackerel, coalfish, pollack, cod, conger, haddock, skate and flounder.
Boats: Dinghies with or without outboard engines can be hired from local

lobster fishermen.
Tackle: Visitors are advised to bring their own.
Bait: Mussels, worms and small crabs can be readily be obtained at low tide in Arinagour Bay.
Season: May to September and later depending on weather.

FORTH AND LOMOND (EAST COAST)

Anglers going afloat from Fife and Forth Harbours are advised to contact the coastguard at Fifeness for weather information. Tel: (01333) 450666 (day or night). All harbours under Forth Port Authorities may charge a launching fee.

Tayport
Tayport, on the Firth of Tay opposite Dundee, in the northernmost part of Fife, enjoys good shore fishing in sheltered waters. There are no hotels but there is a modern caravan and camping site with showers, laundry etc.
Types of fish: Cod, flounder and plaice from shore, with occasional sea trout (permit required).
Bait: Lugworm, ragworm, mussels, cockles and crabs available locally at low water.
Season: April-January.

St. Andrews
St. Andrews is a leading holiday resort with sea angling as one of its attractions. Fishing is mainly from boats, but good sports can be had from the rocks between the bathing pool and the harbour.
Tackle: Messrs J. Wilson & Sons (Ironmongers), 169-171 South Street, St. Andrews KY16 9EE. Tel: (01334) 472477.
Bait: Excellent supplies of Lugworm, ragworm and large mussels can be gathered on the beach.

Boarhill and Kings Barns
Good beach fishing for cod and flatfish.

Anstruther
It is a fishing village with plenty of good boat and beach fishing. A very rocky coastline but can be very rewarding with good catches of cod, saithe, flounder, wrasse and whiting. Be prepared to lose tackle.
Types of fish: Cod, saithe, wrasse, flounder, ling, conger and mackerel.
Boats: Plenty charter boats with local skippers who know all the hot spots.
Bait: Lug, rag, white rag, cockle, crab, mussel which can be dug locally.
Season: Boat - May-October. Beach - September-January.

Pittenweem
The nerve centre of the East Neuk with a large deep water harbour which boats can enter or leave at any stage of the tide. The European Cod Festival is now held there each year and produces large catches of cod. The harbour wall is very popular with young and old alike, with some good catches.
Types of fish: Cod, saithe, flounder, wrasse, ling, conger, whiting, mackerel from boats. Cod, saithe, flounder, wrasse and whiting from beach.
Bait: Lug and rag can be dug locally.
Season: Beach - September-January.

Leven
A holiday resort with about 2 miles of lovely sandy beaches. Beach fishing is very popular with some very good catches.
Types of fish: Flounder, cod, bass, mullet, saithe.
Boats: No charter boats.
Bait: Lug available locally.
Season: July-January.

Buckhaven
A small town on the north side of the Firth of Forth, which is renowned for its boat and beach fishing. The Scottish Open Beach Competition is fished from Buckhaven to Dysart each year with large entries from all over Scotland.
Types of fish: Cod, saithe, flounder, whiting, mackerel from beach. Cod, saithe, flounder, whiting, ling, mackerel and wrasse from boat.
Bait: Lug available at Leven.
Boats: No charter hire.
Season: Boat - June-November. Beach - October-January.

Kirkcaldy
Beach fishing at east and west end of town.
Types of fish: Cod, flatfish, saithe and mackerel.
Bait: Beach off bus station.

Pettycur and Kinghorn
Rock and beach fishing off Pettycur Harbour and

Kinghorn Beach.
Types of fish: Saithe and flatfish.
Boats: Small boats can be launched from beaches.
Bait: Plenty locally. Local caravan sites.

Burntisland
Permission required to fish the beach from harbour to swimming pool.
Types of fish: Saithe, flatfish, small cod.
Boats: None locally
Bait: Lug available locally.

South Queensferry
A picturesque burgh overshadowed by the Forth Bridges, There are 3 launching slips in the area, but currents can be dangerous and local advice should be obtained before setting out in dinghies.
Types of fish: Cod, whiting, coalfish, mackerel, flounder from boat and shore in season.
Bait: Lugworm, ragworm, mussel, cockle, clams and crabs at low water in this area.
Season: May-October.

Edinburgh
Scotland's capital city, on the south of the Forth estuary, has several miles of shoreline. Most of this is sandy, and can produce good catches of flatfish, although codling, Ray's bream, whiting, eels and mackerel can be taken in season from the shore. Best marks are at Cramond, round the mouth of the River Almond, and the Seafield to Portobello area.
Bait: Lugworm, ragworm, mussels cockles and clams from most beaches at low water.
Season: All year round.

Musselburgh
This town stands on the estuary of the River Esk, 6 miles to the east of Edinburgh, overlooking the Firth of Forth. It has a small but busy harbour at Fisherrow, catering mainly for the pleasure craft.
Boats: Enquiries should be made at the harbour. Best shore marks range from Fisherrow harbour to the mouth of the Esk.
Bait: Lugworm, ragworm, mussels, cockles and clams at low water.

Cockenzie
Mullet can be caught around the warm water outfall to the east of Cockenzie Power station and around the harbour. Other species include flatfish, codling and mackerel.

North Berwick
There is good boat fishing out of North Berwick and the coastline between the town and Dunbar is good for shore fishing.
Types of fish: Cod, haddock, plaice, mackerel and coalfish.
Bait: Mussels, crabs and shellfiish of various types available at low water.
Further information from: Information Centre, Quality Street, North Berwick. Tel: (01 620) 892197 January - December.

Dunbar
The coastline from Dunbar to Eyemouth is very popular for rock and beach fishing.
Types of fish: Cod, haddock, flounder, coalfish, mackerel, wrasse and whiting.
Boats: Details can be obtained from The Tourist Information Centre, Dunbar.
Bait: Mussels, lug and ragworm available at low water, and also from tackle dealers.
Season: Best April to October.
Further information from: Information Centre, Town House. High Street, Dunbar.
Tel: (01368) 863353
January - December.

TAYSIDE

Arbroath
Situated on the east coast of Angus, 17 miles north-east of Dundee, Arbroath is easily accessible by road and rail. It is the centre for commercial fishing, and famous for its smokies. Pleasure boats ply for short cruises to local sea cliffs and caves, from the harbour. There are about 10 boats between 15ft and 35ft used for lobster and crab fishing, taking out parties for sea angling.
Types of fish: Cod, coalfish, mackerel, flounder, conger, plaice, haddock and pollack.
Boats: Available through local fishermen and part time lobster and crab fishermen at reasonable prices.

Dundee
Dundee is situated on the estuary of the River Tay and has sea fishing in the city centre, while Broughty Ferry, a suburb of Dundee, Easthaven and Carnoustie, all within easy reach by road and rail, have sea fishing from rocks, piers or from boats. There are good marks around the Bell Rock about 12 miles offshore.
Types of fish: Cod, flatfish from shore plus cod, haddock, coalfish, ling, pouting and plaice from boats.
Bait: Available locally.
Season: All year.

NORTH EAST AND SPEY VALLEY

Moray Firth
The Moray Firth has always been famous for its fishing grounds and most of the towns along the south coastline depend largely on commercial fishing for their prosperity; cod, haddock, flatfish of many kinds, pollack, coalfish and mackerel being landed.

Nairn
Nairn is set on the pleasant coastal plain bordering the southern shore of the Moray Firth. There is a beautiful stretch of sands to the east. Most fishing is done from two small piers at the entrance to the tidal harbour.
Types of fish: Mackerel, small coalfish, pollack, dab and cod.
Boats: One or two, privately owned, will often take a passenger out. Enquiries should be made at the harbour.
Tackle: P. Fraser, 41 High Street, Nairn.
Tel: (01667) 453038.
Bait: Lugworm available on the beach at low water. Mackerel etc., mostly taken on flies.

Lossiemouth and Garmouth
Lossiemouth, a small prosperous town, is a unique combination of white fish centre, seaside, shops and hotels. The angler will find unlimited sport of a kind probably new to him, for off the east and west beaches sea trout and finnock abound, and spinning for these into the sea, especially into the breakers, is a magnificent sport.
Types of fish: Sea trout, conger from the pier, coalfish, flatfish, 6.5 miles of shore fishing. Haddock , cod, plaice and coalfish from boats. Shore fishing - sea trout between harbour and Boar's Head Rock and at the old cement works Garmouth.
Bait: Lugworm on the west beach and the harbour at low water. Also plenty of mussels to be collected. Spinners, Pirks.
Season: Migratory fish season, October. Best months late July, early August.

Buckie
Buckie is a major commercial fishing port on the eastern side of Spey Bay. It has become increasingly popular over the last few years as a tourist area and is well supplied with hotels, golf courses and caravan sites. It offers a varied coastline in the form of sandy beaches and quite spectacular rugged cliff formations.
Types of fish: Cod, coalfish, conger, pollack, mackerel, haddock, whiting and flatfish.
Bait: Lugworm, ragworm, mussels , cockles and crabs freely available along the shoreline eastwards.
Season: April-October. Winter months best for cod.

Cullen
M. V. Rosenberg is a 30ft long, twin-engine cruiser providing pleasure trips and catering for sea anglers (tackle for hire or for sale). The boat is licensed by the Department of Transport and, as such, meets all its survey requirements annually. The vessel, which has all modern aids to navigation, has a certificated skipper. Details may be had from Cullen Marine Services, 27 North Deskford Street, Cullen.
Tel: (01542) 840323.

Portknockie
Portknockie is a quaint little fishing village to the west of Cullen Bay. The small harbour is used by two small mackerel boats.
Types of fish: Excellent rock fishing here for cod, coalfish, and some mackerel from the piers. Good boat fishing for haddock, ling and gurnard.
Boats: There are no boats for hire as such, although

it is possible to get out in two small (18ft) mackerel boats.
Bait: Lugworm and mussels in the harbour at low water.
Further information from: Tourist Information Centre, 17 High Street, Elgin IV30 1EG.
Tel: (01343) 542666/543388.

Portsoy
One of the numerous small towns that line the Banffshire coast. It is a former seaport but the harbour is silting up.
Types of fish: Coalfish and mackerel from the small pier and some good rock fishing east and west for cod. From boats, mackerel, cod, haddock, plaice, coalfish and dab.
Bait: Some lugworm at low water mark.

Gardenstown and Crovie
These are traditional fishing villages. Mackerel are plentiful, June-September. Anglers would be well advised to follow local boats which are fishing commercially.
Types of fish: From shore, coalfish, pollack flatfish conger. From boats - mackerel, cod, haddock, flounder, plaice, conger, dab, catfish, gurnard and ling.
Bait: Available on beach, but local people prefer to use flies.

Fraserburgh
Situated on the north-east shoulder of Scotland, Fraserburgh has the Moray Firth to the west and north and the North Sea to the east. The Burgh was primarily given over to the herring and white fish industry, but has developed as a holiday resort with the decline of commercial fishing in the North Sea. Tickets and permits for game fishing from the beaches can be had at Weelies, Grocer, College Bounds.
Types of fish: Shore- cod, coalfish and mackerel. Boat - as shore.
Bait: Mussels and lugworm can be dug from the beach.
Season: May-October.

Peterhead
Peterhead is an important fishing port situated north of Buchan Ness, the most easterly point of Scotland. Excellent breakwaters, 1900ft and 2800ft long, are the main shore marks for holiday anglers. Access to the breakwaters is dependent on weather conditions and can be restricted when vessels are being worked. A safety access procedure has been agreed with the North Breakwater Sea Angling Society to whom further queries should be directed. However passengers are at times taken out by private boats.
Types of fish: From the pier - mackerel, coalfish, dab and cod. From boats- cod, haddock, dabs, ling, coalfish and mackerel.
Boats: There are a number of privately owned boats which will sometimes take out passengers. Enquiries should be made at the harbour.
Tackle: Available from Robertsons Sports, 1 Kirk Street, Peterhead.
Tel : (01779) 472584
Bait: Lugworm can be dug from shore at low water while mussels can be gathered from the rocks.

Stonehaven
Stonehaven is a holiday resort 15 miles south of Aberdeen on main road and rail routes. Magnificent catches of cod and haddock are taken regularly by boat. Anglers obtain great co-operation from angling boat skippers and local professional fishermen. On either side of Stonehaven there are good rock fishing marks which should be approached with care especially during strong easterly winds.
Types of fish: Cod, haddock, pollack, coalfish, pollack, ling, catfish, plaice and other flatfish, ballan wrasse, cuckoo wrasse, whiting and Norway haddock from boats.
Boats: Boats are available from skipper:
A . McKenzie, 24 Westfield Park, Stonehaven,
Tel: (01569) 763411.
Bait: Mussels available if ordered from skippers of boats.
Season: All year
Further information from: Information Centre, 66 Allardice Street, Stonehaven.
Tel: (01569) 762806 Easter - October.

GREAT GLEN AND ISLE OF SKYE

Isle of Eigg

The Isle of Eigg lies 5m SW of Skye.
Types of fish: Pollack, conger, spurdog, skate, cod, mackerel.
Season: Summer - Autumn.

Isle of Skye

The many lochs and bays around the beautiful Isle of Skye provide ideal facilities for sea angling. There is a great variety of fish, most of which can be caught from the shore because of the deep water found close inshore off rocky shores and headlands. Local residents are very knowledgeable about fishing in their own area Loch-Snizort has now been found to hold a number of large common skate and anglers could well contact these during a session there.

Isle of Skye (Portree)

Portree, the capital of Skye, is situated half way up the east coast of the island. There is a very good harbour and good fishing marks in and around it. Ample free anchorage and berthing available for visiting craft. Slipping, refuelling and watering facilities are easily accessible.
Types of fish: Cod, haddock, whiting, coalfish, pollack and mackerel.
Boats: Greshornish House Hotel, Edinbane, by Portree, Isle of Skye. Tel: (01470) 582266, has one boat available.
Bait: Unlimited mussels and cockles available in tidal area of Portree Bay.
Season: May - September.

Isle of Skye (Camastianavaig by Portree)

To reach this sheltered bay which lies 4 miles south east of Portree, turn off the A850 to Braes. Although local tactics are the use of feathers, bottom fishing with trace or paternoster has yielded heavy bags with skate of 62.5lbs, cod 6 lbs whiting 3lbs, haddock 3lbs, spurdog 12lbs, gurnard 2lbs, pollacks 12lbs coalfish 14lbs , all from boats.
Types of fish: Shore - coalfish, pollack, wrasse and mackerel. Boat - cod, haddock and spurdog.
Tackle: Obtainable at Portree.
Bait: Lugworm at Broadford Bay and Balmeanac Bay. Cockles and mussels at Portree Loch.
Season: June - October

Isle of Skye (Uig)

Uig, a picturesque village amidst some of the finest scenery in the north west, has excellent fishing on its doorstep. Loch Snizort and small islands at its entrance, together with the Ascribe Islands opposite, are well worth fishing. Fishing can be arranged as far round the coast as Score Bay, known to some ring net fishermen as the "Golden Mile" .
Types of fish: Shore - coalfish, mackerel, pollack, conger and dogfish. Boat - coalfish, mackerel, pollack, conger, whiting, haddock, dogfish, flatfish, skate, cod and gurnard.
Boats: Available locally at Uig, Waternish and Kilmuir.
Season: May - September

Isle of Skye (Skeabost Bridge)

Skeabost Bridge is situated 5 miles from Portree at the south east end of Loch Snizort.
Types of fish: There is no shore fishing but many types of sea fish can be caught from boats.
Bait: Available locally.
Season: July - October.

Kyle of Lochalsh

The village of Kyle, on the mainland opposite Kyleakin on the Isle of Skye, there is a railhead and a car ferry link with Skye and the Hebrides.
Types of fish: Conger, coalfish, pollack and whiting from the harbour. Boat - pollack, cod, coalfish, mackerel and whiting.
Tackle: Available from John MacLennan & Co., Marine Stores, Kyle of Lachalsh IV40 8AE Tel; (01599) 534208.
Bait: Mussels from Fishery Pier and clams and cockles at spring tides.
Season: June - September.

NORTH SCOTLAND

Gairloch

Gairloch Bay is very popular with sea anglers. There is good fishing in this lovely sea loch, especially around Longa Island which lies near the entrance to the Loch.

Poolewe and Aultbea
Situated amidst magnificent scenery, the sheltered waters of Loch Ewe offer the sea angler opportunities of fine catches. Suitable accommodation is available in surrounding villages and local advice is always available.
Types of fish: Shore - pollack, coalfish, dab, codling. Boat - haddock, cod, codling, gurnard, skate, whiting, mackerel and flatfish.
Boats: Several boats available locally.
Bait: Mussels, lugworm, cockles, etc., from shore.
Season: April - October incl.

Little Loch Broom
Ten miles north east Aultbea/ Ullapool & The Summer Isles Loch Broom and the waters encircled by the Summer Isles offer excellent sea angling. The banks can be approached from Ullapool, which is an attractive holiday village sited on a peninsula projecting into Loch Broom. The numerous banks and islands offer superb fishing and beautiful scenery in sheltered waters. Many attractions on shore via local shops; hotels and sporting facilities available throughout the season. Achiltibuie, a small village, also gives access to fishing grounds.
Types of fish: Shore - codling, coalfish, conger, pollack, mackerel, dabs, thornbacks, dogfish, flounders and plaice. Boat - as above plus haddock, whiting, wrasse, ling, megrim, gurnard, spurdog and turbot.
Season: June-October inclusive. Big skate best in autumn.

Lochinver
Lochinver is one of the major fishing pons in the north of Scotland. With a population of some 300 inhabitants it has a safe all-tides harbour with excellent shore services, including good moderately - priced accommodation and two fishing tackle shops. Excellent sea fishing within a short distance from the port specialising in jumbo haddock, cod, skate and conger. It is one of the few areas where large halibut are caught. Boats available. A large fleet of fishing vessels operates from the harbour and bait is readily available.
Types of fish: Cod, haddock, whiting, saithe, gurnard, ling, pollack, mackerel, wrasse, conger, skate. Coalfish, pollack, cod and mackerel from the shore.
Tackle: Tackle is available from Lochinver Fishselling Co., Culag Square, Lochinver.
Tel: (01571) 844228.
Season: April - October

Drumbeg
Seven miles north of Lochinver

Caithness
With the prolific fishing grounds of the Pentland Firth, the north of Caithness has built up a reputation as being one of the premier sea angling areas in Scotland. It is now recognised that the chance of taking a halibut on rod and line is better in Pentland waters than anywhere else; more halibut have been taken here than in any other part of the British Isles. The presence of Porbeagle shark in these waters has been proved by the capture of many good heavy specimens, including the world record, with many more hooked and lost. Among the notable fish caught were European halibut records of 194 lbs. in 1974,
215 lbs in 1975, 224 lbs. in 1978 and 234 lbs in 1979. This fish represented a world record catch for the species. The Scottish shore record ling of 12 lbs 4 oz was caught in these waters. With countless numbers of rocky coves and sandy beaches there is much for the shore angler to discover along the whole of the north coast of Scotland. Accommodation is available to suit everyone, from first class hotels, private B & B to caravan and camping sites with full facilities. It is also possible to have a full sea angling package holiday with full board at a hotel and all boat charges included. The number of angling boats available increases each year, but it is still advisable to book boat places in advance.

Thurso and Scrabster
Thurso is the main town on the north side of Caithness and gives access

through Scrabster to the waters of the Pentland Firth, where there are first class fishing grounds. Thurso Bay and the Dunnet Head area are sheltered from prevailing winds and it is reasonably easy for anglers to get afloat to the marks. Scrabster 1.4 miles from Thurso, is the main harbour in northern Caithness. Most of the angling boats are based here. There is also some excellent rock fishing, while conger may be caught from the harbour walls.
Types of fish: Cod, ling, haddock, conger, pollack, coalfish, dogfish, spurdog, plaice, wrasse, mackerel, dab, whiting, rays, halibut and Porbeagle shark.
Tackle: Harper's Fishing Services, 57 High Street , Thurso KW14 8AZ. Tel: (01847) 893179.
Bait: Mussels, lugworm can be gathered at low water, mackerel and squid from fish shops and local fishermen. Most species take lures, feather and rubber eels, etc., and most fishing is done with this artificial bait.
Season: April - November.
Further information from: Caithness Tourist Board, Whitechapel Road, Wick.
Tel: (01955) 602596.
Jan-Dec.
Boat: Paul Gough - (01847) 895009.

Dunnet

Dunnet is situated 8 miles east of Thurso at the end of the famous Dunnet Sands, which are over 2.5 miles long. Few anglers fish this beach, as there is excellent boat fishing nearby. There is plenty of lugworm and the beach is well worth trying.
Types of fish: As for Thurso.
Boats and Tackle: As for Thurso.
Bait: Mussels from the rocks at low tide and lugworm all along Dunnet Sands.
Season: Shore - July and August. Boat - April - November

Keiss

Good shore fishing is to be had around Keiss, a small fishing village between John O'Groats and Wick. It might be difficult to get out in a boat. The shore fishing is from the rocks around Keiss, and from the beach at Sinclair's Bay to the south of the village. Here some very good plaice have been taken and also anglers have caught sea trout while spinning for mackerel.
Tackle: Tackle shops at Wick.
Bait: Mussels and lugworm can be obtained at low tide.

Sutherland and Easter Ross, Brora

Brora is a village situated on the A9, 12 miles south of Helmsdale. There is a small harbour and a few boats are available to sea anglers. There are rail links to Brora from the south and ample hotel accommodation and caravan facilities.
Types of fish: Cod, coalfish, cod, ling, haddock, rays and conger from boats.
Boats: Some owners are willing to take visitors at nominal costs.
Bait: Can be dug locally.
Season: July- September.

Grannies Heilan' Hame, Embo

This is a caravan holiday centre with extensive amenities 2 miles north of Dornoch.
Types of fish: Spinning for sea trout from the beach up to the mouth of Loch Fleet. Coalfish, mackerel and flatfish from the pier. The rocks provide good cod fishing. From boats, coalfish, mackerel, plaice, cod, haddock and whiting at times.
Bait: Lugworm can be dug at the ferry landing area and there are plenty of mussels and cockles near Loch Fleet.
Season: April - September.

Dornoch

Dornoch gives access to the fishing banks off the north coast of the Dornoch Firth. There is good shore fishing from the rocks at Embo, but to get afloat it is necessary to make arrangements in advance. Youngsters can enjoy good fishing from Embo Pier.
Types of fish: Sea trout from shore. Flat fish, haddock and cod from boats.
Boats: Boats are difficult to hire but there are one or two in Embo which is three miles from Dornoch.
Season: April - September.

Tain
Tain lies on the South side of the Dornoch Firth and gives access to excellent sea trout fishing, both shore and boat, in sheltered waters of the Firth.
Types of fish: Shore- wrasse, flatfish, pollack, mackerel. Boat - haddock, cod, skate, mackerel.
Boats: Available in Balintore, 6 miles from Tain and Portmahomack.
Bait: Available from the shore.

Balintore
The village of Balintore, near Tain has over the past 4 years increased in status and is now one of the recognised centres for big catches. Catches of up to 1,000lbs of cod and ling have been made (8 anglers) in a single morning's fishing.
Types of fish: Cod, ling, wrasse, pollack and mackerel.
Season: Mid-April to beginning of November.

Portmahomak
This fishing village is well situated in a small bay on the southern shore of the Dornoch Firth, 9 miles east of Tain and 17 miles from Invergordon to the south. There is a well protected harbour and a good, safe sandy beach.
Types of fish: Cod from the shore. Haddock and cod from boats.
Tackle: Available at Tain.
Season: Spring to Autumn.

North Kessock, Avoch and Fortrose
These villages lie along the north west side of the Moray Firth north of Inverness. This sheltered sea loch provides good fishing.

WESTERN ISLES

The Western Isles
The Western Isles form a north-south chain of islands off the west coast of Scotland. Separated from the mainland by the Minches, much of their rod and line fishing remains to be discovered, not only due to a lack of boats in the area, but also due to lack of communications between and within the islands. Car ferries run from Oban and Ullapool on the mainland and Uig on Skye. Regular air services to Barra, Stornoway, for Lewis and Harris and Benbecula for the Uists.

Isle of Harris (Tarbert)
The largest community on the southern part of the largest Hebridean islands. Tarbert stands on a very narrow neck of land where the Atlantic and the Minch are separated by only a few hundred yards of land. It is the terminal for the car ferry from Uig on Skye and Lochmaddy on North Uist.
Types of fish: Boat - mackerel, ling, coalfish, cod, rays, pollack and conger. Shore - plaice, haddock and flounder.
Boats: Check with Tourist Information Centre, Tarbert.
Tel: (01859) 502011.
Bait: Mussels available on the shore, lugworm, cockles.
Season: May-October.
Further information from: Tourist Centre, Tarbert.
Tel: (01859) 502011.

Isle of Lewis (Stornoway)
Stornoway, the only town in the Outer Hebrides, is easily accessible by air from Glasgow Airport (1 hour) and Inverness (25 mins); there is also a drive-on car ferry service from Ullapool (3.5 hours crossing). Another car ferry service connects Uig (Skye) to Tarbert (Harris), which is only an hour's drive from Stornoway. Stornoway is now recognised as a mecca for sea angling in Scotland. There is an enthusiastic sea angling club with club boats and licensed premises which overlook the harbour. Each August the club runs the Western Isles (Open) Sea Angling Championships. Many skate over the ton have been caught, the heaviest so far being 192 lbs. The Scottish blueshark record of 85.5 lbs. was off Stornoway in August 1972. Visiting anglers may become temporary members of the Stornoway Club (one minute from the town hall) and can make arrangements for fishing trips with club members in the club boats.
Accommodation can be arranged through the Wester Isles Tourist Board, Administration and Information Centre, 26 Cromwell Street,

Stornoway, Isle of Lewis. Tel: (01851) 703088.
Types of fish: Conger, cod, skate, rays, ling, pollack, whiting, dabs, bluemouth, flounder, dogfish, wrasse, haddock.
Bait: Mussels in harbour area; mackerel from local boats.

NORTHERN ISLES

Orkney

The waters around Orkney attract many sea anglers each year as big skate, halibut and ling are there for the taking. Ling of 36 lbs. skate of 214 lbs. taken by Jan Olsson of Sweden and the former British record halibut (161.5 lbs) taken by ex - Provost Knight of Stromness provide the bait which attracts anglers to these waters. The Old Man of Hoy, Scapa Flow and Marwick Head are well-known names to sea anglers. The Brough of Birsay, Costa Head and the Eday and Stronsay Firths are equally well known as marks for big halibut and skate. Fishing from Kirkwall or Stromness, there is easy access to Scapa Flow where wrecks of the German Fleet of the First World War provide homes for large ling and conger. In the fish rich sea surrounding Orkney the angler will find some excellent shore fishing, nearly all of which remains to be discovered. Furthermore skate of over 100 lbs. are still common while specimens of 200 lbs. have been recorded. More halibut have been caught in the waters to the south separating Orkney from the mainland than elsewhere in the U.K. Shark have also been sighted and hooked but none so far have been landed. Around the islands, in bays and firths, there is excellent sport for the specimen fish hunter and the Orcadians are eager to help sea anglers share the sport they enjoy. There is a regular car ferry service from Scrabster (Thurso) to Orkney and daily air services from Edinburgh, Glasgow and other points of the U.K.
Types of fish: Sea trout, plaice, pollack and coalfish, mackerel, wrasse from the shore. Skate, halibut, ling, cod, pollack, haddock; coalfish, plaice and dogfish from the boats.
Tackle: Available from Stromness and Kirkwall.
Bait: Available from most beaches and piers.
Season: June - October.

Shetland

Shetland offers the best skate fishing to be had in Europe; during the years 1970-74 more than 250 skate over 100 lbs. were caught. These included a European record of 226.5 lbs and 12 other skate over 190 lbs. During the same period, Shetland held nine British records, ten Scottish records and six European records, giving some indication that the general fishing is of no mean standard. Halibut and porbeagle of over 300 lbs. have been taken commercially in the Sumburgh area with porbeagle shark now being landed by anglers from this area. The Scottish record of many large porbeagle sharks of up to 450 lbs have been landed here and bigger fish have been taken by commercial boat. Shore fishing remains for the most part to be discovered.
Types of fish: Shore - coalfish, pollack, dogfish, mackerel, dabs, conger and cod. Boat - skate, halibut, ling, cod, tusk, haddock, whiting, coalfish, pollack, dogfish, porbeagle shark, Norway haddock, gurnard, mackerel, cuckoo and ballan wrasse.
Boats: Many boats available for hire throughout the islands. Boats can also be arranged through the Shetland Islands Tourism, Market Cross, Lerwick, Shetland.
Tackle: Available from J.A. Manson, 88 Commercial Street, Lerwick and Cee & Jays, 5 Commercial Road, Lerwick.
Bait: Fresh, frozen or salted fish bait available from fishmongers. Worm bait, crabs etc., from beaches.
Season: Limited to May to October by weather conditions.

Fishing tackle specialists

The following pages feature many of Scotland's best tackle and outdoor clothing suppliers.

Whatever your tackle requirements these retail outlets offer an excellent selection of the best products available.

Many will be able to provide the visiting angler with a wealth of local information and first-hand knowledge of the area. Often fishing permits for local waters are also available from these tackle shops.

All-in-all they represent an ideal starting point for your fishing trip to Scotland.

BRIDUN LURES

Bridun Lures are manufactured in Scotland with only one thought in mind - the angler. At our factory in Tobermory, the very best designs* become great fishing lures.
We pride ourselves on quality workmanship. Lure bodies are polished to a "mirror surface" and finished to produce an outstanding appearance. It's not surprising that Bridun Lures are so popular with anglers:
Rotobait™ Plugs, Hunter™ Spinners, Forktail, Salmon Lures, Ripple Fin, Lance™ Lures, Pike Spoons, Flatty Spoons, Bass Lures, Mullet Hunter, Jack-o-bite™, Flickerbaits™, Flutter Spoons and Flashadders™.
Fish Scotland's great waters with Bridun's great Scottish lures.

BRIDUN

The Lure of Scotland

Our trading address is:
Knotless Fishing Tackle Ltd,
Main Street, Tobermory, Isle of Mull, Argyll,
Scotland PA75 6NU
Telephone: (01688) 302113 Fax: (01688) 302140

*Our firm has won a British Design Award and a Merit Award for Research and Technology

INVERAWE FISHERIES

A SUPER DAY'S SPORT

4 Lochs, stocked daily with prime hard fighting Rainbows. Rod and Net hire, Casting and Fishing Courses.

Beginners most welcome.............

Self Catering Cottages, Smokery Exhibition & Salmon fishing also available.

Call us on (01866) 822446

HARPER'S FISHING SERVICES

57 High Street, Thurso
Tel/Fax: (01847) 893179

For Shakespeare, Daiwa and other leading makes of salmon, trout and sea fishing tackle.

A good selection of books, videos, outdoor clothing, buoyancy aids and most other fishing and field sports goods always in stock.

We now carry a large and varied selection of Army and Navy Surplus Goods, both new and used.

Local Fishing and Boat Hire arranged.

LOCHORE MEADOWS FIFE COUNCIL

Trout fishing on Fife's biggest loch
Stocked with brown & rainbow trout up to 7 lbs

Courses available
Disabled welcome
Excellent facilities including cafe.

Season 1998
1st March - 30th November

Fly fishing only - March-May - Boats available
Fly, Bait & Spinning - June-November

FOR FURTHER INFORMATION AND BOOKINGS
PHONE: (01592) 414312.
FAX: (01592) 414345.
Lochore Meadows Country Park,
Crosshill, by Lochgelly,
Fife KY5 8BA.

WM. ROBERTSON & CO. LTD EST. 1881

GAME FISHING TACKLE SPECIALISTS
61 MILLER STREET GLASGOW G1 1EB
TEL: 0141-221 6687 FAX: 0141-204 4209

- GLASGOW'S MAIN HARDY DEALER -
GAME FISHING TACKLE BY ALL LEADING MAKERS
ORVIS - DAIWA - SHAKESPEARE - MASTERLINE

COME AND VISIT OUR COUNTRY CLOTHING DEPT.
BARBOUR - HOESMAN - MUSTO - HARDY

THE OLD SHOP WITH THE YOUNG IDEAS

- GLASGOW'S MAIN ORVIS DEALER -
FLY FISHING - SPIN FISHING -
SEA FISHING - PIKE FISHING

MAIL ORDER SEND FOR OUR PRICE LIST
WHY NOT COME ALONG AND SEE US AT

ANGLERS' RENDEZVOUS EST. 1962

FISHING TACKLE SPECIALISTS
18 SALTMARKET GLASGOW CROSS
TEL: 0141 - 552 4662 FAX: 0141 - 552 7730

SCOTTISH FEDERATION OF SEA ANGLERS OFFICIALS

Chairman
Mr. David Neil,
3 Roman Road,
Ayr KA7 3SZ.
Tel: (01292) 281945.

Vice Chairmen
Mr. Alastair Forsyth,
26 Trentham Court,
Westhill,
Inverness IV1 2DF.
Tel: (01463) 792412.

Mr. John Taylor,
1/1, 6 Tower Terrace,
Paisley,
Renfrewshire PA1 2JT.
Tel: 0141- 561 8554.

Hon. Treasurer
Mr. Robert Keltie,
76 Stewart Avenue,
Bo'ness,
West Lothian EH51 9NW.
Tel: (01506) 826274.

Fish Recorder
Mr. Gordon Morris,
8 Hurt Avenue,
Kinghorn,
Fife KY3 9XB.
Tel: (01592) 890055.

Coaching Co-Ordinator
Mr. Paul King,
Harbour House,
Hopeman, IV30 2RU.
Tel: (01309) 672161.

Public Relations Officer/Sponsorship
Mr. Brian Burn,
Flat 2, 16 Bellevue Road,
Ayr KA7 2SA.
Tel: (01292) 264735.

Office
Secretary Administrator
S.F.S.A.,
Caledonia House,
South Gyle,
Edinburgh EH12 9DQ.
Tel/Fax: 0131-317 7192.

REGIONAL SECRETARIES

Clyde & Western
Mr. R. Hart,
85 Tobermory Road,
Cathkin,
Glasgow G73 5PS.
Tel: Home: 0141 - 569 6081.
Work: 0141 - 561 1560.

Central
Mr. Jim Beveridge,
72 Appin Crescent,
Kirkcaldy, KY2 6ES.
Tel: (01592) 269474.

West
Mr. I. B. McClymont,
41 Corrie Crescent,
Saltcoats KA21 6JL.
Tel: (01294) 461830.

North East
Mr. Jim Croal,
2 Strachan Avenue,
Westferry Park,
Dundee DD5 1RE.
Tel: (01382) 774794.

Eastern
Mr. Bill Murray,
189 Broomfield Crescent,
Edinburgh EH12 7NH.
Tel: Daytime 0131 - 334 4274.

Highlands & Islands
Mr. Alistair Forsyth,
26 Trentham Court,
Westhill,
Inverness IV1 2DF.
Tel: (01463) 792412.

Also send communications to:
Mr. Willie Mackintosh,
"Schiehallion",
16 Glengarry Road,
Inverness IV3 6NJ.
Tel: (01463) 235850.

Western Isles
Mr. Angus Macdonald,
19 Clachan Biorach,
Tong,
Isle of Lewis HS2 0JD.
Tel: (01851) 703096.

Where to stay

As much as the rivers and lochs of Scotland provide the opportunity for the visitor to enjoy the sport at its best, no holiday can be enjoyed to the full unless a careful selection of accommodation is made. Our 'Where to Stay' section provides an enormous choice of facilities to suit every budget and taste. Scottish landlords and landladies are famed for their hospitality and friendliness. As you will see many of them can provide complete packages which simplify the planning of a sporting holiday. We are sure you will find in this section of the guide, the key to a wonderful visit to Scotland.

Ardbrecknish
LOCH AWE

FREELANCE FISHING HOLIDAYS

British record wild brown trout 25lbs 5oz taken in Ardbrecknish boat Easter 1996..... *There are surely even bigger fish to catch!*
Unrivalled location for all anglers seeking wild brown trout, rainbow trout, char, pike and Autumn salmon. Early 17th century fortified tower house set amidst spectacular mountain glen and lochside scenery. Scottish Tourist Board 4 Crowns Highly Commended and Commended self - catering apartments and cottages. In house public bar and games room, with open log fires, serving excellent bar meals March to October.
Boat hire, fishing tackle, tuition and ghillie services are available at special rates for Ardbrecknish guests.
For non-anglers in the party our own tennis court, nearby golf courses, walking, mountain climbing, cycling and a great variety of birds, flora and fauna provide alternatives whilst waiting the day's catch.

Open all year from £175 to £840 per week for 2-12 persons, Spring and Autumn short breaks are particularly good value.

Call or write for details to:
The Boden Family,
Ardbrecknish House,
South Lochaweside,
by Damally,
Argyll PA33 1BH.
Tel/Fax: (01866) 833223.
e-mail: ardbreck01 @aol.com

The THURSO RIVER

Fishing on one of Scotland's finest fly-only salmon rivers and brown trout fishing on twelve hill lochs are available on attractive inclusive terms to guests staying at:

THE ULBSTER ARMS HOTEL

CAITHNESS KW12 6XY
Telephone: (01847) 831206 or 831641

RAC ** AA **

TRADES DESCRIPTION ACT

The accommodation mentioned in this guide has not been inspected, and the publishers rely on information provided.

The publishers have every confidence in their advertisers but cannot be held responsible for the accuracy of the descriptions published.

GOLF HOTEL

Links Avenue, Powfoot by Annan.
Tel: (01461) 700254
Fax: (01461) 700288
Proprietor: Adam T. Gribbon.

21 comfortable bedrooms all with colour TV, telephone and tea making facilities; 15 luxury bedrooms with bathrooms. Permits available from the hotel for fishing River Annan, only 5 miles away with salmon, trout and sea trout also coarse fishing nearby. Superb cuisine includes local salmon, duck and mouth watering steaks, complemented by extensive wine list. Public bar, luxurious bunker bar. Balconied residents' lounge.

Ashley Courtenay & LesRoutiers Recommended AA ★ ★

DALSTON HOUSE HOTEL

5 Laurieknowe, Dumfries, S.W. Scotland,
Tel: (01387) 254422.

Executive en-suite accommodation. A la carte catering, friendly lounge bar. Ample private parking. Mealtimes to suit. Packages arranged. Ready access to rooms.

Family run establishment with personal, friendly service, excellent cuisine and comfortable accommodation

Welcome to Warmanbie
"A small hotel with a big welcome"
A real fisherman's hotel - free fishing on our private stretch (only 100 yards away) of the River Annan - best fish 39lbs.
Many other stretches available including the rivers Nith and Eden.
Ghillie, freezer, rod/tackle hire/sale available.

Owned and run by the Duncan family, Warmanbie is a Georgian country house hotel overlooking the river, with secluded woodland grounds, extensive lawns, mature trees and walled garden.
With creative cooking, superb bedrooms (two four posters), warm and friendly service, huge breakfasts, home baking, log fires and a good range of malts.....it's not only fishers who will appreciate the warmth of our welcome.

For River Annan fishing details and a colour brochure, write to:
Warmanbie Hotel and Restaurant,
SFF, Annan, Dumfriesshire DG12 5LL
-or telephone/fax (01461) 204015

Scottish Tourist Board Commended

EGON RONAY RECOMMENDED

CULLIGRAN

Glen Strathfarrar
Struy, Nr. Beauly IV4 7JX.

Salmon & trout fishing on the Rivers Farrar and Glass, tributaries of the Beauly. Holiday Cottages. Guided tours of the deer farm/estate. Bicycles for hire. All within a National Nature Reserve.
For Information/Prices
Tel/Fax: (01463) 761285.
Frank & Juliet Spencer-Nairn

Scottish Tourist Board Commended

THE TOMICH Hotel

Scottish Tourist Board

Strathglass, Inverness-shire IV4 7LY

The Tomich Hotel in Strathglass is one of the most beautiful areas in Scotland, among many old forests and glens - noteable of which is Glen Affric.
Tomich is the perfect base for your Highland Holiday especially if you wish to fish the local hill-lochs and rivers. Trout fishing at Tomich has been famous for many years, but has only been available to the public since 1989. The hotel enjoys a substantial reputation with guests and locals alike for delicious food. You can enjoy the heated indoor swimming pool at nearby Guisachan Farm.
For further information please contact:
HUGH STANFORD ON (01456) 415399

Barncrosh Farm Ringford Castle Douglas

Enjoy a peaceful relaxing holiday in beautiful rural surroundings on a farm near coast and hills. Comfortable, well equipped cottages for 2-8. Well heated and fully equipped including bed linen and towels. Colour T.V. Children and dogs welcome. Plenty of fishing all around.
Write or phone for brochure to:

F. S. Ball, Barncrosh Farm, Ringford, Castle Douglas DG7 1TX.
Tel: (01556) 680216 Fax: (01556) 680442

Galloway for your 1998 Holiday

High-quality self-catering accommodation.
About 200 houses throughout South West Scotland.

- ✲ Peaceful Country Cottages
- ✲ Elegant Country Houses
- ✲ Convenient Town Houses
- ✲ Quiet Farm Houses

RIVER FISHING FOR SALMON AND SEA TROUT,
LOCH FISHING FOR COARSE FISH - ESPECIALLY PIKE,
SEA FISHNG FROM SHORE OR BOATS.

For free colour brochure, contact: G. M. THOMSON & CO.,
27 King Street, Castle Douglas, Kirkcudbrightshire DG7 1AB.
Tel: (01556) 504030 (24hr. answering service).
Fax: (01556) 503277.

Tweed Valley Fishing

Here at the Tweed Valley Hotel we pride ourselves on taking care of our fishermen. Traditional Scottish hospitality combined with all the comfort and modern facilities of a country house hotel await our guests.

We have our own private beats for both salmon and trout fishing. We also have private hill lochs allowing you to fish for either stocked rainbows or wild brownies - and the scenery comes absolutely free!

We can provide ghillies for either sole or group use, and fly fishing tuition can be arranged at any time.

Superb restaurant and well-stocked bar with over fifty choice malt whiskies.
Own smokehouse producing fine smoked meats and cheeses.

Tweed Valley Hotel Walkerburn Peebleshire EH43 6AA
Tel: (01896) 870 636 Fax: (01896) 870 639
E-mail: 101325.2512@compuserve.com
To enjoy this Taste of Scotland Hospitality
Telephone Rachel or Les on: (01896) 870 636

The Dunalastair Hotel

Wild Brownies & True Highland Hospitality

Ideally situated on the shores of Loch Rannoch, offering excellent wild brown trout and char fishing, the Dunalastair is the perfect venue for your Highland getaway.
After a long day you will find a relaxed and very friendly atmosphere back at the Dunalastair. All of our twenty rooms are spacious and have been restored to their original appearance. The food is unusual and is complimented by a superb range of fine wines and tasty whiskies. We have two boats on Dunalastair Water, and five boats on Loch Rannoch. Fishing on River Tummel and a

The Dunalastair Hotel
Kinloch Rannoch
Perthshire
Tel: (01882) 632323
Fax: (01882) 632371

Moorfield House Hotel

Coupar Angus,
By Blairgowrie,
Perthshire PH13 9HS.
Tel: (01828) 627303
Fax: (01828) 627339

A privately owned, family run Country House. Centrally located in beautiful Perthshire we offer spacious, comfortable rooms, all with private facilities. We work hard to maintain our excellent reputation for food and make every effort to meet the requirements of all our guests. Ideally located for all types of fishing - loch and river. Permits available locally.
Picnic lunches as requested and facilities available for the ones who don't get away!

LOCH VIEW FARM

There is a south facing lodge, newly built, on the edge of the privately owned Loch at Loch View Farm. Situated in idyllic surroundings with panoramic scenery, two miles from Comrie and six miles from the town of Crieff.
We are ideally situated for Trout Fishing (Brown and Rainbow), and offer Bank or Boat fishing at an excellent price of only £6 per person per day.
Tastefully furnished to a high standard it provides an excellent relaxing base.
Centrally heated lodge with all modern amenties all linen and towels provided.
With all this on your doorstep - WHY GO ANYWHERE ELSE ?

FOR FURTHER INFORMATION PLEASE CONTACT:
Mr Wallace Booth (Snr),
Loch View Farm,
Mill of Fortune, Perthshire PH6 2JE or Telephone: (01764) 670677

FARLEYER HOUSE HOTEL

"Affordable Luxury"

Farleyer House Hotel,
Aberfeldy,
Perthshire PH15 2JE.
Tel: (01887) 820332.
Fax: (01887 829430.

Farleyer House has secured prime fishing on several famous beats of the River Tay for 1998.
Stay in total comfort, enjoy the best food Perthshire has to offer and fish some of the best water on the Tay. Prices start from £295 for a three day break including Dinner in our Bistro Restaurant, accommodation in the Ghillies Cottage and fishing.
Spey casting courses also available.
Suites and family rooms are also available.

BUNRANNOCH HOUSE

Kinloch Rannoch, Perthshire PH16 5QB

Lovely Victorian house set in 2 acres of grounds on the outskirts of Kinloch Rannoch. A warm welcome awaits you, together with a complimentary tea tray of home cooking on arrival. Comfortable accommodation includes 3 double, 2 twin and 2 family rooms, most en-suite. All rooms have uninterrupted highland views and tea/coffee making facilities. Two guest lounges. Fire Certificate. Fishing, walking, cycling, bird-watching, boating and horse riding provide ample choice. Log fires and good cooking. S.T.B. 2 Crowns Commended.

For further details contact:
Mrs. J. Skeaping on (01882) 632407

BIRNAM HOUSE HOTEL

Perth Road, Birnam, Dunkeld PH8 0BQ
Tel: (01350) 727462 Fax: (01350) 728979
Open Jan-Dec

Scottish Tourist Board
COMMENDED

27 dble/twin
1 family
all with private bath & shower

B & B per person
Single - £32.00-£45.00
Dbl/Twin-£25.00-£35.00
DB & B-£25.00-£45.00
EM 6 p.m.- 9 p.m.

Set in the ancient village of Macbeth the Birnam House Hotel offers 28 newly refurbished, en-suite bedrooms with satellite television, radio, direct dial telephone, trouser press, hairdryer and hospitality tray. Lift to all floors, superb cuisine at affordable prices. Wide range of fine wines, whiskies and beers. Relaxing surroundings with friendly, attentive service. Open all year. Ideal base for touring, sightseeing, walking, fishing and relaxing.

all bedrooms with satellite/cable TV

THE ROMAN CAMP
COUNTRY HOUSE HOTEL

The Roman Camp sits on the north bank of the River Teith amongst 20 acres of mature and secluded gardens.

The house was built as a hunting lodge for the Dukes of Perth in 1625. We have 3/4 mile river running through our gardens, enabling guests to fish for wild brown trout and salmon on our private beat. The hotel can also arrange fishing on the many lochs and other private beats surrounding Callander.

The Roman Camp Country House Hotel, Callander FK17 8BG
Tel: (01877) 330003 Fax: (01877) 331533

Overscaig Loch Side Hotel

An attractive Hotel situated on the bank and amid spectacular scenery of Loch Shin within 16 acres of grounds in picturesque countryside of Sutherland on the A838 trans country route from Lairg to Durness.

Recently refurbished to a very high standard with all rooms en-suite.

Sutherland Lochs are legendary, with fishermen coming from all over the world to fish for brown trout.

The Overscaig Hotel is a renowned fishermans post, with fishing rights and boats on Lochs Shin, A' Ghriama and Loch Merkland.

AA ★★

OVERSCAIG LOCHSIDE HOTEL
LOCH SHIN, By LAIRG,
SUTHERLAND IV27 4NY
TEL: (01549) 431203

Scottish Tourist Board COMMENDED ★★★★

The Anglers' Retreat INCHNADAMPH HOTEL

Assynt, by Lairg, Sutherland IV27 4HN.
Tel: (01571) 822202 Fax: (01571) 822203

Looking across the waters of Loch Assynt or to the mountains beyond, Inchnadamph enjoys one of the most spectacular lochside settings, in a land famed for its breathtaking scenery.

Visitors enjoy true Highland hospitality in the welcoming atmosphere found only in a family run hotel.

Savour the finest Scottish cuisine selected from fresh, local produce. Sample our connoisseur malts in our cozy lounge bar and relax by roaring open fires.

A favourite haunt of anglers - 19 beats available - brown trout and salmon fishing offered free to hotel guests.

BEN LOYAL HOTEL

Tongue, Sutherland IV27 4XE

The Ben Loyal provides the warmth of welcome and comfortable, quality accommodation you deserve, that is so rare in these parts.

The restaurant has "Taste of Scotland" dinners, recently awarded an AA Rosette, using the best local produce and our own grown salad, vegetables and herbs. Ideally situated in the middle of the north coast, this Highland Oasis is perfect for either the relaxing or active holiday.

Scottish Tourist Board Commended. "Les Routiers Casserole Award Winner" - for the 4th year.
One of Scotland's "PUBS OF GOOD TASTE" AA ROSETTE AWARD - the only one in a hundred miles and many other guides we're not allowed to say!
CONTACT MEL OR PAULINE COOK ON Tel: (01847) 611216 Fax: (01847) 611212

S.W. SCOTLAND

✓✓✓✓ ▸▸▸ THISTLE COMMENDATION

Cock Inn Caravan Park

AUCHENMALG : NEWTON STEWART : WIGTOWNSHIRE : SCOTLAND

Peaceful, select Caravan Park adjacent pleasant little beach and small Country Inn. Panoramic view across Luce Bay. Bathing, Sailing, Sea Angling etc. Also Bungalow all year round.

● GOLF ● PONY TREKKING ● FISHING

Modern toilet block, showers, freezing facilities, shaver points and all facilities

Shop on site Sauna Bar meals available at the Inn

FULLY SERVICED HOLIDAY CARAVANS FOR HIRE

TOURERS WELCOME E.H.U.

Please send for brochure or telephone

(01581) 500227

CORSEMALZIE HOUSE HOTEL

AA ★★★ RAC ★★★ Scottish Tourist Board COMMENDED

Come and relax in the beautiful Galloway countryside. We have 10 miles of salmon/trout fishing on the Rivers Bladnoch and Tarff for exclusive use by our guests. Good Spring and Autumn salmon runs. **New 23 acre trout loch. Boats available.** Stay in our secluded country house and enjoy good food, wines and every comfort. Good rough shooting also available. Golfing arrangements.

Write or phone for brochure.

Port William, Newton Stewart DG8 9RL.
Tel: (01988) 860254.
Fax: (01988) 860213.

ISLE OF LEWIS

SCALISCRO AND NORTH EISHKEN ESTATES

Superb wild brown trout, salmon and seatrout fishing on many lochs amidst beautiful Hebridean scenery.
Excellent red deer stalking and rough shooting.

Scaliscro Lodge Hotel

Spectacularly situated overlooking the sea.
Privacy, seclusion and tranquillity guaranteed.
Homely food and good wines.
Luxury, self-contained cottage (sleeps 8) also available.
For further information please contact:

The Estates Office, Scaliscro,
Uig, Isle of Lewis HS2 9EL
Tel: (01851) 672325
Fax: (01851) 672393

LOCHMADDY HOTEL

LOCHMADDY, ISLE OF NORTH UIST HS6 5AA

FOR FURTHER INFORMATION CONTACT:
JOHN COLES
RESIDENT PROPRIETOR
TEL: (01876) 500331/2 - FAX: (01876) 500210

Enjoy Hebridean hospitality with comfortable accommodation and good home cooking at the Lochmaddy Hotel.

With countless hill and machair lochs producing wild brown trout, North Uist offers anglers possibly the greatest variety of gamefishing to be found in Scotland. Salmon run from Spring to Autumn, with spectacular Summer runs. Sea trout can be found in the sea pools from late spring, running into the lochs from July to October.

Addresses	Type of Accommodation	Type of Fishing	Permits Available	Drying Facilities	Freezing Facilities	Price p.p. B & B or B.B.E.M.	Special Features

HOTELS & GUEST HOUSES

Addresses	Type of Accommodation	Type of Fishing	Permits Available	Drying Facilities	Freezing Facilities	Price p.p. B & B or B.B.E.M.	Special Features
ARGYLL **Dalmally** A.J. Burke (Mr.), "Orchy Bank", Dalmally, Argyll PA33 1AS. Tel: (01838) 200370.	Guest House Listed Comm.	Salmon Trout Pike	Yes	Yes	Yes	B. & B. from £18.00	Two miles from Loch Awe on bank of River Orchy.
Ford J.V. Boardman (Miss), Ford Hotel, Ford by Lochgilphead, Argyll. Tel: (01546) 810273.	Hotel Grading Pending	Trout Pike Loch	Yes	Yes	Yes	B. & B. from £22.50 p.p.p.n.	Restaurant. Bar. Close to Loch Awe. Comfortable rooms.
Islay of Islay Ian Brown (Mr.), Machrie Hotel & Golf Links, Port Ellen, Isle of Islay, Argyll. Tel: (01496) 302310.	Hotel S/C 3 Crowns	Salmon Trout	Ask	Yes	Yes	B. & B. from £26.50	Warm, friendly hotel serving excellent food. Has one river and loch.
Frank T. Spears (Mr.), Port Askaig Hotel, Isle of Islay, Argyll PA46 7RD. Tel: (01496) 840245. Fax: (01496) 840295.	Hotel 3 Crowns Comm.	Brown Trout	Yes	Yes	Yes	B. & B. from £29.00 p.p. B.B.E.M. from £44.75 p.p.	7 lochs with boats. Fly fishing only.
BERWICKSHIRE **Earlston** McPherson (Mr.), Red Lion Hotel, The Square, Earlston, Berwickshire. Tel: (01896) 848279.	Hotel 1 Crown Comm.	Trout Salmon	Yes	No	Yes	B. & B. Single £18.00 Double £35.00	A friendly hotel situated near excellent rivers for fishing. Warm welcome.
CLACKMANNANSHIRE **Alloa** Dunmar House Hotel, Dunmar Drive, Alloa, Clackmannanshire FK10 2EN. Tel: (01259) 214339	Hotel Waiting Inspection	Rainbow Trout Brown Trout	Yes	No	No	B. &. B. from £37.50	Lovely listed building which has been totally refurbished to a high standard. Dunmar is in the heart of Braveheart country.

Addresses	Type of Accommodation	Type of Fishing	Permits Available	Drying Facilities	Freezing Facilities	Price p.p. B & B or B.B.E.M.	Special Features
DUMFRIESSHIRE **Auchencairn** Swift (Mr.), Solwayside House Hotel, Auchencairn, Dumfriesshire. Tel: (01556) 640280.	Hotel 3 Crowns Comm.	Trout Salmon Sea Fishing Coarse	Ask	Yes	Yes	B.B.E.M. from £30.00	Family run providing excellent comfortable accommodation. Home cooked food. Ideal location for fishing in south west Scotland.
Dumfries G. Ford (Mr. & Mrs.), Brae House Country Guest House, Crocketford Road, (A75), Crocketford, by Dumfries, Dumfriesshire DG2 8QE. Tel: (01556) 690253.	Guest House 2 Crowns Comm.	Salmon Trout Loch Sea Fishing	From Local Tackle shops Ask	Yes	Yes	B. & B. £18.00 B.B.E.M. £28.00	Charming 18th century country house, with wonderful views over Galloway hills. 7 miles from Dumfries. Just off A75. Fishing enthusiast host.
Nick Robinson (Mr.), Cowans Farm Guest House, Kirkgunzeon, Dumfries, Dumfriesshire DG2 8JY. Tel: (01387) 760284.	Guest House Award Pending	Coarse Fishing	Yes Free to Residents	No	Bait only	B. & B. from £18.00 p.p.p.n.- 2 nights. E.M. from £8.00.	Skill testing fishing for carp (to 13lbs), tench, roach, bream and rudd.
Moniaive Craigdarroch Arms Hotel, High Street, Moniaive, Dumfriesshire DG3 4HN. Tel: (01848) 200205.	Hotel Award Pending	River Loch Coarse	Yes	Yes	Yes	B. & B. £20.00	Warm, friendly atmosphere. Fishing within short travelling distance.
INVERNESS-SHIRE **Invergarry** Peter Thomas (Mr.), Ardochy Lodge, Glengarry, Invergarry, Inverness-shire. Tel: (01809) 511232.	Hotel 3 Crowns Highly Comm.	Brown Trout Arctic Char	Yes	Yes	Yes	B. & B. from £29.50 B.B.E.M. from £39.50	Family run hotel with boats available on Lochs Garry and Inchlaggan.
Kincraig L.E. Rainbow (Mrs.), Ossian Hotel, The Brae, Kincraig, Kingussie, Inverness-shire PH21 1QD. Tel: (01540) 651242 Fax: (01540) 651633.	Hotel Lic. 4 Crowns Comm.	Trout Salmon On Loch & River	Bank/ boat permits	Yes	Ye	B. & B. from £19.50 - £29.5	Family run hotel. Beautiful lochside village. Good food and wines.

Addresses	Type of Accommodation	Type of Fishing	Permits Available	Drying Facilities	Freezing Facilities	Price p.p. B & B or B.B.E.M.	Special Features
KIRKCUDBRIGHTSHIRE **Castle Douglas** D. Fulton (Mr.), Kings Arms Hotel, St. Andrew Street, Castle Douglas, Kirkcudbrightshire. Tel: (01556) 502626.	Hotel 4 Crowns Appr.	All types	Ask	es	Yes	B. & B. £26.00 B.B.E.M. £34.50	Personal service. Excellent food. Packed lunches. Secure parking. Late bar.
McIntosh (Mr.), Douglas Arms Hotel, King Street, Castle Douglas, Kirkcudbrightshire. Tel: (01556) 502231. Fax: (01556) 504000.	Hotel 3 Crowns Comm.	Coarse Game Trout Pike	Yes	Yes	Yes	B. & B. £28.00- £33.00 Single £26.00 - £31.00 Double	Privately owned hotel in market town. Secure under cover parking. Cosy bar and restaurant.
Twynholm Gilbert (Mr.), Burnbank Hotel, 1 Kirkbrae, Twynholm, Kirkcudbrightshire. Tel: (01557) 860244.	Hotel	Coarse Game Sea	Yes	Yes	Yes	B. & B. £17.00 p.p.p.n.	A small family run hotel situated in the heart of Dumfries and Stranraer. Ideal for coarse sea and game fishing. Experts available for good advice.
PERTHSHIRE **Pitlochry** Kathleen Shepherd, Poplars Hotel, 27 Lower Oakfield, Pitlochry, Perthshire PH16 5DS. Tel: (01796) 472129.	Hotel 3 Crowns Comm.	Salmon Trout Game	Local Angl- ing Club	Yes	Yes	B. & B. from £19.00 B.B.E.M. from £31.00	Spacious Victorian building set in a large garden with outstanding views of the Tummel Valley.
MORAYSHIRE **Keith** Ross (Mr.), Ugie House Hotel, Church Road, Keith, Morayshire. Tel: (01542) 887671.	Hotel 3 Crowns Comm.	Trout Salmon Sea Trout	Yes	Yes	Yes	£27.50 Single	Recently refurbished villa in the 18th century town of Keith. Superbly situated for for fishing, golf and of course the famous Scotch Whisky Trail.
SUTHERLAND **Tongue** Stephanie Mackay (Mrs.), Rhian Guest House, Tongue, Sutherland IV27 4XJ. Tel: (01847) 611257.	Guest House Lic. 3 Crowns Comm	Salmon Sea Trout Brown Trout	Ask	Yes	Yes	B. & B. £18 - £20 B.B.E.M.	Secluded guest house. Relaxed atmosphere, excellent cuisine, wines and matts. Close to local lochs and Kyle of Tongue.

Addresses	Type of Accommodation	Type of Fishing	Permits Available	Drying Facilities	Freezing Facilities	Prices p.p. B & B or B.B.E.M.	Special Features
SCOTTISH ISLANDS **Orkney** **Birsay** I. Clouston (Mrs.), Primrose Cottage, Birsay, Orkney KW17 2NB. Tel/Fax: (01856) 721384.	Guest House 2 Crowns Comm.	Trout	Yes Free to Residents	Yes	Yes	B. & B. £13 - £18 B.B.E.M. + £8	Overlooking Marwick Bay. Good food and a friendly welcome.
Westray Stout (Mr.), Cleaton House Hotel, Westray, Orkney. Tel: (01857) 677508. Fax: (01857) 677442.	Hotel 3 Crowns Highly Comm.	Wild Brown Trout	Yes	Yes	Yes	B. & B. £30.00 Single £27.50 Twin	Superb walking and bird-watching. Hotel set in splendid isolation. Bar meals from £3.50 and a la carte £20.00.
Isle of Skye **Struan** John Mulford (Mr.), Ullinish Lodge Hotel, Struan, Isle of Skye IV56 8FD. Tel: (01470) 572214. Fax: (01470) 572341	Hotel Comm	Salmon Brown Trout Sea Trout	Free to Residents	Yes	Yes	B. & B. £25.00 - £35.00 B.B.E.M. £44.50 - £54.50	Fishing on two rivers and three hill lochs.

Addresses	Type of Accommodation	Type of Fishing	Permits Available	Drying Facilities	Freezing Facilities	Prices p.p. B & B or B.B.E.M.	Special Features

SELF CATERING

Addresses	Type of Accommodation	Type of Fishing	Permits Available	Drying Facilities	Freezing Facilities	Prices p.p. B & B or B.B.E.M.	Special Features
ABERDEENSHIRE **Aboyne** Elizabeth Crothers (Mrs.), Glen Tanar Estate, Brooks House, Glen Tanar, Aboyne, Aberdeenshire AB34 5EU. Tel: (013398) 86451/86305. Fax: (013398) 86047.	Cotts. 3 Crowns Highly Comm. 5 Crowns Highly Comm.	Salmon Sea/ rainbow Trout	Yes Day or Week	Yes	Yes	From £150	Tastefully furnished, well equipped self catering cottages set in beautiful countryside on private estate.
ARGYLL **Appin** D. Mathieson, Appin House Apartments and Lodges, Appin House, Appin, Argyll PA38 4BN. Tel: (016317) 30207. Fax: (016317) 30567.	Apts Lodges 3 Crowns Comm. 4 Crowns Highly Comm.	Sea Loch River (Fly)	Yes	Yes	No	From £130 - £375	Peace and privacy with beautiful views.
Loch Awe J.C. Soar (Mr.), Sonachan House, Portsonachan, by Dalmally, Argyll PA33 1BN. Tel: (01866) 833240. Fax: (01866) 833241.	Flats House Chalets Mobile Homes Comm. to Highly Comm. 4 Crowns	Brown Trout Rainbow Trout Pike Perch Char Sea Trout Salmon	On Site	On Site	On Site	On Application	Boat hire. 1/3 mile shore. UK Record Brown Trout (25lbs 6oz) by one of their visitors.
BANFFSHIRE **Buckie** The Manager, Letterfourie, Buckie, Banffshire AB56 2JP. Tel: (01542) 832298.	Flats 5 Crowns Comm.	Sea River	Yes	Yes	Yes	From £180 - £630 weekly	Private 300 acre estate. Tennis. Coast 3 miles. Spey 7 miles.

Addresses	Type of Accommodation	Type of Fishing	Permits Available	Drying Facilities	Freezing Facilities	Prices p.p. B & B or B.B.E.M.	Special Features
INVERNESS-SHIRE **Boat of Garten** B. Gillies (Mr.), Boat of Garten Caravan Park, Boat of Garten, Inverness-shire PH24 3BN. Tel: (01479) 831652.	Cabins Thistle 5 Ticks	River Loch	Yes	Yes	Yes	From £87 - £355	River Spey, golf, tennis. Steam railway all within walking distance.
Kincraig David Kinnear (Mr.), Dalraddy Holiday Park, by Aviemore. Write to: Alvie Estate Office, Kincraig, Kingussie, Inverness-shire PH21 1NE. Tel: (01540) 651255. (01479) 810330.	F'hse 4/5 Crowns	Salmon Sea Trout Pike Char Trout	Yes	Yes	Yes	From £300 - £500	Variation of lochs and river fishing.
MORAYSHIRE **Grantown-on-Spey** A. Laing (Mrs.), Logie House, Forres, Morayshire IV36 OQN. Tel: (01309) 611278.	Lodge Cottage 3/4 Star Comm.	Brown Trout	Free	Yes	Yes	From £170 - £1,100 per house per week	Lodge sleeps 16. Cottage sleeps 4. Peaceful setting on lochside. Bank fishing free. Boats for hire.
PERTHSHIRE **Bridge of Cally** J. Farmer (Mrs.), Persie Mains, Bridge of Cally, Blairgowrie, Perthshire PH10 7LQ. Tel: (01250) 886250.	Cotts 4 Crowns Highly Comm.	Loch Trout River Salmon	Yes	Yes	Yes	From £150 -£350	Quality accommodation on a Highland estate. Superb views/amenities.
Comrie Wallace Booth (Snr), Loch View Farm, Mill of Fortune, Comrie, Perthshire PH6 2JE. Tel: (01764) 670677.	House Award Pending Apt.	Fly only	Yes	Yes	Yes	On Application	Unique site, with own rowing boat ten feet from lochside.

Addresses	Type of Accommodation	Type of Fishing	Permits Available	Drying Facilities	Freezing Facilities	Prices p.p. B & B or B.B.E.M.	Special Features
Pitlochry Stewart (Mr.), Milton of Fonab Caravan Site, Bridge Road, Pitlochry, Perthshire PH16 5NA. Tel: (01796) 472882. Fax: (01796) 474363.	Static C'vans 4 Ticks & Thistle	Trout Salmon	Yes	Yes	Yes	On Application	On banks of River Tummel. Couples and families only.
ROSS-SHIRE **Gairloch** H.M. Garrioch (Mrs.), The Old School, Old School Road, Opinan, Gairloch, Ross-shire IV21 2AT. Tel: (01445) 741206.	House 4 Crowns Comm.	Loch Sea River	No	Yes	Yes	From £160 - £350	Large garden. Gas cook-ing/ Central heating inclusive.
SUTHERLAND **Brora** P. Sowerby (Mr.), c/o Mrs. M.F. Sowerby, Balnacoil Cottage, Brora, Sutherland. Tel: (01408) 621219.	Cottage 4 Crowns Deluxe	Salmon Trout	Yes	Yes	Yes	From £295 - £425 per week	Spectacular loch and hill views. Fishing on doorstep. Central heating and double glazing.
Kinbrace M. Wigan (Mr.), Borrobol, Kinbrace, Sutherland KW11 6UB. Tel: (01431) 831264.	House B'low	Wild Brown Trout on Loch	Yes	No	Yes	From £226 - £270 House £254 - £329 B'low	Privacy, scenery, boat on loch, birdlife and deer. Private estate.
WIGTOWNSHIRE **Newton Stewart** Eric Hyslop (Mr.), Borgan, Bargrennan, Newton Stewart, Wigtownshire DG8 6SR. Tel: (01671) 840247.	Cotts 4 Crowns Comm.	Salmon Trout Sea Trout	Yes	Yes	Yes	From £175 - £265	Exclusive salmon/sea trout fishing available. Central base for all fishing pursuits.

KEY TO MAPS

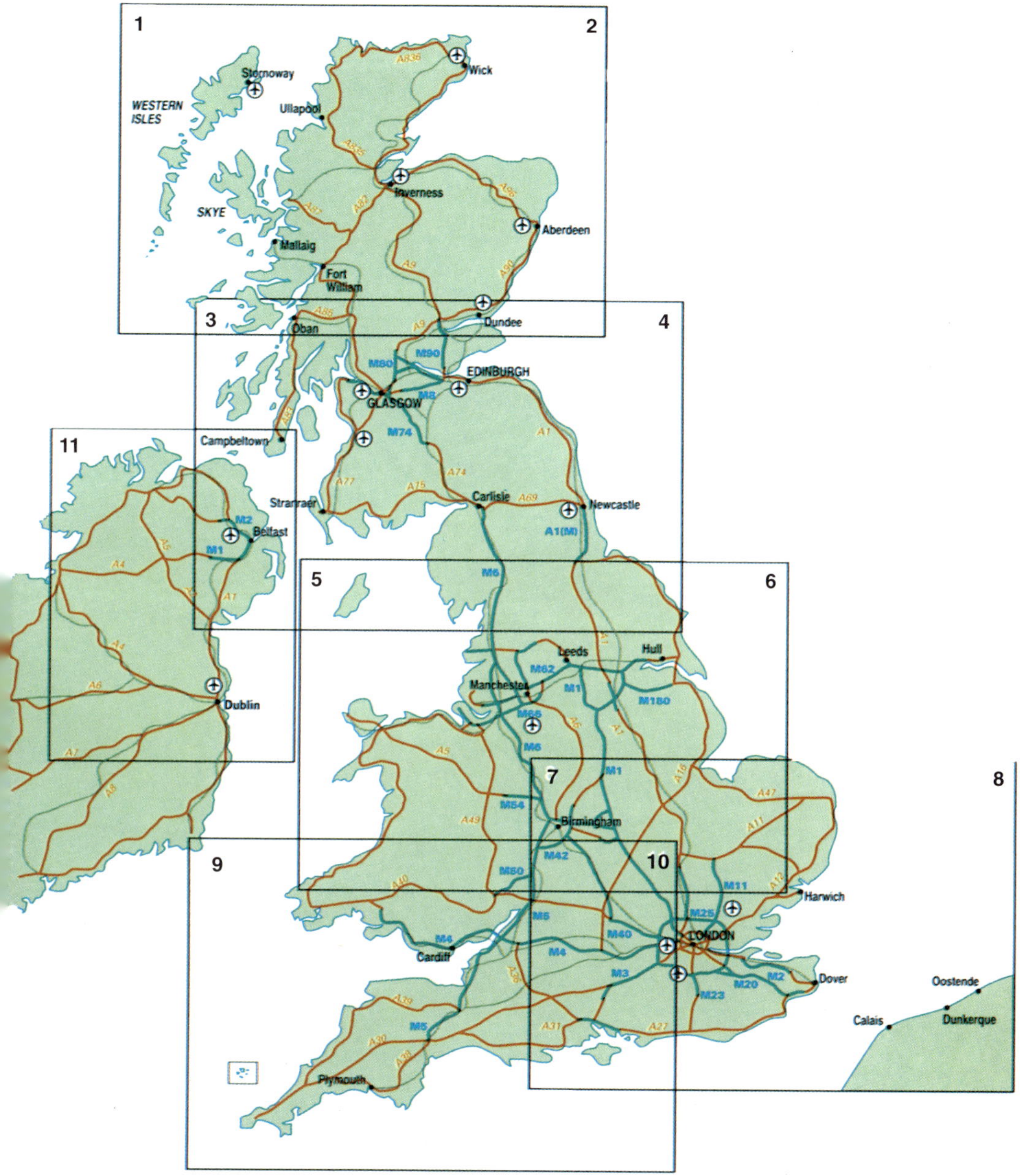

All maps on pages 1-11 are 20 miles to 1 inch

0 10 20 30 40 Miles

0 10 20 30 40 50 60 Kilometres

OUTER HEBRIDES
Butt of Lewis
Port of Ness
Borve
Galston
North Tolsta
Tolsta Head
Barvas
Gallan Hd.
Carloway
Uig
Callanish
Garynahine
Tiumpan Head
Portnaguran
Stornoway
Balallan
Scarp
LEWIS
Limervoy
Taransay
Tarbert
Toe Hd.
Shiant Is.
Scalpay
Pabbay
Leverburgh
HARRIS
Rodel
THE MINCH
Point of Stoer
Scourie
Kylestrome
Kylesku
Lochinver
Inverkirkaig
Suilven
Rubha Coigeach
Summer Is.
Achiltibuie
Ullapool
Greenstone Pt.
Gruinard Bay
Gruinard
Rubha Reidh
Melvaig
Aultbea
Poolewe
Dundonnell
Gairloch
L. Maree
Kinlochewe
Torridon
Achnasheen
Shieldaig
Applecross
Kishorn
Lochcarron
Auchnashellach
Loch Carron
Toscaig
Plockton
Stromeferry
Kyle of Lochalsh
Kyleakin
Dornie
L. Mullardoch
Kylerhea
Glenelg
Shiel Bridge
Cluanie
L. Cluanie
Kinloch Hourn
Tomdoun
Inverie
Loch Quoich
NORTH UIST
Lochmaddy
Clachan
Carinish
Monach Is..
Gramisdale
Creagorry
Benbecula
Carnan
SOUTH UIST
Lochboisdale
Daliburgh
Kilbride
Ludag
Eriskay
Barra
Castlebay
Sandray
Pabbay
Barra Hd.
Rubha Hunish
Kilmaluag
Vaternish Point
Staffin
Uig
Dunvegan Head
Rona
L. Pooltiel
Bernisdale
Skeabost
Dunvegan
Portree
Raasay
Struan
Bracadale
Sligachan
Scalpay
Talisker
Carbost
Laib
Cuillin Hills 3309
Broadford
L. Eynort
Isleoronsay
L. Eishort
Soay
Canna
Ardvasar
Rum
Point of Sleat
Mallaig
Morar
Arisaig
L. Morar
Eigg
Muck
Glenfinnan
Gulvain
Lochailort
Kinlocheil
Lochy Bridge
Spean Bridge
Kinlochmoidart
Fort William
Dalelia
Loch Shiel
BEN NEVIS 4408
Pt. of Ardnamurchan
Mingary
Salen
Strontian
North Ballachulish
Coll
Sorisdale
Arinagour
Onich
Inversanda
Glencoe
Tobermory
Ballachulish
Glen Coe
Calgary
Duror
Camasnacroise
Tiree
Scarinish
Hynish
Lochaline
Portnacroish
Port Appin
Ulva
Salen
Lismore
Staffa
Gruline
Craignure
New Selma
Lochdonhead
Connel
Loch Etive
MULL
Oban
Taynuilt
Iona
Lochbuie
Dalmally
Fionnphort
Bunessan
Kerrera
Firth of Lorn
Kilninver
Cladich
Fasdale
A857
A858
A859
A865
A837
A835
A832
A896
A890
A87
A855
A863
A850
A851
A830
A861
A82
A884
A849
A828
A85
1

Head
Stroma
John o' Groats
Duncansby Hd.
Strathy Point
Strathy
Scrabster
Mey
Dunnet
Dounreay
A836
Thurso
Castletown
A838
Bettyhill
Melvich
Reay
Keiss
A9
Tongue
Sinclair's Bay
Ben Hope 3040
A836
A882
Reiss
Noss Head
Watten
Wick
Forsinard
A895
A9
A897
Altnaharra
Ben Kilbreck 3154
Latheron
Lybster
Morven 2313
Kinbrace
Dunbeath
Overscaig
Berriedale
L. Shin
Helmsdale
A9
Lairg
A837
A839
Brora
Rosehall
Golspie
Invershin
Bonar Bridge
Embo
Ardgay
Dornoch
Kincardine
Edderton
Portmahomack
Aultnamaig
Tain
Moray Firth
A9
Balintore
Wyvis
Alness
Invergordon
Evanton
Hopeman
Lossiemouth
Cromarty
Burghead
Dingwall
Kinloss
Buckie
Portsoy
Banff
Fraserburgh
Fortrose
Fort George
Nairn
Elgin
Llantryde
Cullen
Macduff
Conon Br.
A96
Forres
Mosstodloch
Cornhill
A92
Avoch
Auldearn
Fochabers
A97
A98
Rathen
North Kessock
A941
Gordonstown
A952
A939
Rothes
Crimond
Beauly
Cawdor
A940
Dallas
Aberchirder
New Pitsligo
St. Fergus
Keith
A95
Inverness
Craigellachie
Mintlaw
Longside
A96
Turriff
A833
Dufftown
Peterhead
Moy
Huntly
A92
Boddam
Dores
Spey
A95
Ballindalloch
Hatton
A9
A941
Grantown on Spey
A920
Fyvie
Methlick
Tomatin
Cruden Bay
Drumnadrochit
Errogie
Cromdale
A952
Ness
Foyers
Dulnain Bridge
Rhynie
Oldmeldrum
A975
Newburgh
A97
Insch
Carrbridge
Loch
Tomintoul
Lumsden
Inverurie
Whitebridge
Nethy Bridge
Bridge of Alford
Newmachar
Aviemore
Alford
Strath Spey
A939
A944
A92
Balmedie
Monadhliath Mts.
Strathdon
Kintore
Don
Dyce
A9
Kingussie
Cock Bridge
A944
Dunecht
Skene
Aberdeen
Kincraig
A97
Cults
Newtonmore
Peterculter
Aboyne
A939
A93
Banchory
Dee
Laggan
A86
Crathie
A93
Cove Bay
Braemar
A93
Ballater
A90
MOUNTAINS
Bridge of Feugh
A957
Muchalls
A889
Bridge of Dye
Dalwhinnie
Lochnagar
Stonehaven
Laggan
GRAMPIAN
Beinn Dearg
Devil's Elbow
Glenbervie
A90
Forest of Atholl
L. Ericht
Dalnaspidal
A93
Fordoun
Fettercairn
A9
Spittal of Glenshee
Inverbervie
Gourdon
Calvine
Blair Atholl
Laurencekirk
South Esk
Glen Shee
Kinloch Rannoch
A924
Lair
Trinafour
Brechin
A90
Glenisla
St. Cyrus
Pitlochry
Kirkmichael
L. Rannoch
L. Tummel
Kirriemuir
Montrose
Farnell
Moor
Aberfeldy
Forfar
A9
A93
A932
Inverkeilor
A827
Friockheim
Kenmore
Blairgowrie
Glamis
A92
Dunkeld
Tay
Coupar Angus
Muirdrum
Arbroath
Amulree
A822
A90
Ardeonaig
Loch
Killin
Bankfoot
Meikleour
Carnoustie
2
A94
Stanley
Dundee
Barry
Lochearnhead
St. Fillans
Broughty Ferry
Methven
A9
New Scone
A90
Newport on Tay
A85
A85

Firth of Lorn
Easdale
Kilninver
Kilmelford
Cladich
Crianlarich
Balquhidder
Loch Earn
St. Fillans
Comrie
Strathyre
Ben Vorlich
Ardlui
Loch Awe
Inveraray
Cairndow
Inversnaid
Loch Katrine
Callander
Greenloaning
Dunblane
Bridge of Allan
Ford
Furnace
Crarae
Kilmartin
Strachur
Arrochar
Tarbet
Aberfoyle
Lochgoilhead
Finnart
Loch Lomond
Doune
Kippen
Stirling
Colonsay
Scalasaig
JURA
Crinan
Lochgilphead
Garelochhead
Luss
Drymen
Arnprior
Fintry
Oronsay
Ardlussa
Ardrishaig
Ardentinny
Shandon
Gartocharn
Campsie Fells
Strathblane
Denny
Kilsyth
Ardnave Pt.
Bunnahabhainn
Port Askaig
Lagg
Keillbeg
Otter Ferry
Colintraive
Dunoon
Greenock
Port Glasgow
Helensburgh
Dumbarton
Milngavie
Falkirk
Cumbernauld
Feolin Ferry
Craighouse
Kilberry
Tarbert
Tighnabruaich
Rames
Innellan
Gourock
Inverkip
Clydebank
Renfrew
Glasgow
ISLAY
Bridgend
Bowmore
BUTE
Rothesay
Wemyss Bay
Lochwinnoch
Paisley
Rutherglen
Motherwell
Portnahaven
Skipness
Claonaig
Clachan
Kilchattan
Largs
Millport
Barrhead
Giffnock
Hamilton
Gigha Is.
Lochranza
Fairlie
Kilbirnie
Beith
Newton Mearns
East Kilbride
Wishaw
Carluke
Port Ellen
Ardbeg
Ardminish
Tayinloan
Grogport
Corrie
Dalry
Lugton
Stonehouse
Cara Is.
Pirnmill
W. Kilbride
Ardrossan
Kilwinning
Kilmaurs
Stewarton
Larkhall
Glenbarr
Carradale
ARRAN
Brodick
Saltcoats
Stevenson
Fenwick
Strathaven
Dreghorn
Irvine
Newmilns
Kirkmuirhill
Lanark
Saddell
Lamlash
Kilmarnock
Galston
Darvel
Lesmahagow
Troon
Loans
Blackwaterfoot
Whiting Bay
Machrihanish
Campbeltown
Prestwick
Monkton
Mauchline
Muirkirk
Douglas
Ayr
Auchinleck
Cumnock
Alloway
Pladda
Coylton
New Cumnock
Abington
Maybole
Patna
Leadhills
Southend
Turnberry
Kirkoswald
Straiton
Dalmellington
Kirkconnel
Sanquhar
Wanlockhead
Mull of Kintyre
Sanda Is.
Mennock
Girvan
Carronbridge
Ailsa Craig
Carsphairn
Moniaive
Pinwherry
Ballantrae
Barrhill
Dalry
NORTH CHANNEL
New Galloway
Newbridge
Ken Bridge
Bargrennan
Maxwelltown
Kirkcolm
Cairnryan
Crocketford
New Luce
Newton Stewart
Cairnsmore of Fleet 2329
Crossmichael
Laurieston
Stranraer
Kirkcowan
Castle Douglas
Dalbeattie
Portpatrick
Glenluce
Creetown
Ringford
Wigtown
Twynholm
Gatehouse of Fleet
Sandhead
Kirkinner
Kirkcudbright
Auchencairn
Rockcliffe
Luce Bay
Wigtown Bay
Borgue
Port William
Dundrennan
Port Logan
Whithorn
Drummore
Isle of Whithorn
Mull of Galloway
Burrow Hd.
Solway
St. Bees
Pt. of Ayre
Jurby
Bride
Ballaugh
Ramsey
Kirk Michael
Snaefell 2034
Maughold Hd.
Peel
Laxey
St. John's
ISLE OF MAN
Glenmaye
Onchan
Douglas
Port Erin
Port St. Mary
Castletown
A816
A819
A83
A815
A82
A85
A84
A81
A811
M9
A886
A814
A846
A847
A8
M80
A891
A80
A761
A78
M8
M73
M74
A736
A77
A726
A841
A71
A76
A70
A713
A7
A702
A714
A712
A762
A711
A75
A718
A716
A747
A746
A710
A3
A2
A1
A5

Broughty Ferry
Newport on Tay
New Scone
A9
A90
Leuchars
Newburgh
St. Andrews
Bridge of Earn
Abernethy
A914
A91
Cupar
Auchtermuchty
Fife Ness
Glenfarg
A91
Falkland
A915
Largoward
Crail
Milnathort
A911
Glenrothes
Lundin Links
A917
Anstruther
Kinross
Windygates
Leven
Elie
Pittenweem
M90
Lochgelly
Buckhaven & Methil
Buddon Ness
A92
Cowdenbeath
Kirkcaldy
North Berwick
A921
Kinghorn
Burntisland
Gullane
Inverkeithing
N. Queensferry
Aberlady
A198
Dunbar
Queensferry
Edinburgh
Prestonpans
A1
E. Linton
Cockburnspath
Musselburgh
Tranent
Haddington
East Calder
A720
Dalkeith
Grantshouse
Eyemouth
A702
Penicuik
A68
Berwick upon Tweed
Tweedmouth
Carlops
A701
Leadburn
Moorfoot Hills
Heriot
Duns
A703
Romanno Bridge
A7
Swinton
Eddleston
A697
Greenlaw
Stow
Lauder
Blyth Bridge
Peebles
A68
Eccles
Coldstream
Holy Is. (Lindisfarne)
Clovenfords
Barmoor
Broughton
A72
Galashiels
Bamburgh
Innerleithen
Melrose
Kelso
Belford
Tweed
Seahouses
Selkirk
Newtown St. Boswells
Doddington
Wooler
Tweedsmuir
Embleton
Ashkirk
Teviot
Bonjedward
A1
A708
A7
Jedburgh
A697
Hawick
Alnwick
Cheviot Hills
Bonchester Bridge
A68
Whitingham
Coquet
Amble
Teviothead
Rothbury
Moffat
Byrness
Felton
Rochester
Eskdalemuir
Longhorsley
Otterburn
Newbiggin-by-the-Sea
A7
West Woodburn
Morpeth
Newcastleton
Langholm
Bellingham
Blyth
A709
A696
Belsay
Seaton Burn
Lockerbie
A1
N. Tyne
Colwell
Whitley Bay
Canonbie
Ponteland
Tynemouth
Ecclefechan
M74
A68
Newcastle
Wallsend
A75
Longtown
Haydon Bridge
Heddon-on-the-Wall
South Shields
Annan
A74
Greenhead
A69
Ryton
Jarrow
Gretna
A6071
Hexham
Prudhoe
Boldon
A7
Brampton
A69
Haltwhistle
Riding Mill
Gateshead
Kirkbride
A686
A692
Sunderland
Silloth
Carlisle
Warwick
S. Tyne
Shotley Bridge
Chester le Street
Washington
Houghton-le-Spring
Abbey Town
Wigton
Thursby
Consett
A691
Castleside
Hetton-le-Hole
Seaham
Alston
Lanchester
Easington
Aspatria
A596
M6
A6
A68
Neville's Cross
Durham
Peterlee
A595
Tow Law
A686
Wearhead
Crook
A19
Sheraton
Bothel
Melmerby
Cross Fell 2390
Ferryhill
Spennymoor
Langwathby
Hartlepool
Kilnhill
Greystoke
Sedgefield
Cockermouth
Bishop Auckland
Penrith
Temple Sowerby
A1(M)
A177
Wolviston
Redcar
Saltburn
A66
Tees
West Auckland
Pooley Bridge
Clifton
A688
A68
Stockton on Tees
A5086
Portinscale
Keswick
Appleby
Piercebridge
Middlesbrough
Barnard Castle
Guisborough
Brough
Patterdale
Yarm
A66
Shap
Bowes
Greta Bridge
Darlington
Egremont
M6
Stokesley
Kirkby Stephen
A591
A19
Cleveland Hills
A66
A172
Scotch Corner
Ambleside
A685
A595
Skelwith Br.
Entercommon
Gosforth
A6
Tebay
Richmond
A167
A684
North York Moors
Windermere
Coniston
A1
Northallerton
Bowness
A591
Ravenglass
Sedbergh
Leeming Bar
Kendal
A684
Leyburn
A19
Broughton
A592
Hawes
Wensley
Kirkbymoorside
Bootle
Lowick
Newby Br.
Levens Br.
Bedale
Thirsk
Helmsley
Pickering
Silecroft
Aysgarth
A170
Whicham
Lindale
Crooklands
Busby Stoop
Sproxton
Millom
Grenodd
A590
Milnthorpe
Kirkby Lonsdale
Masham
A1
Ulverston
A6
Buckden
Topcliffe
A65

St. Bees Head
Egremont
A595
Gosforth
Ravenglass
Bootle
Whicham
Millom
Broughton
Silecroft
Coniston
Skelwith Br.
Ambleside
Windermere
Bowness
A591
Kendal
A592
Lowick
Newby Br.
Levens Br.
Crooklands
Lindale
Greenodd
A590
Milnthorpe
A6
M6
Ulverston
Barrow-in-Furness
Walney Island
Morecambe
Carnforth
Claughton
Heysham
Lancaster
Morecambe Bay
Cockerham
Fleetwood
Cleveleys
A586
Blackpool
Barton
M55
Kirkham
A584
Lytham St. Annes
Lytham
Preston
Tarleton
Leyland
Southport
Rufford
Chorley
A570
A59
Ormskirk
A565
M58
Aintree
Bootle
St. Helens
Liverpool Bay
Birkenhead
Hoylake
Prescot
M57
Wallasey
Heswall
Liverpool
Runcorn
Widnes
M53
Ellesmere Port
Welsh Corner
A55
Queensferry
Northop
Mold
Hawarden
Chester
Tarvin
A51
Northwich
Winsford
A49
Tarporley
A494
Rossett
A483
Ridley
A41
A534
Wrexham
Marchwiel
Nantwich
Audlem
Overton
Whitchurch
A525
Market Drayton
Ruabon
Chirk
Gobowen
Ellesmere
A495
Oswestry
Whittington
Queens Head
A5
Nesscliffe
Hodnet
A53
Shawbury
Shrewsbury
A458
Wellington
Telford
Middletown
Welshpool
Cressage
Much Wenlock
Church Stoke
Lydham
Church Stretton
Morville
Craven Arms
Bromfield
Leintwardine
Ludlow
A4117
Knighton
Tenbury Wells
Leominster
Pt. of Ayre
Jurby
Bride
Ballaugh
A3
Ramsey
Kirk Michael
Snaefell 2034
A2
Maughold Hd.
Peel
Laxey
St. John's
ISLE OF MAN
Glenmaye
A1
Onchan
A5
Douglas
Port Erin
Port St. Mary
Castletown
Calf of Man
Cemaes Bay
Amlwch
Carmel Hd.
Holyhead Bay
A5025
Red Wharf B.
Holyhead
Valley
ANGLESEY
Holy I.
Menai Br.
Gt. Ormes Hd.
Llandudno
Colwyn Bay
Prestatyn
Rhyl
Mostyn
Rhuddlan
Holywell
Penmaen mawr
Conwy
Abergele
St. Asaph
Trefnant
Llanfairfechan
A548
A543
Denbigh
A525
Bangor
Port Dinorwic
Bethesda
A470
Caernarfon
Llanrwst
Ruthin
Caernarfon Bay
Menai Str.
Snowdon 3561
Capel-Curig
Betws-y-coed
Pentre-Foelas
Cerrig-ydrudion
Gwyddelwern
Corwen
Druid
Llangollen
A487
A499
Beddgelert
Blaenau-Ffestiniog
Llanaelhaiarn
Peninsula
Tremadog
Ffestiniog
A4212
Lleyn
Y Flor
Criccieth
Porthmadog
Pwllheli
Trawsfynydd
A494
Harlech
Tremadog Bay
Llanbedr
A496
Llanuwchllyn
Ganllwyd
Llanelltyd
Dolgellau
Llanymynech
Llanfyllin
Bardsley
Pencilan Hd.
Barmouth
A493
Dinas Mawddwy
Llangadfan
Llwyngwril
Minffordd
Mallwyd
Llangelynin
Cemmaes
Llanfair Caereinion
Cemmaes Rd.
Tywyn
Pennal
Machynlleth
Carno
Garthmyl
CARDIGAN BAY
Aberdyfi
Newtown
Borth
Talybont
Caersws
Kerry
Llanidloes
Aberystwyth
Ponterwyd
A44
Dyffryn Castell
Llangurig
Llanfarian
A4120
Llanbadarnfynydd
Llanrhystud
Llanbister
Rhayader
A488
Crossgate
Penybont
New Radnor
Aberaeron
Llandrindod Wells
A482
Tregaron
Newbridge on Wye
MOUNTAINS

Darlington
Bowes
Greta Bridge
Yarm
Stokesley
Lythe
Sleights
Richmond
Scotch Corner
Entercommon
Cleveland Hills
North York Moors
Saltergate
Burniston
Northallerton
Scalby
Scarborough
Wensley
Leyburn
Leeming Bar
Kirkbymoorside
Helmsley
Sproxton
Pickering
Brompton
Seamer
Filey
Aysgarth
Bedale
Thirsk
Busby Stoop
Staxton
Sherburn
Masham
Rillington
Hunmanby
Buckden
Topcliffe
Easingwold
Ripon
Dishforth
Malton
Threshfield
Barton Hill
Yorkshire Wolds
Burton Agnes
Bridlington
Bridlington Bay
Shipton
Ripley
Hellifield
Bolton Bridge
Blubberhouses
Knaresborough
Fridaythorpe
Harrogate
Bainton
Great Driffield
Skipton
Addingham
Wetherby
York
Pocklington
Hornsea
Ilkley
Otley
Collingham
Long Marston
Barnaby Moor
Harewood
Bramham
Tadcaster
Escrick
Keighley
Bingley
Shipley
Horsforth
Seacroft
Bradford
Leeds
Monk Fryston
Selby
Barlby
Burnley
Queensbury
Halifax
Hebden Br
Castleford
Howden
South Cave
Hull
Hedon
Withernsea
Dewsbury
Brotherton
Rawcliffe
Todmorden
Sowerby
Pontefract
Snaith
Goole
Barton upon Humber
New Holland
Partrington
Ripponden
Huddersfield
Wakefield
Barnsdale Bar
Crowie
Immingham
Kilnsea
Rochdale
Askern
Thorne
Scunthorpe
Grimsby
Spurn Head
Cleethorpes
Hatfield
Gt. Limber
Manchester
Woodhead
Penistone
Barnsley
Brigg
Stalybridge
Flouch
Wortley
Mexborough
Doncaster
Hibaldstow
Chister
Moffram
Stocksbridge
Hyde
Glossop
Rotherham
Lincoln Wolds
Saltfleet
Stockport
Barnby Moor
Gainsborough
Market Rasen
Ludford
Louth
Hazel Grove
New Mills
Sheffield
Faldingworth
Mablethorpe
Swallow Nest
Ranby
East Retford
Langworth
Wragby
Burwell
Dronfield
Worksop
Baumber
Macclesfield
Barlborough
Buxton
Staveley
Cuckney
Luxford
Newton upon Trent
Lincoln
Bardney
Chesterfield
Market Warsop
Ollerton
Partney
Burgh-le-Marsh
Rowsley
Clay Cross
Horncastle
Pleasley
Carlton on Trent
Spilsby
Congleton
Matlock
Mansfield
Skegness
Matlock Bath
Stretton
Newark-on-Trent
Hanley
Alfreton
Stickney
Wainfleet All Saints
Rainworth
Ambergate
Ripley
Old Leake
Stoke-on-Trent
Belper
Eastwood
Leadenham
Mayfield
Ashbourne
Heanor
Sleaford
Heckington
Boston
Longton
Nottingham
Ilkeston
Bingham
Bottesford
Upper Tean
Brailsford
Stapleford
Radcliffe
Grantham
Threekingham
Swineshead
Uttoxeter
Derby
West Bridgford
Donington
Sutterton
Sudbury
Long Eaton
The Wash
Sandon
Hatton
Castle Donington
Burton upon Trent
Stafford
Kegworth
Bourne
Spalding
Holbeach
South Woo
King's Bromley
Swadlincote
Woodville
Melton Mowbray
Rudeley
Ashby de la Zouch
Loughborough
Stretton
Cannock
Mountsorrel
Market Deeping
Wisbech
Lichfield
Crowland
Measham
Oakham
Great Casterton
Stamford
Glinton
Thorney
Downham Market
Walsall
Sutton Coldfield
Leicester
Billesdon
Earl Shilton
Oadby
Guyhirn
Peterborough
Eye
March
Narborough
West Bromwich
Birmingham
Hinckley
Whittlesey
Nuneaton
Elton
Corby
Halesowen
Stonebridge
Oundle
Chatteris
Husbands Bosworth
Coventry
Rugby
Alconbury Hill
Ely
Hagley
Kettering
Rothwell
Thrapston
Kenilworth
Dunchurch
Raunds
Huntingdon
Bromsgrove
Stoneleigh
Irthlingborough
Wellingborough
Higham Ferrers
Rushden
Kimbolton
Godmanchester
Stretham
Warwick
Leamington Spa
Buckden
Fenstanton
Daventry
Northampton
St. Neots
Caxton Gibbet
M1
M5
M6
M18
M40
M42
M62
M180
M621
A1(M)
A1
A6
A14
A15
A16
A17
A19
A46
A47
A50
A52
A57
A59
A61
A63
A64
A65
A66
A166
A170
A171
A165
A614
A616
A617
A630
A631
A638
A1033
A1079
6

Nottingham
Derby
Stafford
Loughborough
Leicester
Melton Mowbray
Grantham
Walsall
Birmingham
West Bromwich
Coventry
Rugby
Nuneaton
Hinckley
Halesowen
Bromsgrove
Warwick
Leamington Spa
Stratford upon Avon
Daventry
Northampton
Wellingborough
Kettering
Corby
Oakham
Stamford
Peterborough
Spalding
Bourne
Holbeach
Wisbech
Downham Market
Ely
Huntingdon
St. Neots
Cambridge
Bedford
Milton Keynes
Buckingham
Banbury
Evesham
Cheltenham
Chipping Norton
Bicester
Aylesbury
Leighton Buzzard
Dunstable
Luton
Hitchin
Letchworth
Stevenage
Baldock
Royston
Hertford
Welwyn Garden City
St. Albans
Hemel Hempstead
Watford
Harlow
Bishop's Stortford
Stansted
Witney
Oxford
Swindon
Abingdon
Didcot
Wantage
Henley on Thames
High Wycombe
Beaconsfield
Maidenhead
Windsor
Slough
Heathrow
Uxbridge
Reading
Newbury
Marlborough
Devizes
Basingstoke
Camberley
Farnborough
Aldershot
Farnham
Guildford
Woking
Epsom
Dorking
Reigate
Redhill
Gatwick
Crawley
Horsham
Haywards Heath
Tunbridge Wells
LONDON
Enfield
Edmonton
Hendon
Romford
Brentwood
Croydon
Bromley
Richmond
Kingston upon Thames
Andover
Salisbury
Winchester
Southampton
Eastleigh
Romsey
Fareham
Portsmouth
Gosport
Havant
Chichester
Petersfield
Bognor Regis
Littlehampton
Worthing
Shoreham by Sea
Brighton
Hove
Lewes
Newhaven
Seaford
Eastbourne
Lymington
Bournemouth
Poole
Christchurch
Newport
Ryde
Cowes
Sandown
The Wash
M1
M4
M6
M40
M25
M3
M27
M11
M23
M42
M45
M20
M26
A1(M)
A3(M)
7

Cley
Sheringham
Cromer
A149
Holt
A148
Roughton
Fakenham
North Walsham
Aylsham
Sea Palling
A140
A149
Stalham
Bawdeswell
Rollesby
Attlebridge
Caister-on-Sea
A47
Horsham St. Faith
East Dereham
Honingham
Acle
Great Yarmouth
A47
Norwich
Blofield
Wymondham
A146
Gorleston-on-Sea
A11
A143
Attleborough
Long Stratton
Ellingham
Lowestoft
A140
Bungay
A146
Beccles
A143
Kessingland
Thetford
A1066
Diss
A144
Wrentham
Halleston
Scole
Botesdale
Blythburgh
Ixworth
Peasenhall
Yoxford
Bury St. Edmonds
Dennington
A140
A45
A1120
Saxmundham
Stowmarket
Wickham Market
A12
Aldeburgh
A45
Needham Market
Claydon
Woodbridge
Ipswich
Felixstowe
Manningtree
A12
Colne
Elmstead Market
Harwich
The Naze
Colchester
Walton-on-the-Naze
A133
Clacton-on-Sea
West Mersea
Blackwater
Foulness Pt.
Foulness Island
Southend-on-Sea
Shoeburyness
Sheerness
Isle of Sheppey
Westgate
Margate
Leysdown
Herne Bay
Birchington
Broadstairs
Whitstable
A299
A253
Faversham
A28
Sarre
Ramsgate
M2
A2
Sturry
A257
Sandwich
Canterbury
Wingham
A20
Bridge
A256
Deal
A28
Barham
A2
Ashford
A260
A20
Dover
Sandgate
Folkestone
A2070
A259
Hythe
Dymchurch
New Romney
Rye
Littlestone-on-Sea
Winchelsea
Lydd
Dungeness
Oostende
Middelkerke
Westende
Koksijde
De Panne
N63
Dunkerque
N1
Diksmuide
Calais
Gravelines
N56
D916
Roesel
A19
N65
Guines
Cap Gris Nez
Ardres
N1
D928
N43
Marquise
Cassel
A25
D933
Boulogne
8
St-Omer
© Baynefield Carto-Graphics Ltd. 1995
Roub
le Portel
N42
Hazebrouck
Desvres

Tregaron
Llanarth
Temple Bar
Post-mawr
A487
Lampeter
Cardigan
Newcastle Emlyn
Llanybydder
Pumsaint
Strumble Hd.
Goodwick
A487
Newport
Eglwyswrw
Llandysul
Llandovery
Fishguard
Crymmych Arms
Newport B.
Alltwalis
Llanwrda
St. David's Hd.
St. David's
A487
A40
A478
A485
Ramsay I.
Llandusili
Carmarthen
A40
Llandeilo
St. Brides Bay
Haverfordwest
Canaston Bridge
A40
Whitland
A48
Llanddarog
A483
St. Clears
Skomer
A4076
Narberth
Laugharne
Cross Hands
Ammanford
Johnston
A477
A484
Kidwelly
Pontardawe
Milford Haven
Neyland
Kilgetty
Pendine
Llanelli
Pontardulais
Skokholm
Pembroke
Tenby
Carmarthen Bay
Burry Port
M4
A465
Loughor
Swansea
Caldey
Gower Peninsula
Llanrhidian
St. Govan's Hd.
Knelston
Rhossili
Mumbles
Port Talbot
Port Eynon
Porthcawl
Bristol Ch
Lynmouth
Ilfracombe
Lundy
Lee
Combe Martin
Parracombe
Blackmoor Gate
A361
A39
A399
Braunton
Bideford Bay
Appledore
Barnstaple
Hartland Pt.
Instow
South Molton
Westward Ho!
A377
A361
Hartland Quay
Clovelly
Bideford
A39
Umberleigh
Buck's Mills
Great Torrington
Morwenstow
A361
A388
A386
Chulmleigh
Kilkhampton
Merton
Lapford
Bude
Stratton
A3072
Hatherleigh
A377
Bude Bay
Holsworthy
Bow
Crediton
Okehampton
Whiddon Down
A30
A39
Bridestowe
Chagford
ISLES OF SCILLY
Davidstow
Launceston
Lifton
A30
Dartmoor
Bryher
St. Martin's
Camelford
Lydford
Samson
Tresco
A386
Widecombe-in-the-Moor
Hugh Town
St. Mary's
Milton Abbot
A382
Annet
Gugh
Trevose Hd.
Padstow
A30
A388
St. Agnes
Bodmin Moor
Tavistock
Callington
A390
Ashburton
Watergate B.
A39
St. Columb Major
Yelverton
Bodmin
Buckfastleigh
Newquay
Liskeard
Plymouth
South Brent
A390
A38
Bugle
Saltash
Totnes
Lostwithiel
Ivybridge
A38
Mitchell
Fraddon
St. Blazey
Devonport
Plymstock
St. Austell
Looe
Modbury
A30
Fowey
Polperro
Yealmpton
Probus
Grampound
St. Austell B.
Whitesand B.
The Sound
A379
St. Ives Bay
Redruth
Truro
Tregony
Bigbury-on-Sea
Kingsbridge
St. Ives
A39
Gorran Haven
Thurlestone
Hayle
Camborne
Veryan B.
Salcombe
Penzance
A30
Penryn
C. Cornwall
Marazion
A394
St. Just
A30
A394
Falmouth
Sennen Cove
Newlyn
Helston
Land's End
A3083
Lizard
Lizard Pt.

Llandrindod Wells
Builth Wells
Kington
Lyonshall
Leominster
Worcester
Inkberrow
Alcester
Stratford upon Avon
Wellesbourne
Staverton
Daventry
Whitney
Willersley
Newton
Bromyard
Great Malvern
Malvern Wells
Trumpet
Pershore
Evesham
Norton
Bidford
Mickleton
Ettington
Mollington
Towcester
Blisworth
Hay-on-Wye
Glasbury
Hereford
Ledbury
Newtown
Sedgeberrow
Broadway
Shipston on Stour
Banbury
Warmington
Llyswen
Broonllys
Talgarth
Wormbridge
Black Mountains
Pontrilas
St. Weonards
Ross on Wye
Tewkesbury
Bishop's Cleeve
Moreton in Marsh
Long Compton
Adderbury
Brackley
Chipping Norton
Baynards Green
Tingewick
Coombe Hill
Winchcomb
Gloucester
Huntley
Cheltenham
Stow on the Wold
Enstone
Middleton Stoney
Bicester
Winslow
Trelower
Crickhowell
Pandy
Abergavenny
Whitchurch
Lea
Minsterworth
Andoversford
Shipton under Wychwood
Woodstock
Gilwern
Monmouth
Brynmawr
Tredegar
Newnham
Hardwicke
Birdlip
Northleach
Burford
Witney
Abersychan
Pontypool
Llanhilleth
Mountain Ash
Lydney
Cambridge
Stroud
Cirencester
Fairford
Bampton
Eynsham
Oxford
Wheatley
Tintern
Crumlin
Newbridge
Cwmbran
Chepstow
Caerleon
Stone
Dursley
Nailsworth
Lechlade
Faringdon
Kingston Bagpuize
Abingdon
Stokenchurch
Dorchester
Wallingford
Crosskeys
Tetbury
Crudwell
Cricklade
Highworth
Shrivenham
Steventon
Didcot
Henley on Thames
Caerphilly
Newport
Aust
Alveston
Chipping Sodbury
Malmesbury
Swindon
Wantage
East Ilsley
Streatley
Goring
Nantgarw
second Severn crossing open 1996
Whitchurch
St. Mellons
Cardiff
Avonmouth
Marshfield
Wootton Basset
Wroughton
Ogbourne St. George
Aldbourne
Pangbourne
Reading
Bristol
Chippenham
Cold Ashton
Avebury
Marlborough
Hungerford
Thatcham
Penarth
Barry
Clevedon
Quisgate
Keynsham
Box
Calne
Beckhampton
Newbury
Theale
Aldermaston
Wokingham
Weston-Super-Mare
Pensford
Bath
Melksham
Devizes
Bleadon
Farrington
Gurney
Trowbridge
Pewsey
Upavon
Burnham-on-Sea
Cheddar
East Brent
Beckington
Litchfield
Basingstoke
Hook
Bridgewater Bay
Frome
Westbury
Netheravon
Wells
Highbridge
Weyhill
Andover
Whitchurch
Odiham
Nether Stowey
Williton
Shepton Mallet
Warminster
Heylesbury
Amesbury
Pilton
Longbridge Deverill
Stapleford
Lopcombe Corner
Crowcombe
Street
Deptford
Barford St. Martin
Stockbridge
Sutton Scotney
Alton
Othery
Kings Worthy
Taunton
Langport
Mere
East Knoyle
Wilton
Salisbury
Winchester
New Alresford
Milverton
Ilchester
Sparkford
Wincanton
Coombe Bissett
Henstridge
Shaftesbury
Chandler's Ford
West Meon
Wellington
Blackdown Hills
Ilminster
Sherborne
Fordingbridge
Romsey
Eastleigh
Ower
Waterloo Cross
Yeovil
Southampton
Crewkerne
Blandford Forum
Ringwood
Lyndhurst
Hythe
Fareham
Wimborne Minster
Brockenhurst
Fawley
Titchfield
Havant
Spetisbury
Beaulieu
Gosport
Honiton
Axminster
Charmouth
Maiden Newton
Puddletown
Bere Regis
Lytchett Minster
Trickett's Cross
Christchurch
Lymington
Cowes
East Cowes
Portsmouth
Bridport
Poole
Milford on Sea
Ryde
Sidford
Lyme Regis
Winterbourne Abbas
Dorchester
Bournemouth
Yarmouth
Fishbourne
Newport
Sidmouth
Wareham
Freshwater
Shalfleet
Sandown
Budleigh Salterton
Osmington
Wool
The Needles
Shanklin
Corfe Castle
Swanage
Chale
Ventnor
Lyme Bay
Chesil Beach
Weymouth
St. Albans Hd.
Durlston Hd.
ISLE OF WIGHT
Niton
St. Lawrence
Isle of Portland
Easton
Bill of Portland
M4
M5
M50
M40
M3
M27
A3(M)

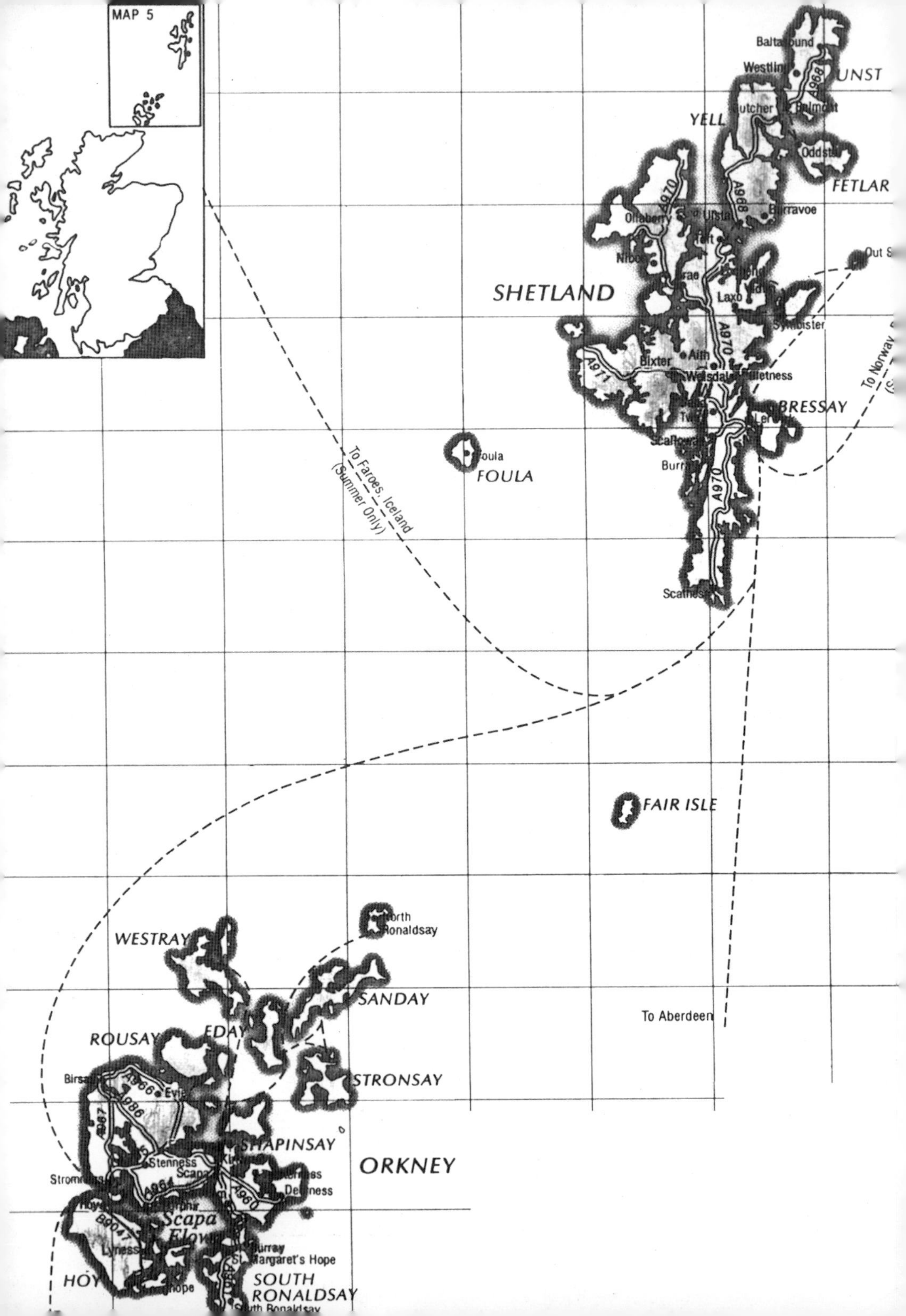
MAP 5
UNST
YELL
FETLAR
A968
A970
Ollaberry
Ulsta
Burravoe
SHETLAND
Laxo
Symbister
Bixter
Aith
A971
Weisdale
BRESSAY
To Norway
Foula
FOULA
To Faroes, Iceland
(Summer Only)
Burra
FAIR ISLE
To Aberdeen
North
Ronaldsay
WESTRAY
SANDAY
ROUSAY
EDAY
STRONSAY
A966
Evie
A986
A967
SHAPINSAY
ORKNEY
Stenness
Scapa
Deerness
A964
A960
Scapa
Flow
B9047
Lyness
Burray
St. Margaret's Hope
HOY
SOUTH
RONALDSAY